OUT & ABOUT

• WALKING GUIDES TO BRITAIN •

No 2

The Lake District
and North East England

MARSHALL CAVENDISH

First published in Great Britain in 1995 by
Marshall Cavendish Books, London
(a division of Marshall Cavendish Partworks Ltd)

ISBN 03190 057 47

British Library Cataloguing in Publication Data:
A catalogue record for this book is available from the British Library

Printed and bound in Dubai, U.A.E.

Some of this material has previously appeared in the Marshall Cavendish partwork OUT & ABOUT

CONTENTS

Introduction to OUT & ABOUT • WALKING GUIDES TO BRITAIN •

Walking has become one of the most popular pastimes in Britain. To enjoy walking, you don't need any special skills, you don't have to follow rules or join expensive clubs, and you don't need any special equipment – though a pair of walking boots is a good idea! It is an easy way of relaxing and getting some exercise, and of enjoying nature and the changing seasons.

The OUT & ABOUT WALKING GUIDES TO BRITAIN will give you ideas for walks in your own neighbourhood and in other areas of Britain. All the walks are devised around a theme and range in length from about 2 to 9 miles (3.25 to 14.5 km) and in difficulty from very easy to mildly strenuous. Since each walk is circular, you will always be able to get back to your starting point.

Devised by experts and tested for accuracy, all the walks are accompanied by clear, practical instructions and an enlarged section of the relevant Ordnance Survey map. The flavour of the walk and highlights to look out for are described in the introductory text.

LOCAL COLOUR

Background features give you extra insight into items of local interest. The OUT & ABOUT WALKING GUIDES TO BRITAIN relate legends, point out unusual architectural details, provide a potted history of the lives of famous writers and artists connected with a particular place, explain traditional crafts still practised by local artisans, and uncover the secrets behind an ever-changing landscape.

DISCOVER NATURE

One of the greatest pleasures in going for a walk is the sense of being close to nature. On the walks suggested in the OUT & ABOUT WALKING GUIDES TO BRITAIN, you can feel the wind, smell the pine trees, hear the birds and see the beauty of the countryside. You will become more aware of the seasons – the life cycles of butterflies, the mating calls of birds, the protective behaviour of all creatures with their young. You will see the beginning of new life in the forests and fields, the bluebell carpets in spring woodlands, the dazzling beauty of rhododendron bushes in early summer, the swaying cornfields of summer and the golden colours of leaves in autumn. The OUT & ABOUT WALKING GUIDES TO BRITAIN tell you what to look out for and where to find it.

NATURE WALK

Occasional nature walk panels. will highlight an interesting feature that you will see on your walk. You will learn about natural and manmade details in the landscape, how to tell which animal or bird has nibbled the cones in a pine forest, what nurse trees are and what a triangulation point is.

FACT FILE

The fact file will give you at-a-glance information about each walk to help you make your selection.

- general location
- map reference for Ordnance Survey map with grid reference for starting point
- miles 0 1 2 3 4 5 6 7 8 9 / kms 0 1 2 3 4 5 6 7 8 9 10 11 12 13 14 15 length of the walk in miles and kilometres
- time needed if walking at an average speed
- character of the walk: easy/easy with strenuous parts/mildly strenuous; hills to be climbed and muddy or dangerous areas are pointed out
- P parking facilities near the start of the walk
- T public transport information
- facilities for refreshment, including pubs serving lunchtime meals, restaurants, tea rooms and picnic areas
- WC location of toilets
- historic sites

ORDNANCE SURVEY MAPS

All the walks in the OUT & ABOUT WALKING GUIDES TO BRITAIN are illustrated on large-scale, full-colour maps supplied by the Ordnance Survey. Ordnance Survey are justifiably proud of their worldwide reputation for excellence and accuracy. For extra clarity, the maps have been enlarged to a scale of 1:21,120 (3 inches to 1 mile).

The route for each walk is marked clearly on the map with a broken red line, and the numbers along the route refer you to the numbered stages in the written directions. In addition, points of interest are marked on the maps with letters. Each one is mentioned in the walk directions and is described in detail in the introductory text.

ABOVE: *Colourful narrowboats are always an attractive feature on inland waterways.*

COUNTRYWISE

The countryside is one of our greatest resources. If we treat it with respect, we can preserve it for the future.

Throughout the countryside there is a network of paths and byways. Some are former trading routes, others are simply the paths villagers took to visit one another in the days before public transport. Most are designated 'rights of way': footpaths, open only to people on foot, and bridleways, open to people on foot, horseback or bicycle. These paths can be identified on Ordnance Survey maps and verified, in cases of dispute, by the definitive map for the area, held by the relevant local authority.

THE LAW OF TRESPASS

If you find a public right of way barred to you, you may remove the obstruction or take a short detour around it. However, in England and Wales, if you stray from the footpath you are trespassing and could be sued in a civil court for damages. In Scotland, rights of way are not recorded on definitive maps, nor is there a law of trespass. Although you may cross mountain and moorland paths, landowners are permitted to impose restrictions on access, such as during the grouse-shooting season, which should be obeyed.

If you are following a public right of way and find, for example, that your path is blocked by a field of crops, you are entitled to walk the line of the footpath through the crops, in single file. Farmers are required, by law, to restore public rights of way within 14 days of ploughing. However, if you feel uncomfortable about doing this and can find a way round, then do so. But report the matter to the local authority who will take the necessary action to clear the correct route.

RIGHT: *The stunning patchwork of fields surrounding the picturesque village of Widecombe in the heart of Dartmoor makes a beautiful setting for the famous annual fair.*
BELOW: *Brown hares boxing in spring are a fascinating sight.*

It is illegal for farmers to place a bull on its own in a field crossed by a right of way (unless the bull is not a recognized dairy breed). If you come across a bull alone in a field, find another way round.

COMMONS AND PARKS

There are certain areas in England and Wales where you may be able to wander without keeping to paths, such as most commons and beaches. There are also country parks, set up by local authorities for public recreation – parkland, woodland, heath or farmland.

The National Trust is the largest private landowner in England and Wales. Its purpose is to preserve areas of natural beauty and sites of historic interest by acquisition, holding them in trust for public access and enjoyment. Information on access may be obtained from National Trust headquarters at

THE COUNTRY CODE

- **Enjoy the countryside, and respect its life and work**
- **Always guard against risk of fire**
- **Fasten all gates**
- **Keep your dogs under close control**
- **Keep to public footpaths across farmland**
- **Use gates and stiles to cross fences, hedges and walls**
- **Leave livestock, crops and machinery alone**
- **Take your litter home**
- **Help to keep all water clean**
- **Protect wildlife, plants and trees**
- **Take special care on country roads**
- **Make no unnecessary noise**

ABOVE RIGHT *Carelessness with cigarettes, matches or camp fires can be devastating in a forest.*

36 QueenAnne's Gate, London SW1H 9AS
Tel: 071-222 9251.

Most regions of great scenic beauty in England and Wales are designated National Parks or Areas of Outstanding Natural Beauty (AONB). In Scotland, they are known as National Scenic Areas (NSAs) or AONBs.

Most of this land is privately owned and there is no right of public access. In some cases, local authorities may have negotiated agreements with landowners to allow walkers access on mountains and moors.

CONSERVATION

National park, AONB or NSA status is intended to provide some measure of protection for the landscape, guarding against unsuitable development while encouraging enjoyment of its natural beauty.

Nature reserves are areas set aside for conservation. Most are privately owned, some by large organizations such as the Royal Society for the Protection of Birds. Although some offer public access, most require permission to enter.

THE RAMBLERS ASSOCIATION

The aims of the Ramblers Association are to further greater understanding and care of the countryside, to protect and enhance public rights of way and areas of natural beauty, to improve public access to the countryside, and to encourage more people to take up rambling as a healthy, recreational activity. It has played an important role in preserving and developing our national footpath network.

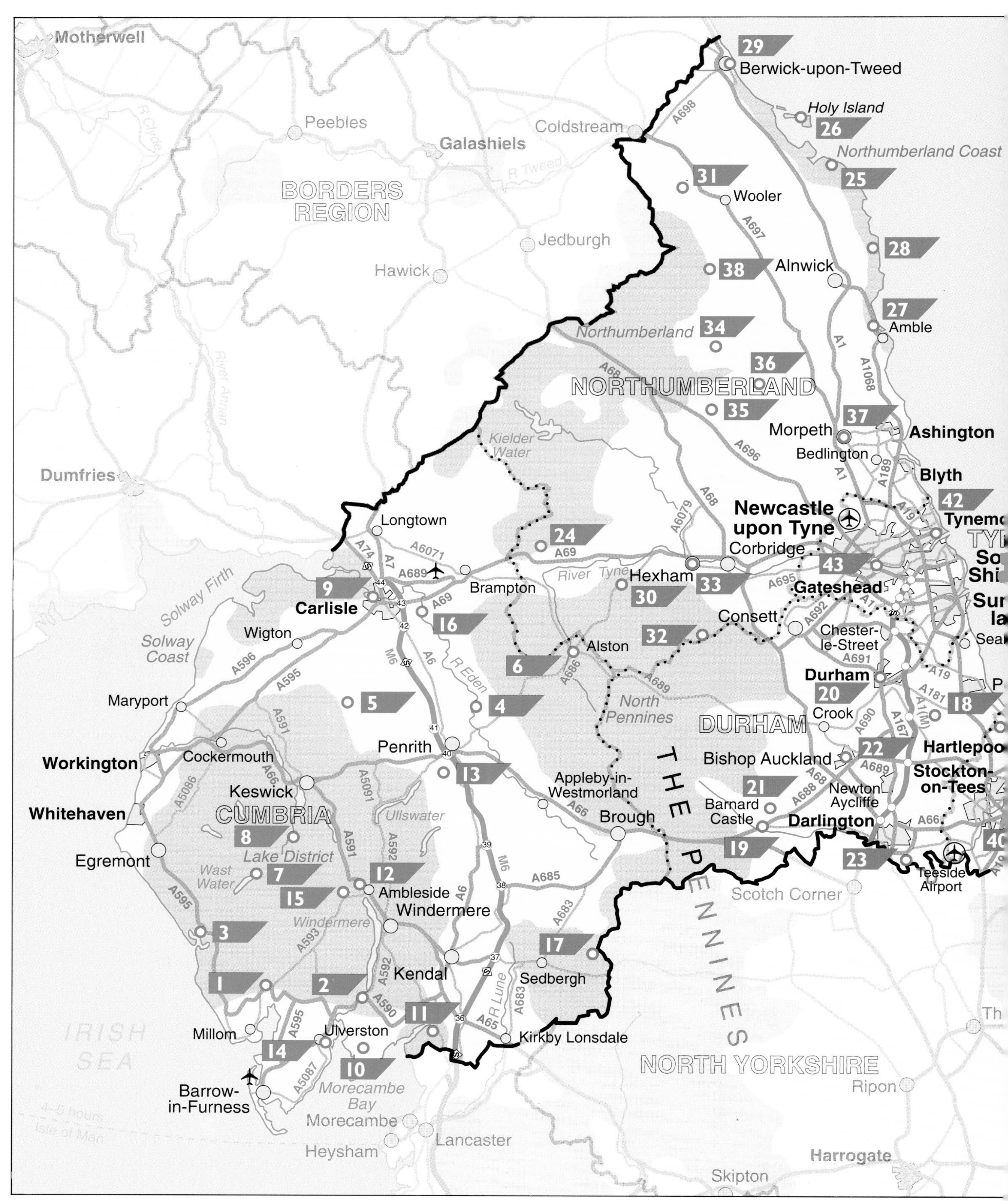
Motherwell
Berwick-upon-Tweed
Holy Island
Northumberland Coast
Peebles
Coldstream
Galashiels
BORDERS REGION
Wooler
Jedburgh
Hawick
Alnwick
Amble
Northumberland
NORTHUMBERLAND
Morpeth
Ashington
Bedlington
Blyth
Kielder Water
Dumfries
Newcastle upon Tyne
Longtown
Corbridge
Hexham
Brampton
Gateshead
Carlisle
Solway Firth
Consett
Wigton
Chester-le-Street
Solway Coast
Alston
Durham
North Pennines
Maryport
Crook
DURHAM
Penrith
Cockermouth
Workington
Bishop Auckland
Hartlepool
Keswick
Appleby-in-Westmorland
Stockton-on-Tees
CUMBRIA
Newton Aycliffe
Whitehaven
Ullswater
Barnard Castle
Brough
Darlington
Egremont
Lake District
West Water
Ambleside
Windermere
Scotch Corner
Teesside Airport
THE PENNINES
Kendal
Sedbergh
Millom
Ulverston
Kirkby Lonsdale
IRISH SEA
NORTH YORKSHIRE
Morecambe Bay
Barrow-in-Furness
Morecambe
Ripon
Lancaster
Heysham
Harrogate
Skipton

The Lake District & North East England

All the walks featured in this book are plotted and numbered on the regional map (left) and listed in the box below.

1 Dunnerdale Fells
2 An Elizabethan Topiary Garden
3 The Riches of Ravenglass
4 The Vale of Eden
5 John Peel Country
6 Gills and Valleys
7 Wasdale Head
8 The Borrowdale Valley
9 A Quiet Port
10 Sands of Time
11 Underlaid Wood
12 Where Wordsworth Wrote
13 The Castle and the Hall
14 The Common and the Shore
15 The Tarn and the Water
16 East and West of Eden
17 The Falcons of Mallerstang
18 Taking the Nature Trail
19 The Tees Valley
20 The Proud Towers
21 A Village on the Tees
22 Valley of the Prince Bishops
23 In Search of the Cheshire Cat
24 In Hadrian's Footsteps
25 The Castle on the Rock
26 High-Tide Island
27 A Medieval Stronghold
28 The Coastal Path
29 Above the Last Bastions
30 By the Banks of the Allen
31 Yeavering Bell's Twin Peaks
32 Along Shildon Burn
33 Historic Hexham
34 Drake Stone
35 From Peel to Pen
36 Crags and Conifers
37 Bridges and Bagpipes
38 Village, Ash and Spout
39 Along the Cleveland Coast
40 The Hollow Hill
41 Hart to Hart
42 Call of the Sea
43 Old Newcastle

USING MAPS

Although the OUT & ABOUT WALKING GUIDES TO BRITAIN give you all the information you need, it is useful to have some basic map skills. Most of us have some experience of using a motoring atlas to navigate by car. Navigating when walking is much the same, except that mistakes are much more time and energy consuming and, if circumstances conspire, could lead to an accident.

A large-scale map is the answer to identifying where you are. Britain is fortunate in having the best mapping agency in the world, the Ordnance Survey, which produces high-quality maps, the most popular being the 1:50,000 Landranger series. However, the most useful for walkers are the 1:25,000 Pathfinder, Explorer and Outdoor Leisure maps.

THE LIE OF THE LAND

A map provides more than just a bird's eye view of the land; it also conveys information about the terrain – whether marshy, forested, covered with tussocky grass or boulders; it distinguishes between footpaths and bridleways; and shows boundaries such as parish and county boundaries.

Symbols are used to identify a variety of landmarks such as churches, camp and caravan sites, bus, coach and rail stations, castles, caves and historic houses. Perhaps most importantly of all, the shape of the land is indicated by contour lines. Each line represents land at a specific height so it is possible to read the gradient from the spacing of the lines (the closer the spacing, the steeper the hill).

GRID REFERENCES

All Ordnance Survey maps are overprinted with a framework of squares known as the National Grid. This is a reference system which, by breaking the country down into squares, allows you to pinpoint any place in the country and give it a unique reference number; very useful when making rendezvous arrangements. On OS Landranger, Pathfinder and Outdoor Leisure maps it is possible to give a reference to an accuracy of 100 metres. Grid squares on these maps cover an area of 1 km x 1 km on the ground.

GIVING A GRID REFERENCE

Blenheim Palace in Oxfordshire has a grid reference of **SP 441 161.** This is constructed as follows:

SP These letters identify the 100 km grid square in which Blenheim Palace lies. These squares form the basis of the National Grid. Information on the 100 km square covering a particular map is always given in the map key.

441 161 This six figure reference locates the position of Blenheim Palace to 100 metres in the 100 km grid square.

44 This part of the reference is the number of the grid line which forms the western (left-hand) boundary of the 1 km grid square in which Blenheim Palace appears. This number is printed in the top and bottom margins of the relevant OS map (Pathfinder 1092 in this case).

16 This part of the reference is the number of the grid line which forms the southern (lower) boundary of the 1 km grid square in which Blenheim Palace appears. This number is printed in the left- and right-hand margins of the relevant OS map (Pathfinder 1092).

These two numbers together (SP 4416) locate the bottom left-hand corner of the 1 km grid square in which Blenheim Palace appears. The remaining figures in the reference **441 161** pinpoint the position within that square by dividing its western boundary lines into tenths and estimating on which imaginary tenths line Blenheim Palace lies.

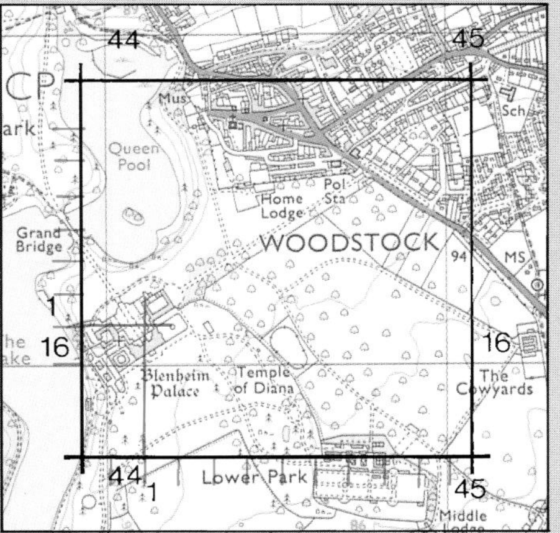

DUNNERDALE FELLS

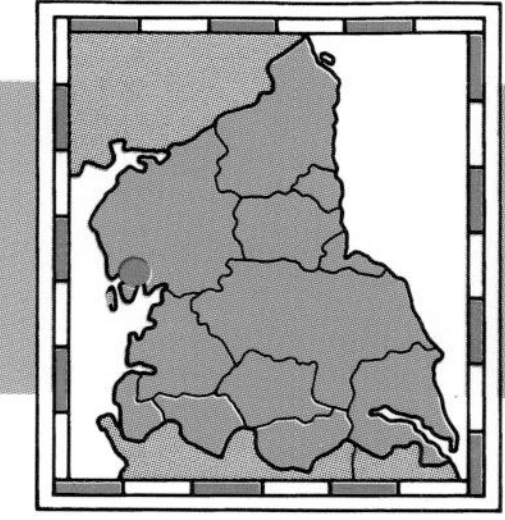

Woodland and open country near Duddon Bridge

Dunnerdale is one of the loveliest dales in Cumbria, and its wooded slopes, open fells and drystone walls make for varied and interesting walking at all times of the year. The River Duddon, rising high on Wrynose Pass, flows southwestwards through this beautiful landscape of contrasts which offers quiet shady paths leading through dense woodlands, the expanse of the open fell and industrial relics of a bygone age.

PAST INDUSTRY

In Furnace Wood, at the lower end of Dunnerdale, lies Duddon Bridge iron furnace Ⓐ. Ironmakers built it in 1736 and it is now magnificently restored. In those days the furnace workers used charcoal for smelting. The site was chosen because of the oak, hazel and birch at hand in Furnace Wood Ⓑ. Seven tons (7.1 tonnes) of wood were needed to produce 1 ton (tonne) of charcoal. Only by using charcoal could the smelters achieve the heat required

FACT FILE

Duddon Bridge, near Broughton-in-Furness on the A595

Pathfinder 625 (SD 08/18), grid reference SD 197882

miles 0 1 2 3 4 5 6 7 8 9 10 miles
kms 0 1 2 3 4 5 6 7 8 9 10 11 12 13 14 15 kms

Allow 2½ hours

One steep climb. Woodland and fell paths can be muddy. Walking boots recommended

In lay-by on fell road off the A595

Café and pubs in and near the square, Broughton-in-Furness

JOHN WATNEY

STEPHEN DALTON/NHPA

JOHN WATNEY

▲ Duddon valley drops away below Furnace Wood, which contains beech, oak and hazel trees (hazel catkins inset).
◄ The last bridge over the River Duddon before it flows into the estuary and into the Irish Sea.

to smelt the iron ore, which was transported to the furnace by barge and then packhorse.

On the open fell, on a crop of limestone, stands a well-preserved lime-kiln Ⓓ. It was built by limestone burners who needed limestone to fuse the metals in the iron furnace. The slow-burning fire was fanned by huge bellows, operated by a water wheel.

Criss-crossing the fells, drystone walls Ⓒ form boundaries between farms and pastures. They were built after land enclosures in the 18th century to stop stock from wandering. Gangs of wallers went from farm to farm, building miles of wall by placing stone upon stone without using mortar to hold them in place. They camped beside the walls to avoid trudging across the land each day to continue their hard and never-ending work.

BIRDWATCHING

In the woodlands the chiff-chaffs can be heard constantly calling their name from about March onwards. Soon after, willow warblers fill the air with their sweet songs. Blackcaps quickly follow, together with whitethroats and garden warblers. At all times of the year, jays, green and spotted woodpeckers, treecreepers and mixed flocks of tits can be seen. Grey wagtails regularly

THE WALK

DUDDON BRIDGE – FURNACE WOOD

The walk begins in the lay-by at the signpost to Duddon Bridge iron furnace.

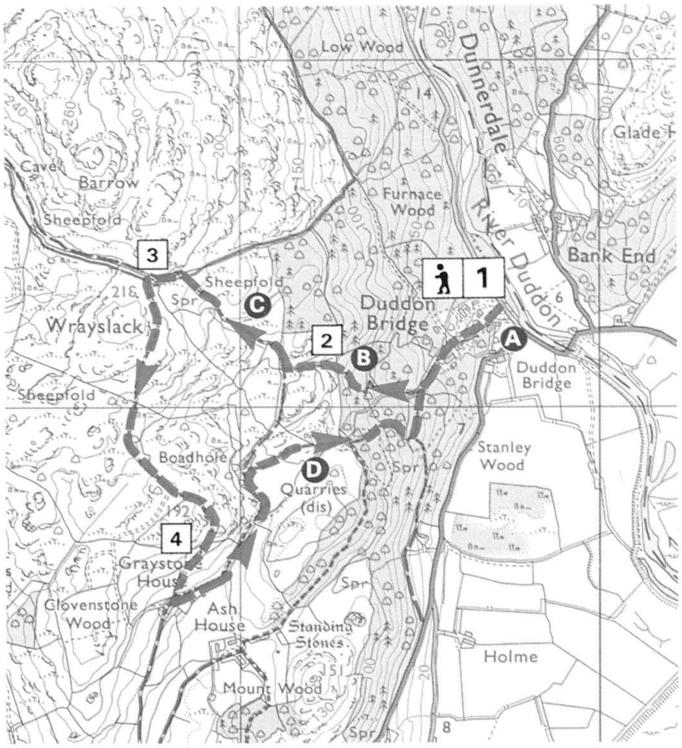

1 Walk along the bridlepath from the lay-by to the entrance of the furnace **A**. Enter the enclosure and wander around the buildings, imagining the noise, smell and activity of 250 years ago.

2 Return to the bridleway. Follow the blue waymark and turn left into the trees. Cross the hotel driveway and continue up the waymarked path. When the path branches (just before a stream), bear right, following the blue arrow. The path climbs relentlessly through oak woodland **B**. It disappears for a short time, but you continue ahead where another distinct path soon appears. Go up this attractive leafy way, which zigzags to reduce the gradient. Follow the waymarks to a gate marked Boadhole with a blue arrow on it.

3 Go through the gate on to open fell. Follow the path through bracken and past rowan, hawthorn, gorse and birch as it zigzags again. Take care in summer as the bracken grows very high. Continue along the path until it forks. Take the arrowed path on the right (white arrows painted on a slab of slate and placed on either side) until a wall is reached **C**. Turn right, and, with the wall on your left, follow the track between two walls and when the wall on the right finishes continue ahead, keeping close to the left-hand one. After the last waymark on this part of the walk continue to a gate in the fell wall. Turn left and after about 60 yards (55 metres) turn left again through another gate. Take the faint, grassy track ahead, which eventually leads to another gate. Go through this gate, and follow track beside the wall on the left.

4 Keep to the track as it curves to the left and then to the right before going through another gate to Graystone House. Do not pass between the farm buildings but turn left and walk up the steadily climbing farm track. Pass through two gates to reach the farm buildings of Boadhole. Cross the ladder stile, and after 50 yards (45 metres) cross the ladder stile on the right. Pass to the right of a small pond. Look right to beyond the hedge to see a well-preserved lime-kiln **D**. Follow the stream in the direction of some trees. Cross the wall by another ladder stile and enter the wood. Then turn right and where the path branches and is waymarked white, take the left fork. The waymarked track drops steadily downhill before levelling out to continue to the track just above the hotel. Turn right, cross the driveway, and walk through the trees to return to the start of the walk.

raise their broods on the banks of the little stream which runs near the site of the furnace.

On the fell, look for buzzards circling overhead, where they use the rising air currents to gain height. A pair of crows may mob these predators or a small flock of meadow pipits could hustle these birds of prey. Kestrels can be seen searching the fell slopes for mice and cuckoos fly low between the hawthorn bushes. In winter the redwings and fieldfares arrive, chatter noisily in the tree tops and then fly down to the fell to hunt for insects. The large-bodied curlew with its white rump and down-curving beak is resident all year.

▲ *Arrows painted on slate mark the way through bracken for part of the route. (right) Wild flowers grow beside the restored 18th-century iron furnace, now as quiet as its surroundings.*

JOHN WATNEY

AN ELIZABETHAN TOPIARY GARDEN

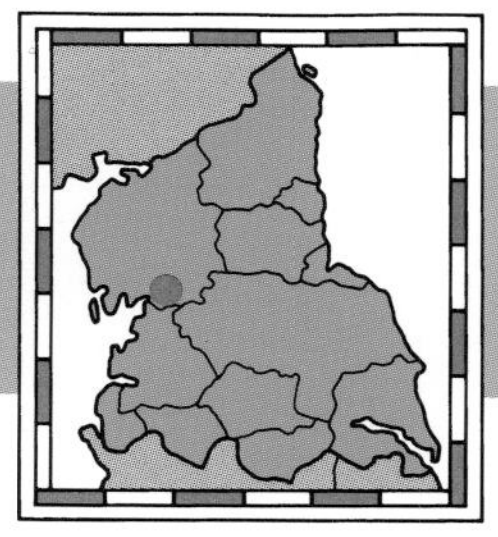

2

J. ALLAN CASH

JOHN WATNEY

◀ *Box and yew have been clipped into cones, pyramids, corkscrews and many strange shapes, in the topiary garden at Levens Hall (below left), an Elizabethan house with a 13th-century tower.*

From Levens Hall along the route of the old Lancaster-Kendal canal

Levens Hall (A), where the walk starts, is an Elizabethan mansion house situated in the scenic countryside of southern Cumbria. The house is surrounded by its famous topiary garden, and across the road is Levens Deer Park, which has a Public Right of Way through it. The route winds through grassland and woods of lime, beech, oak, ash and elm. The River Kent, turbulent in places, can be heard through the trees. The black fallow deer keep their distance; and the deer sanctuary (B) is out of bounds to the public, to protect the animals.

Beyond the park, a stone parapet gives a good view over a series of falls and a natural limestone salmon leap (C). On the opposite bank are the remains of one of the earliest gunpowder mills (D), while further up river are some far more substantial ruins of a bigger gunpowder mill (E), now overgrown.

RIVERSIDE PATHS

A small suspension footbridge takes the path over to the east bank of the river and then upstream above the ravine where the water alternates between cascades over great limestone slabs and still, dark pools. At one point there is a clear view through trees to the foundations of the dam which once diverted water into a leat to feed the water wheels of the gunpowder mill. There are rudimentary paths down to the water's edge, and giant hogweed grows in clusters along the banks and on islets; many of these plants are over 12 feet (3.6 metres) tall. At Hawes Bridge a quick visit can be made through a small, iron gate to see a waterfall (F) from a platform of limestone slabs.

Crowpark Bridge spans the dried-up bed of the Kendal Canal. The walk follows the old towpath to Sedgwick, with sweeping views over the Kent valley. In some places farmers have filled in the canal so that only the towpath shows where it once flowed, while elsewhere, its bed has been colonised by grasses, wild flowers and bushes. It is easy to see that it was a wide and deep canal. Unlike the narrow canals of most of our inland waterways system, this one (opened in 1819 and

FACT FILE

- Levens Bridge, 5 miles (8km) south of Kendal, Cumbria
- Pathfinder 627 (SD 48/58), grid reference SD 496852
- miles 0 1 2 3 4 5 6 7 8 9 10 miles / kms 0 1 2 3 4 5 6 7 8 9 10 11 12 13 14 15 kms
- 4 hours
- Mostly flat, but slippery under the trees after rain, and wet in long grass. Suitable all year and for children
- P Off clearway on wide verge north of Levens Bridge opposite Lawrence House Farm. Car park at Levens Hall for visitors to house (closed Friday, Saturday, October–Easter)
- T Bus service connecting Levens Bridge with Lancaster, Carlisle, Arnside and Keswick
- At Levens Hall for visitors
- WC Shop in Sedgwick

THE WALK

LEVENS BRIDGE – SEDGWICK

The walk begins outside the gates to Levens Hall **A** *at the gap stile on the north side of Levens Bridge, on the A6.*

1 Cross the stile and follow the grass path through the deer park for about ¾ mile (1.2 km) to a sign reading 'No exit beyond this point'. Bear left to the stone steps up to a gap stile in a stone wall.

2 Turn sharp right and walk down beside a stone wall along the edge of the deer sanctuary **B** through another stile in a stone wall. Keep straight ahead across the corner of a field to a third stile which leads on to a country lane beside a house called Park Head.

3 Turn right and walk down to the end of the lane and round the walkway under the A591 viaduct over the River Kent and past the salmon leap **C**. On the other side, walk up the continuation of the lane beside the river to Force Bridge, where gunpowder mill ruins can be seen **D**.

4 Do not cross the bridge but go straight ahead until arriving at a smaller lane on the right.

5 Turn right down this lane and continue until reaching a suspension footbridge on the right which crosses the river. On the way there is a lane on the left which leads to the 14th-century National Trust Sizergh Castle and Gardens.

6 Keep straight on past the suspension bridge for about 300 yards (270 metres) to the visitors' car park and office of the caravan site in Low Park Wood. Beside this are the remains of a big gunpowder mill **E**.

7 Retrace your steps to the path which crosses the suspension bridge and turn left, keeping close to the river all the way to Hawes Bridge, where there is a waterfall **F**. Ignore a larger footpath which veers to the right. There are several stiles and fences to climb.

8 At Hawes Bridge turn right up Natland Lane.

9 Just before Crowpark Bridge, pass through a small gate on the left and turn right (south) down the clearly defined towpath of the dried-out canal, past Larkrigg Spring wood **G**, and continue over several stiles to Sedgwick.

10 From the aqueduct **H** at Sedgwick, walk down steps into the village, cross the road and walk down the road signposted Hincaster. At the junction with the road from Force Bridge, continue to the left and cross the bridge over the A591. Turn right into the lay-by among trees just beyond the bridge.

11 Cross the gap stile in the stone wall at the bottom of the lay-by and walk down the centre of the oak avenue **J** all the way to the stile at the end of the park. Cross the stile on to the A6 and cross this road for Levens Hall car park, or turn right over the bridge to the start.

drained in 1955) allowed small, coastal ships from Glasson Dock to reach the canal basin in Kendal.

A DESERTED BRIDGE

One of the most attractive sections of this walk is through Larkrigg Spring G, a small wood where the canal bed has become part of the floor of the wood. The path then emerges into a huge field and in the very middle stands a solitary ivy- and hawthorn-clad bridge, a relic of the busy waterway.

On the outskirts of Sedgwick the canal has again been colonised by trees. The towpath continues over a stone aqueduct H in the centre of the village from which 36 steps lead down to the main street.

Sedgwick Manor, a gothic-style mansion, is now converted into apartments. It was rebuilt by William Wakefield, the owner of the Sedgwick gunpowder mill, in 1866. It was here that his daughter Mary gave her first public performance as a singer on the tennis court, in 1885. She founded the Mary Wakefield Festival, now the Wakefield Choral Competition, which is a biennial event in Kendal.

The route continues to a back entrance into Levens Park. From here it is a delightful walk through one of England's finest avenues of oaks I to Levens Bridge and Levens Hall. The park and avenue were laid out in the late 17th century by Monsieur Guillaume Beaumont who had been gardener to James II. The attraction on this side of the park is not the deer but the pretty, brown-faced Bagot goats which feature on the Bagot coat of arms. They are the descendants of the goats which Richard I brought back from the Crusades, or so the story goes. He stayed a while with the Bagot

JOHN WATNEY

▲ *The River Kent runs through a deep cut between the trees of Levens Deer Park, where grazing sheep and black fallow deer live happily together. (inset) Further upstream, a suspension footbridge joins the leafy river banks.*

JOHN WATNEY

A riverside footpath below a small stone bridge, Hawes Bridge, which is a popular place with salmon fishermen.

family at Levens Hall and made them a present of a pair of goats, from which has grown the prolific and friendly herd which now eat everything in the park that is not fenced off from them.

On Sunday afternoons and bank holidays the smell of oil and sounds of hissing and whistling steam pervade the air as the Hall's collection of engines, tractors, a wagon and a car are in steam. The Hall and Gardens are closed on Fridays, Saturdays and Sunday mornings, and close at 5pm every afternoon.

◀Dark-faced and white-bodied, the Bagot goats roam the ground of Levens Hall, still the home of the Bagot family. The working model steam collection and full-sized engines (below) are displayed at the house. Once crossing the busy waterway of the Lancaster-Kendal canal, this bridge (below left) now stands in a field with only a small path running beneath it.

A History of Danger

Gunpowder was first manufactured in Cumbria in 1764 and the last mill closed in 1937. Before 1764 gunpowder was made mainly in the south for military purposes. As the mining industry grew the need for a coarser gunpowder from a local source became desperate.

It was John Wakefield (1738–1811), a local Quaker, who had the idea of harnessing the power of the swift waters of the River Kent to grind gunpowder for mining use. In 1790, he built a mill at Force Bridge, the remains of which can be seen from the bank of the river.

Gunpowder in its simplest form is a mixture of saltpetre, sulphur and charcoal, ground to a powder. In this state it ignites rapidly and, if confined, its rapid combustion acts as an explosive. In the 18th century no material was allowed near a gunpowder mill that might cause an explosion; however, accidents were common and gunpowder milling was a very hazardous industry.

◀ Ruins of Sedgwick gunpowder mill. Gunpowder was milled for blasting or for propelling missiles for about 600 years until the mid-19th century when nitroglycerine was discovered.

MANSELL COLLECTION

THE RICHES OF RAVENGLASS

3

CUMBRIA

ALL PHOTOS JOHN WATNEY

FACT FILE

Ravenglass, off the A595, on the south-west Cumbrian coast

Outdoor Leisure Map 6, grid reference NY 086964

miles 0 1 2 3 4 5 6 7 8 9 10 miles
kms 0 1 2 3 4 5 6 7 8 9 10 11 12 13 14 15 kms

Allow 2 hours

Woodland tracks and field paths, some gentle climbs. Stout shoes or boots recommended as there could be mud on forest tracks after rain. Care should be taken on the main road

P Large car park, well signed, in Ravenglass

T British Rail Cumbrian Coast Line between Lancaster, Barrow and Carlisle (except Sundays)

WC Refreshments and toilets at Ravenglass and Eskdale Railway Station. Ratty Arms pub and Pennington Arms Hotel in Ravenglass serve bar meals. Refreshments available at Muncaster Castle (open April-October, closed Fridays)

To a steam railway, a castle known to Shakespeare's Fool and a working watermill

On Lakeland's coast, to the west of the Cumbrian mountains, the village of Ravenglass Ⓐ is situated on an estuary of three small rivers: the Esk, the Mite and the Irt. This easy walk, which begins in the village, takes in a water-powered corn mill, a narrow-gauge steam railway, a Roman bath house and a castle which is still a family home.

The Romans established an important naval base at Ravenglass in the 2nd century, as it was a safe port from which to service the military zone around Hadrian's Wall. The little harbour was also popular with 18th-century smugglers who brought contraband tobacco and French brandy to shore in small boats away from the prying eyes of the excisemen. The main village street leads up from a shingle beach and is paved with smooth sea-rounded pebbles. With long rows of cottages, it still has the atmosphere of a Cumbrian fishing village.

FULL STEAM AHEAD

Affectionately called 'Little Ratt', the Ravenglass and Eskdale Railway Ⓔ is a 15-inch (38-cm) narrow-gauge steam railway. It was originally built to a 3-feet (91-cm) gauge to carry granite from quarries at the top of Eskdale to the port of Ravenglass, but in 1915 it was modified to the smaller gauge and rebuilt as a tourist line. Having escaped closure in the 1960s, thanks to the efforts of the late Lord Wakefield and an enthusiastic preservation society, it now has 12 superb, small-scale but powerful steam and diesel locomotives. With its trains of open carriages it is one of the most popular and best-loved narrow-gauge railways in the British Isles.

◀ Muncaster Castle contains many art treasures owned by the Pennington family. 'Little Ratty' (below) transports visitors along Eskdale.

The Roman bath house in Ravenglass, one of many such sites in Cumbria.

THE WALK

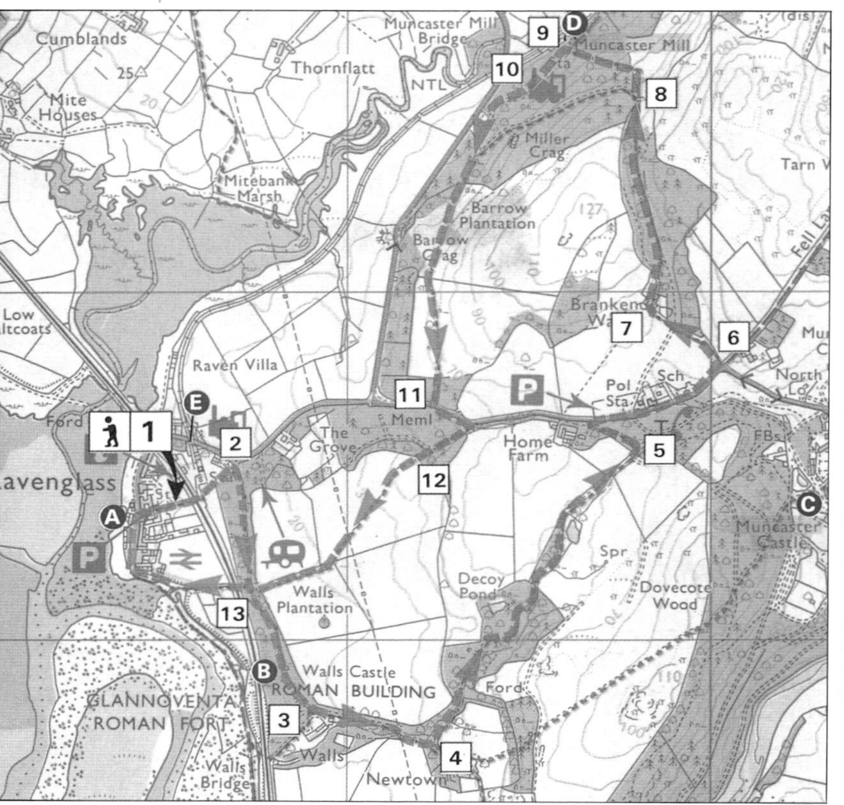

RAVENGLASS – MUNCASTER MILL

The walk begins in the public car park at Ravenglass **A**, *alongside Ravenglass Station.*

1 Leave the car park and cross the footbridge over the railway, passing the children's playground with the terminus of the Ravenglass and Eskdale narrow-gauge railway **E** on the left. Follow the path to its junction with a narrow lane by the main road.

2 Turn right along the lane for about 1/2 mile (800 metres), passing the Roman bath house **B**.

3 At the fork take the track left signposted to Newtown Cottage.

4 Take the next track left, at a footpath sign. This leads past the remains of recently felled woods to a pond (often dry) on the right. Keep ahead through a gate towards the woods.

5 Where the track meets a gate that leads into the grounds of Muncaster Castle **C** do not go through but turn left, following the track as it winds past farm buildings to the main road. Turn right and walk past the Muncaster Castle car park and entrance.

6 Where the main road bends right, go through the gate on the left, along the signposted track towards Branken Farm.

7 Go through the gate into the farmyard and go right at the bridleway sign. Continue through a wooded valley behind the farm.

8 Where the track bends left, look for a narrower track to the immediate right of a holly tree. It is the middle of a total of three paths forming a three-pronged way, which bears steeply downhill to Muncaster Mill **D**.

9 Where the tracks cross, turn right to the mill entrance. Return the same way, but do not climb back up the hill left – keep directly ahead on the signposted permissive track back to Ravenglass.

10 Follow this track as it climbs uphill, giving fine coastal views including a glimpse of Sellafield power station. Keep ahead to the main road

11 Turn left on the main road for about 100 yards (80 metres) before crossing to a stile (signposted) on the right and a path that bears diagonally right through the woods.

12 Where the path emerges from the woods, keep in the same direction down a long, sloping field to a gate near the bottom corner of the field ahead. Turn right along the field edge to a gate into the lane.

13 Almost opposite, an enclosed path leads to a tunnel under the railway towards the sea and the end of the village main street for the car park.

Muncaster Mill has been restored to full working order; the grain is stone-ground.

Along the route there is the only surviving part of the Roman fort of Glannoventa. Strategically important to the Romans, it was developed at Ravenglass to protect the harbour. The Roman bath house **B** is a remarkable building and is the tallest surviving free-standing Roman building in Britain, with substantial masonry and well-built walls and doorways, which rise to 12 feet (3.6 metres) in height. It is now in the care of English Heritage and is open to the public.

Less than 1 mile (1.6 km) from Ravenglass is Muncaster Castle **C**. Altered in the 1860s to become a country house, it is set in magnificent gardens, celebrated for superb rhododendrons and azaleas. Among the paintings in the house is a portrait of Tom Skelton, one of Shakespeare's actors, and a jester, who probably gave his name to 'tomfoolery'.

WATER POWER

Muncaster Mill **D**, on the banks of the River Mite, is a beautifully restored traditional Cumbrian water mill, probably dating from the 18th century, but rebuilt in Victorian times. The machinery can be viewed in action, as can the water courses, millwheel and the drying floor. The mill is open daily, except Saturday, from April to October. A variety of wholemeal flours and semolinas are on sale.

The Vale of Eden

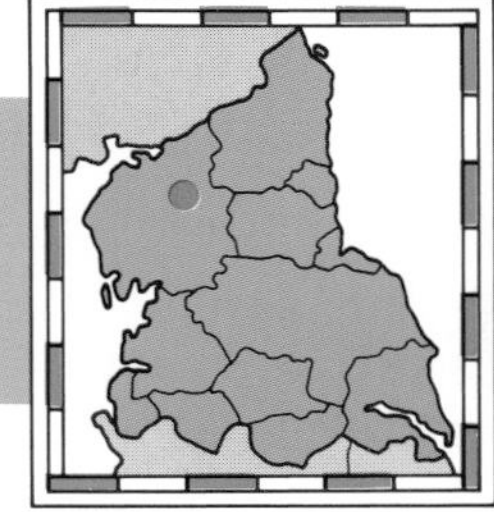

4

CUMBRIA

JOHN WATNEY. INSET: HEATHER ANGEL

▲ *Lacy's Caves are carved into a Gothic-style folly. Butterbur (inset) thrives on damp ground by riversides.*

Through unspoilt countryside in north-east Cumbria

FACT FILE

- Little Salkeld, 9 miles (14.4 km) north-east of Penrith
- Pathfinder 577 (NY 43/53), grid reference NY 565361
- miles 0 1 2 3 4 5 6 7 8 9 10 miles / kms 0 1 2 3 4 5 6 7 8 9 10 11 12 13 14 15 kms
- Allow 3 1/2 hours
- Can be muddy in parts. Only 1 mile (1.6 km) of uphill road. Slippery by Lacy's Caves
- P Around the village green in Little Salkeld
- Shepherds Inn, Langwathby, 1 mile (1.6 km); Prospect Hill Hotel, Black Bull Inn and The Crown Inn at Kirkoswald, 3 miles (4.8 km). Penrith has hotels, cafés, toilets

Far away from the tourist areas of Cumbria, yet with clear views of the Lakeland mountains and the highest part of the Pennines, lies the Vale of Eden. This walk leads through the valley and encompasses two quiet sandstone villages, the River Eden, industrial archaeology, a rich man's folly and the second largest Megalithic site in Britain after Stonehenge.

Little Salkeld Ⓐ, at the start of the walk, is a red sandstone village with a large 19th-century Hall, largely concealed behind ivy-clad walls. More accessible is the restored 19th-century working water mill Ⓖ, which can be visited by appointment with the miller. There is a mill shop selling organic flour, porridge oats and oatmeal.

To the west of the village runs the Settle-Carlisle railway, opened in 1876. Part of the route is very close to the line, so there is a chance of a close-up view of a steam train on its way to or from Carlisle. The walk goes through what were the sidings Ⓑ of the Longmeg gypsum and anhydrite mine. The first material is used in plaster of Paris and plasterboard, the latter for making sulphuric acid. There are rusting notices, which will interest railway buffs. Today, photographers cross the silent sidings to take close-up shots of the steam trains.

The path now follows the track of a long-gone mine tramway perched on a ledge with a steep, wooded drop, down to sheep meadows on one side and a rock escarpment rising on the other. To the left the railway curves away towards Carlisle over a spectacular viaduct **C**, 137 feet (41 metres) long and 60 feet (18 metres) high, which spans a curved broad reach of the Eden and took four years to build.

PAST POWER

On the right of the path the rock face is shored up with ancient timbers and there are vestiges of inclined planes and unloading bays for the tubs which came down from the mines to the tramway in the last century: this is industrial archaeology at its best. From the river comes the sound of roaring water where it bubbles over a wide, rock-strewn weir. Half-submerged in the water are the ruins of a substantial turbine house, which produced electricity to augment the steam power used in the mines and plaster works above. On the opposite bank stands the empty building of the old corn mill.

ALL PHOTOS JOHN WATNEY

▲ *In the 19th century, many wealthy landowners like Colonel Lacy built 'ruins' and follies on their estates, principally to entertain their guests.*

▶ *The old cornmill building overlooks the racing waters of the Little Gill's natural weir. The Carlisle-Settle railway has crossed the River Eden on the spectacular stone arched viaduct (below) for over 100 years.*

The way continues to follow the river bank, which is colourful with Himalayan balsam and butterbur, and passes between the beeches and oaks of Cave Wood. Then five caves appear, cut into a sandstone cliff, which drops sheer to the water. These were hewn out of the soft rock for the eccentric Colonel Samuel Lacy, the owner of Salkeld Hall, in about 1867, and they are still named after him. Some say Lacy's Caves **D** were wine cellars, others that he employed a man to live in them as a hermit. It is easy to imagine the Colonel using the caves as a romantic venue for summer parties. Each gives a different view of the river and all are interconnecting.

GLASSONBY

The walk continues through a young plantation of Norway spruce, yew, cypress and sycamore, and then across pastures sloping down to the river to meet the Glassonby-Kirkoswald road. Bird life along the riverside includes pheasants, rooks and lapwings. There is a steep walk up to Glassonby village **E** but to

THE WALK

LITTLE SALKELD – GLASSONBY

The walk begins at the triangular village green in Little Salkeld **A** .

1 Park on one of the side roads off the green and take the right fork past the end wall of Salkeld Hall into a farm road, which is by a large sign saying 'PRIVATE ROAD No unauthorised vehicles Public Footpath Only'.

2 Walk the full length of the private road beside the Settle-Carlisle railway line until stopped by a road barrier and sign 'PRIVATE Long Meg'.

3 Turn sharp left down a track signposted 'Lacy's Caves and Daleraven', beside an electricity sub-station. Follow the path between wire fences across the site of the railway sidings **B** and on into the trees opposite the railway viaduct **C** . Continue past the remains of mine workings, which are on your right. The weir is on your left.

4 Shortly after passing the weir look for a very small, overgrown path to the remains of the turbine house beside the weir. But avoid this path when the ground is wet and slippery and take particular care if you have young children with you. Follow the original path to continue through Cave Wood alongside the river to Lacy's Caves **D** .

5 At the point where the path climbs up over a cliff, take the narrow path to the left to the first of Lacy's Caves. Avoid walking round the outside of the entrances as the narrow sandstone ledge is very slippery when damp, and the water is deep and fast-flowing below.

6 Retrace your steps to the main path. Climb over the top of the cliff and then walk down through the plantation and across the pastures to the gate on to the road by Daleraven Bridge.

7 On the road, turn right and walk up the 3/4-mile (1,200-metre) road to Glassonby **E** .

8 In Glassonby, keep to the right round the tiny village green and follow the signposted road to Little Salkeld, passing the forge on your right (the blacksmith does not work full time). Shortly after Glassonby Hall (a large house with an enclosed courtyard) continue past another house for 200 yards (180 metres), then turn right by a stone barn up a track to Addingham Church of St Michael.

9 At the rear of the churchyard follow the footpath out of the gate and over a field. Go over a farm road and then cross fields keeping the wall on your right. You will pass through two gates, finally arriving in the field where Long Meg and her Daughters **F** stand.

10 Leave the standing stones and continue on the same path, which here becomes a lane. Turn left at the first junction, then carry on to the crossroads on the Glassonby-Little Salkeld road. Turn right for a short, downhill walk back to the village green. The public house marked on the map is no longer licensed. The Mill **G** is at the southern end of the village by the bridge that crosses Little Gill.

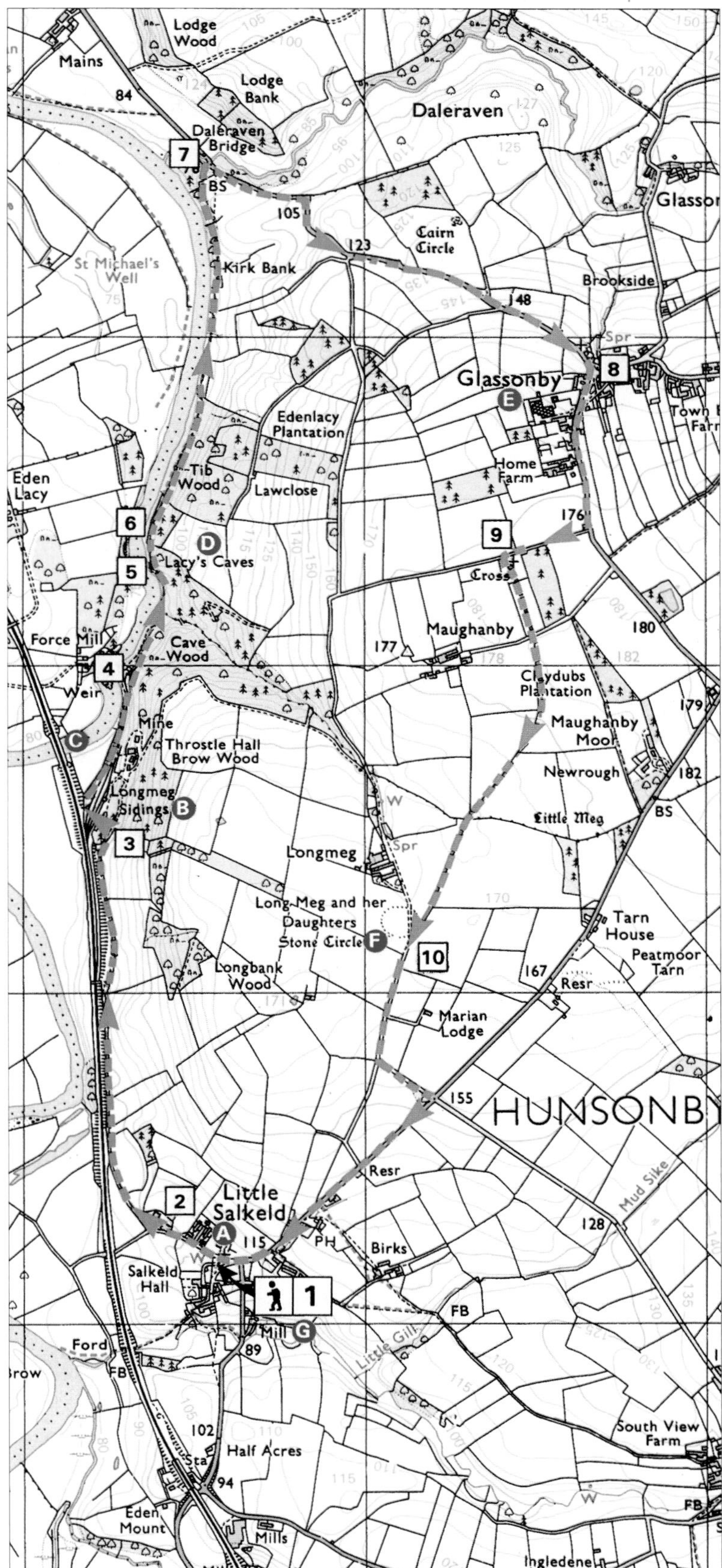

◀ *The Celtic cross in the churchyard of St Michael's. The Viking tombstone in the porch is about 1,000 years old.*

▲ *The 18th-century watermill in Little Salkeld is restored to working order. It contains a shop and an exhibition.*

compensate for the steepness there are superb views of the Pennines, particularly Cross Fell, the highest point in the chain.

Glassonby itself is small and sleepy, and has a working smithy. The church nearby is Addingham Church of St Michael. Part of the church dates back to 1200, but its origins go back to Saxon times. Addingham was an Anglo-Saxon settlement and the church takes its name from the village founded on the banks of the River Eden in the 7th century. The village was washed away in 1350 when the river unexpectedly changed its course.

In the porch of the church, there is a Viking 'hog back' tombstone, two parts of a 14th-century cross shaft and two coffin lids decorated with early Christian emblems. These were recovered from the river in 1913. Standing in the churchyard is a well-preserved hammerhead cross, with four holes and carved scrolls, thought to be Anglo-Saxon. The path through the churchyard goes to Long Meg and her Daughters Ⓕ.

STONE LEGEND

Colonel Lacy wanted these standing stones cut up and made into milestones, but when his workmen started on the job a great storm blew up. In alarm, the workmen fled, believing the storm to be a sign that the Druids were angry at the desecration of their temple.

The walk back to Little Salkeld is rewarded by panoramic views. To the left, there is Cross Fell, Knock, Dufton and Murton Pikes; the Howgills lie ahead and on the right are the Lakeland mountain peaks.

Long Meg and her Daughters

Long Meg and her Daughters, built about 1750 BC, is a younger site than Stonehenge. Like the more famous Stone Age circle, it is presumed to have been used as an astronomical tool.

Astronomical observations at a stone circle were probably used as a calendar to record seasonal changes (particularly important for crop growing), times for festivals or mystic rights, and the transit and phases of the moon. Such stone circles – abundant in Cumbria – are popularly associated with Druids. They were thought of as magicians and held great power.

Long Meg is the second largest neolithic circle in the country. Standing outside the circle, Meg is a single, 15-foot (4.5-metre) megalith. The name possibly derives from a well-known woman who lived in London in the time of Henry VIII. She was extraordinarily tall and her name, Meg, was applied to anything which was unusually tall. Another theory is that Meg could be a corruption of the ancient word 'magus' or magician.

When people attempt to count the stones the totals reached are mysteriously inconsistent, usually between 63 and 69. The legend is that if anyone gets the figure right either the stones will come to life as the daughters of the witch Meg, or the devil will appear.

Viewed from the centre of the circle, at the winter solstice, the sun sets directly behind Long Meg.

John Peel Country

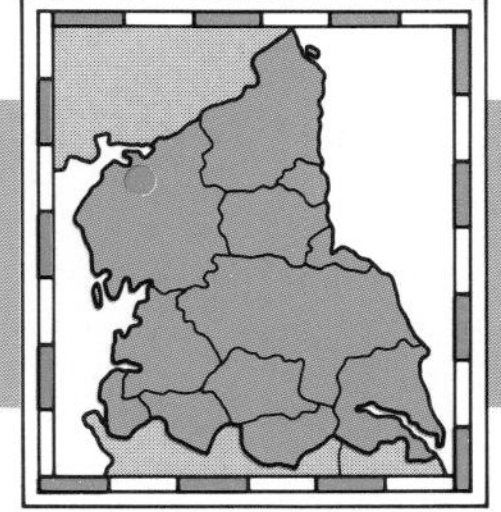

A riverside walk below the northern fells of Cumbria

The walk begins in Hesket Newmarket Ⓐ, which was a flourishing market town in the 18th century and the home of many of the miners who worked in the surrounding hills. The 1750 cross, an open-sided building, still stands and a bear-baiting ring can be traced beside it. In its heyday there were 16 pubs; now it is a quiet village with just one remaining pub called the Old Crown Ⓑ.

CATS AND CURRIES

This is a hostelry of great character with its own brewery producing four beers, its own lending library, innumerable cats and a restaurant specializing in Indian dishes.

FACT FILE

- Hesket Newmarket, 16 miles (25 km) south-west of Carlisle
- OS Pathfinders 576 (NY 24/34) and 576 (NY 23/33), grid reference NY 340386
- miles 0 1 2 3 4 5 6 7 8 9 10 miles / kms 0 1 2 3 4 5 6 7 8 9 10 11 12 13 14 15 kms
- Allow 4 hours
- Muddy and slippery in the wet
- P Free in Hesket Newmarket
- Pub and village shop in Hesket Newmarket. Pub, village shop, tearooms, hotel and restaurant in Caldbeck
- WC

JOHN WATNEY INSET ROGER THOMAS/AQUILA

▲*The thick woodland around tumbling Whelpo Beck, above the Howk gorge, makes the perfect habitat for the treecreeper (inset), whose hooked claws help it climb tree trunks.*

The route leads along a high path through woods above the River Caldew until it joins the Cald Beck at Waters Meet Ⓒ. Waters Meet is a tranquil spot in the sylvan setting of a small wood made almost an island by the Caldew's meandering curves and the Cald Beck that flows into it. During dry spells this stretch of river disappears down swilly holes and that is the time to leave the path and walk beside the river bed to search for fossils in the limestone. In winter and after heavy rain it is a river of tumbling white water.

At this point on the route you can either follow the bridlepath through the heavily forested Parson's Park, or follow the beck itself. Both ways lead to Caldbeck village Ⓓ

In tne village, of immediate interest is John Peel's large, ornate

THE WALK

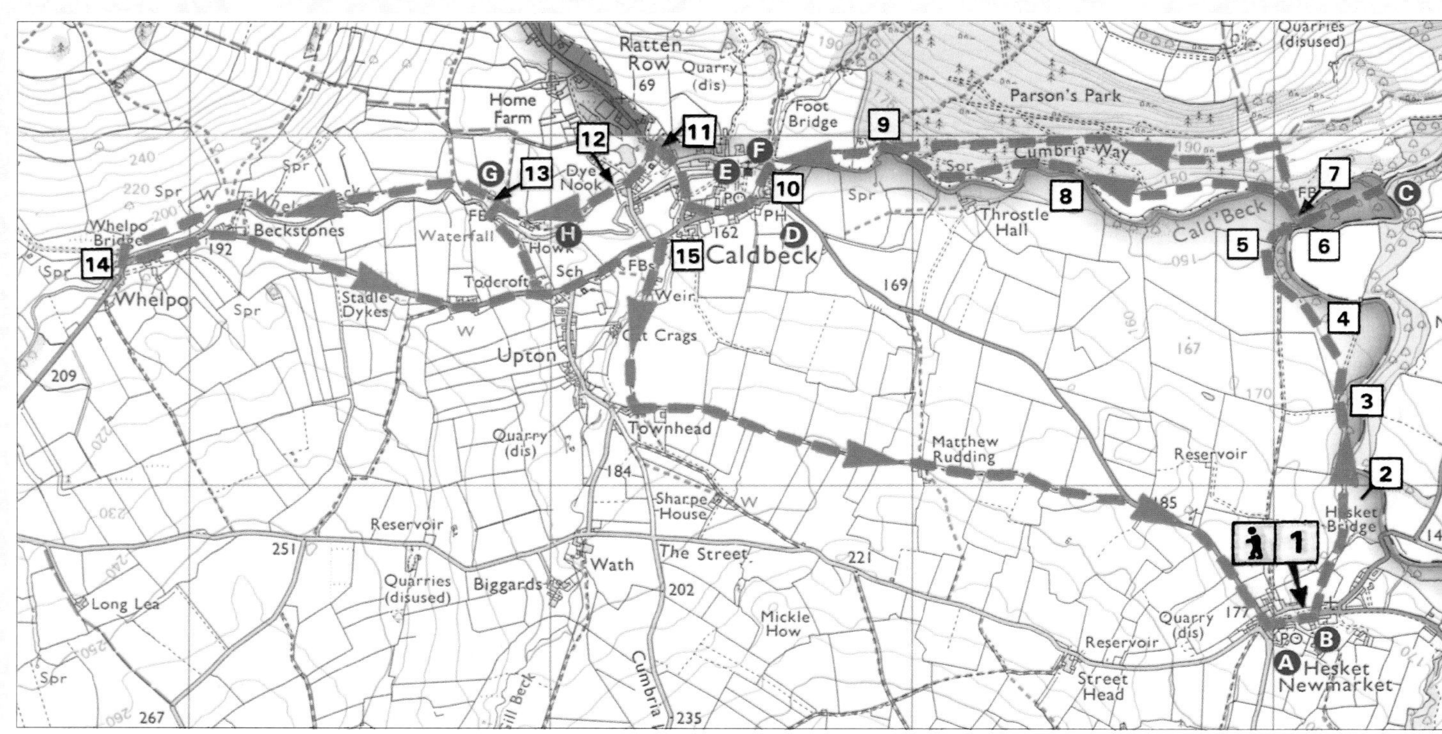

HESKET NEWMARKET – CALDBECK

The walk starts at the kissing gate across the village green opposite the Old Crown **B** *in Hesket Newmarket* **A**.

1 Follow a tiny beck (stream) along the edge of a field to a wooden footbridge and another kissing gate. (There are many of these along the walk to Caldbeck.)

2 Through the gate, turn right and go along a short slope, through another gate, then turn sharp left alongside a barbed wire fence at the top of a steep slope and down to the beck. The narrow path continues north between trees, through several gates and alongside first the beck, then the Caldew River. When the slope eases go down to walk along the flat ground beside the river until the way is blocked by a limestone escarpment butting out into the river.

3 Go through a gate into a field. Make for the corner of wire fencing ahead, then strike off diagonally across the field to the left aiming for a couple of isolated trees on high ground. Ignore the bridge straight ahead.

4 At the two trees bear a little to the right past a white painted post, go through another gate into trees. Follow the path down nine stone steps, along a path through trees, then through a gate and out into an open field.

5 Walk down the right hand curve of a grass ridge to a gate and stile on the edge of a wood. The Cald Beck flows on one side of the ridge, the Caldew on the other.

6 Enter the wood over the stile and, keeping the sound of water on either side, go to the far end of it where the waters meet **C**. Return through the wood.

7 Cross the painted footbridge over the Caldew. Here there is a choice of walking up a slope directly ahead to join the forestry bridlepath to Caldbeck, or staying beside the Cald Beck (the path is like a sheep track across water meadows) until reaching a cattle bridge over the beck. Do not cross.

8 To the right look for a low point in a wire fence beside the ruins of a stone building. A splodge of red paint and the letter 'G' on a stone indicate where there is a stepping stone on either side. Go through the wire and proceed to the left along the path which runs along the bottom of a forest-clad slope, Parson's Park, to a rickety double stile then on to open ground round a drainage works.

9 Follow the service road into the village, cross the stone bridge behind the church and go through a gate into the churchyard of St Kentigern's **E**.

10 Leave by a gate on the east side into a lane to Priest's Mill **F**. Follow the road to Wigton.

11 Turn left through the car park then up to the right towards a duck pond. Turn left along the lane (before reaching the duck pond) for 50 yards (45 metres).

12 Keep straight ahead through a painted wooden door between two stone buildings. A discreet sign on the wall of the right-hand one says 'To the Howk'. Cross a yard and follow the path which leads first to the remains of the bobbin mill **G** and then up a series of steps through the Howk **H** to a footbridge above the main waterfall.

13 At this point the walk can be shortened by about 2 miles (3.2 km) by going over the bridge into the field beyond, then over a stile at the far side on to the road outside Caldbeck. If you proceed past the footbridge, however, the path continues over some stiles beside the beck all the way to Whelpo Bridge.

14 Cross Whelpo Bridge and walk along the south side of the beck, first on a grass bank, then on the road, until past the school on the outskirts of Caldbeck.

15 On the right-hand side of the road, at the start of a row of cottages, follow a sign marked 'Cumbria Way'. Continue past Steadman's Yard along a path beside a modern house to a weir and footbridge. Cross the bridge, go straight up a short steep bank to a stile into a field. On a clear day aim for High Pike, the highest point on Caldbeck Fells, or follow the power-line posts to the opposite side of the field and cross the wall. Turn left along the lane to Matthew Rudding Farm. Cross the step stile in the stone wall at the north end of the farm buildings and, keeping close to the hedges, cross four fields and three stiles to the steps in a stone wall by the Caldbeck-Hesket Newmarket road. Turn right to return to village.

◀*The bridleway through Parson's Park in Caldbeck where John Peel would once have ridden.*

ALL PHOTOS JOHN WATNEY

▲*Below the village, the Cald Beck is broad and tranquil. Above, it is a swirling torrent.*

gravestone in the graveyard of St Kentigern's Church. The church is dedicated to the saint who visited Caldbeck in 553 on hearing that the fells people were heathens. He is remembered by St Mungo's Holy Well, from which water is still fetched for the font.

RESTORATION

The church dates back to the early 12th century. It has been continuously altered and enlarged over the intervening centuries, the last restoration being as late as 1933.

Nearby stands Priest's Mill (F), which was built in 1702 by the rector of Caldbeck and last used as a crushing and saw mill.

It now contains a restaurant, small mining museum, gift shop, antiquarian bookshop, woodwork shop and photographic gallery. The waterwheel has been renovated and on fine days it is a favourite spot for watching the river and the gently turning wheel.

At the opposite end of the village is the Old Smith, now a craft and coffee shop, and across the road is Mr Strong the local clogmaker. The Third World Shop may come as a surprise in this fell village.

ODDFELLOWS

The Oddfellows Arms is the last of 17 public houses that were open in Caldbeck in the middle of the 19th century. It is named after the Oddfellows subscription movement which gave out benefits to widows, orphans and the sick. Also in the village are the remains of Lords wheat mill, built in 1671, and the old brewery of 1810. But of all the many sites in this diverse village the most interesting are the bobbin mill (G) and the Howk (H).

The Howk is a limestone ravine with the Cald Beck (now called Whelpo Beck) running through it. Beside the Howk stands the substantial remains of a bobbin mill built in 1857. It claimed to have the largest

◀*St Kentigern's in Caldbeck is a solid Norman church. In its graveyard you will find John Peel's ornate headstone. He died in the churchyard in 1854, at the age of 78, after falling from his horse.*

John Peel

'D'ye ken John Peel
With his coat so grey'

Everybody knows the song, but what of the man?

He was a rumbustious fellow who is not remembered as ever having done anything but hunt and drink. As a young man he eloped to Gretna Green with Mary White, but the girl's family forgave them and the mother endowed her daughter with land which brought an income of about £500 a year. It was enough for John Peel to be able to indulge full time in his passion for hunting. In the field he mixed with men well above his rank, but he was accepted as being the best huntsman.

He became a local legend in his lifetime and was credited with setting out at dawn and riding 50-60 miles (80-96 km) a day. Hunting in those parts was on foot and mounted, and his livery was a grey coat, as in the song. The song was written by a local woollen manufacturer, John Woodcock Graves. John Peel was born in Caldbeck, died in 1854 at the age of 78 after falling off his horse, and is buried in Caldbeck churchyard.

MARY EVANS PICTURE LIBRARY

A legend in his own lifetime, John Peel's foxhunting exploits live on in song.

waterwheel in the country. This measured 42 feet (12.6 metres) in diameter. The wood used by the mill was local birch and elder, dried for one year in what is called the 'drying shed'. The bobbin mill closed in 1920 and the giant iron wheel was melted down to be used in the manufacture of armaments for the war effort in 1940.

'Howk' is Norse for 'to scoop out' and, over the centuries, that is what Whelpo Beck has done, creating a gorge with several waterfalls and two phenomena — Fairy Kettle and Fairy Kirk. Kettle is a big rock cauldron whose sides are polished by the swirling waters. Kirk is a cavern where the falls can be heard but not seen. Steps up the gorge provide viewing platforms of the Howk.

Mature trees growing out of its rock faces form a near-impenetrable canopy in summer, so the waters of the beck are best seen in winter when in spate and the branches are bare. However, in summer, shafts of sunlight penetrate the dense canopy, spotlighting the falls and pools, and giving the place a sense of mystery.

WATER MEADOWS

Above the Howk the beck flows level again through water meadows between bowing willows to Whelpo Bridge. The walk back to Hesket Newmarket passes the site of Factory House, once a woollen mill. It was here that the coarse grey cloth for John Peel's coat would have been woven. The last leg of the walk is along a lane and across some fields to the road into Hesket Newmarket. There are expansive views south to the Caldbeck Fells and, to the north, overviews of Caldbeck village.

►*The remains of the bobbin mill, which once boasted the largest waterwheel in the country. The wheel was melted down to make armaments during World War II.*

▲***The Priests' Mill was built in 1702 as a saw mill and crusher. It is now a museum, gallery and shop.***

Gills and Valleys

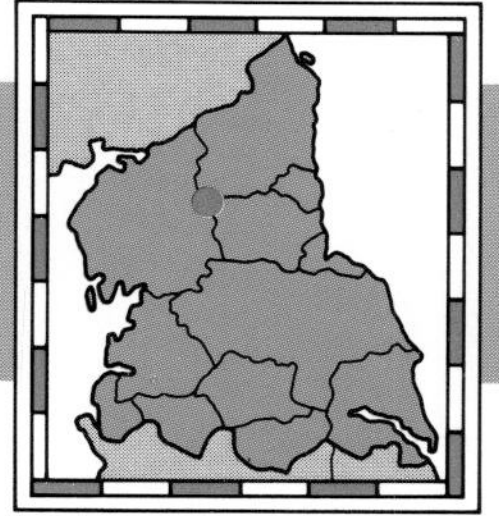

6

By woods and streams through the South Tyne valley

Alston is the highest market town in England, situated amidst the sweeping landscapes of the North Pennines. With magnificent views over the South Tyne valley towards the highest Pennine fells, the walk passes 18th-century hill farms which are still in use, ancient drystone walls and fields grazed by hardy sheep. The route crosses a delightful wooded gill, or ravine, and returns along a section of the Pennine Way. In summer, there is a wealth of interesting flora and upland birds.

ALMSHOUSES

From the top of Alston's main street, beside the Methodist chapel Ⓐ, a narrow lane leads out of the town between the drystone walls and a few outlying cottages. The path reaches Fairhill Cottages Ⓑ, which were once almshouses, and then follows a track to Fairhill Farm Ⓒ, a typical old farmhouse with ventilation slits in the side of the barn instead of windows.

Annat Walls Ⓔ is another farm settlement, with 18th-century buildings and spring water pouring into a stone well beside the track. The fields here are grazed by sheep and cut during summer for hay and silage. There are good views of the Penrith road as it climbs up towards Hartside Pass, which is frequently snowbound in winter.

Alston's history is dominated by the development of mining and agriculture in the area. For centuries

SIMON FRASER

▼*The 18th-century farm buildings at Annat Walls were built from locally quarried limestone.*

DEREK FORSS. INSET: LAURIE CAMPBELL/NHPA

▲*The market town of Alston is the highest in England. The flowers and leaves of the coltsfoot plant (inset) have medicinal properties and have often been used in expectorants.*

FACT FILE

- Alston, Cumbria, 22 miles (35 km) south-west of Hexham
- Pathfinder 569 (NY 64/74), grid reference NY 719462
- miles 0 1 2 3 4 5 6 7 8 9 10 miles / kms 0 1 2 3 4 5 6 7 8 9 10 11 12 13 14 15 kms
- Allow 2 hours
- Good paths, country lanes and fields. Wear trainers or walking boots. Muddy in places in wet weather
- P On Alston main street
- T Bus services from Hexham, Haltwhistle and Penrith
- Cafés and pubs in Alston, including the Country Kitchen and the Blue Bell Inn

THE WALK

ALSTON – BLEAGATE

The walk starts from the Methodist chapel (A) in Alston.

1 Follow the lane between the Swan's Head and the Chapel until it divides behind the Chapel. Take the left fork of the path and follow it to a small road at Fairhill Cottages (B). Turn left, then right and take the rough track to Fairhill Farm (C). Pass a disused quarry (D) on the left and continue to Annat Walls (E).

2 Continue uphill, go through a gate, and follow a fence on your right alongside a conifer plantation, then cross a stile beside an oak tree. Cross another field with a wall on the right, then go through an opening in wall ahead and follow a fence on your right. Descend into the wooded valley of Nattrass Gill (F) and cross the footbridge over a tributary stream. Climb up to a stile leading into fields again. Follow a line of trees to your left across the field ahead to another stile with High Nest (G) about 100 yards (90 metres) away to the right. At the next stile there is a wooden signpost pointing back to Alston.

3 Turn left, then right, onto a lane which continues for about ½ mile (800 metres) to Bleagate (H). Cross the farmyard in Bleagate to a gate and stile, and turn right along the Pennine Way. The path now continues through fields and stiles on a well-trodden grassy path to Nattrass Gill, where there is a footbridge (J). Continue past a plantation on the left. Follow the path above the River South Tyne with newly planted trees on the steep bank beside the path, and mature woodland further on towards Alston. On the edge of Alston, pass the youth hostel (K). Join a road above the main A689, then climb steps leading to a narrow lane between the hospital and the school. Follow the lane up the hill to the chapel to return to the starting point.

the mining communities produced lead and silver, and many of the miners had smallholdings. It was a hard life, and all that remains of those days are old spoil heaps, mineworkings and ruined farmsteads. The farming life of Alston Moor continues today, with a quarter of the working population involved in agriculture. Some of the old farmsteads have been converted into residential or holiday cottages, but there are still some small, private coal mines in the area.

Where the path descends into Nattrass Gill (F) there is a lush growth of primroses, cowslips, ferns and mosses. Waterfalls tumble through the sheltered woods of rowan, hazel, sycamore and birch. In the spring there are strong-smelling ramsons (wild garlic), wood sorrel, pansies, lady's mantle, wild raspberries and strawberries and a variety of ferns.

The footpath climbs steeply out of the gill and back into open country, across fields with clumps of rushes, tiny tormentil flowers and white eyebright. Some of the loveliest yet commonest sights of spring are the tumbling flight displays of the lapwings with their distinctive 'pee-wit' call.

The route soon joins a quiet lane leading to Bleagate (H). The name of this old farming settlement can be found in 13th-century documents. It means, aptly, 'pasturage for cattle'. There is a good view over the valley to the Black Burn. To the south stands the plateau of Cross Fell, the highest point in the Pennines at 2,930 feet (893 metres).

SIMON FRASER

◄*Natrass Gill tumbles and cascades its way past a cluster of marsh marigolds, which thrive near fresh water.*

WASDALE HEAD

7

CUMBRIA

DEREK FORSS, INSET:HELLIO & VAN INGEN/NHPA

Through mountains high above the deepest lake in England

Wastwater is England's deepest lake – at 258 feet (79 metres) below the surface, its bed is actually lower than sea level. Driving towards Wasdale Head, the first view is across the lake to the great crumbling scree slopes, 2,000 feet (610 metres) high, which have been slowly slipping into the lake since a glacier undercut the fellside thousands of years ago. Fingers of the ice-age glacier also scoured out the deep grooves of Mosedale, Styhead and Lingmell, closing in at Wasdale Head.

On this short, low-level walk around Wasdale Head, you are surrounded by the dramatic crags of Yewbarrow, Great Gable, Kirk Fell, and Scafell Pike, which at 3,206 feet (980 metres) is the highest point in England. After walking a little distance towards the lake, you join a path parallel to the Mosedale beck, at the foot of Yewbarrow. The grassy slopes provide sparse grazing for Herdwick sheep.

FORMIDABLE CRAGS

There are good views Ⓐ of Great Gable and Kirk Fell, formed from a great dome of Borrowdale volcanic rock. Great Gable is an imposing, pyramid-shaped mountain. At 2,949 feet (900 metres) high it stands apart from the surrounding ranges and its formidable crags have made it one of the most rewarding peaks for climbers. The rock faces below the summit include named ascents such as Eagle's Nest Ridge, Napes Needle, the Innominate Crack and Kern Knotts Crack.

A left turn between dry stone walls takes you into Mosedale. After a short climb uphill, there is a good view back to Wasdale Head, showing the pattern of fields Ⓑ bounded by drystone walls. A liberal scattering of boulders from the nearby fells was an invitation to the medieval settlers to use them for buildings and to enclose fields.

The fields' patterns are a clue to

◀*Great Gable is a pyramid-shaped mountain that rises 2,949 feet (900 metres) above Wastwater. Teal (above), which are typical 'dabbling' ducks, are the smallest in Britain.*

FACT FILE

- Head of Wastwater, south-west area of Lake District
- Outdoor Leisure Map 6, grid reference NY 186085
- miles 0 1 2 3 4 5 6 7 8 9 10 miles / kms 0 1 2 3 4 5 6 7 8 9 10 11 12 13 14 15 kms
- Allow up to 2 hours
- Grassy and stony paths and tracks. Take care on damp slopes by waterfalls. Strong shoes are recommended
- P By Green at end of road
- Public bar at Wasdale Head Hotel; food at weekends
- WC Near Wasdale Head Hotel

THE WALK

WASDALE HEAD

The walk begins from the Green at the end of the Wasdale Head road.

1 From the Green, walk back along the road towards the lake.

2 Cross the little bridge — 'Down in the Dale Bridge' — then turn right, and go through the kissing gate in the fence on the right. Walk forward along a grassy path which runs above the Mosedale Beck, with views Ⓐ of Great Gable. Continue along this path, which becomes stonier, crossing two little becks and going through a gate, until you are opposite the Wasdale Head Hotel on the far bank.

3 Continue left along the broad stony track between drystone walls. Pass through a kissing gate, next to a five-barred gate (marked 'Waterfalls and Ritson's Force'). Climb upwards along the grassy path following the wall on the right. From here, there are good views back to the medieval field patterns Ⓑ of Wasdale Head.

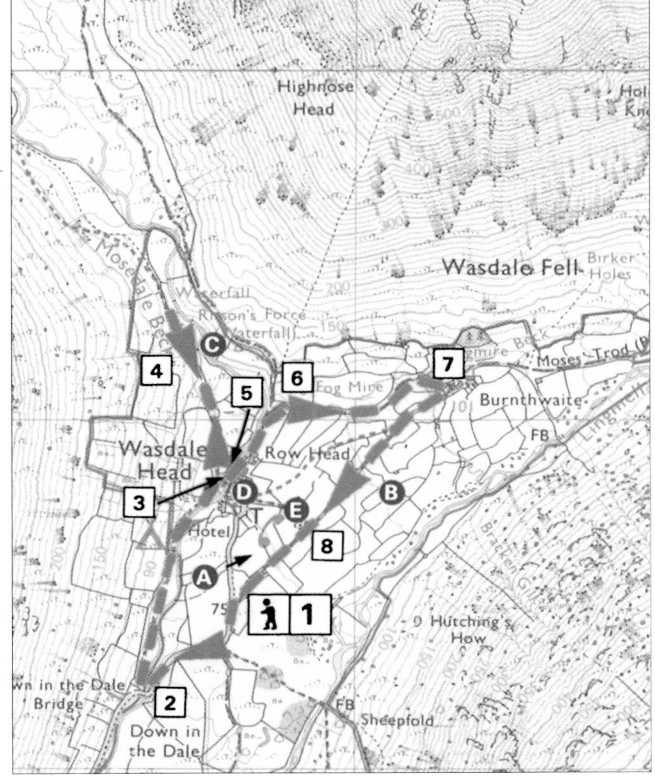

4 By a solitary larch tree turn right, passing between the end of a stone wall and a wire fence. Cross the stony, mossy area through the copse of larch trees, down to Ritson's Force Ⓒ, a series of small waterfalls on the Mosedale Beck (care needed above the rocky gorge). Return by the same route to Stage 3 opposite the Hotel.

5 Cross Row Bridge Ⓓ, a small packhorse bridge, and turn left to walk along the broad, stony track beside the beck. The path crosses a little beck and begins to rise.

6 Watch for a smaller path forking to the right. Take this path following another beck (Fogmire Beck). Cross the beck (right) by a plank bridge. Cross and recross the beck by three more bridges, and go through a wooden gate. Cross another bridge, and walk on between stone walls towards the farm buildings.

7 Follow the barn wall to the left, then go through the gate on the right into the farmyard of Burnthwaite. Walk through the farmyard, join the track, and turn right to leave Burnthwaite. Continue along the track until you come to the tiny church Ⓔ among the yew trees.

8 From the church, rejoin the track and continue on to the start.

◀*Around the area where 'Down in the Dale Bridge' crosses Mosedale Beck a glacier once rolled, leaving flat land.*

BOTH PHOTOS JOHN WATNEY

their age. Early field systems were small and irregular in shape, and the boundary walls meandered around natural obstacles. These old walls often trace corners in a curve instead of a right angle. After the Enclosure Acts, maps were marked out geometrically, making it easier to calculate the area to be allotted to each person. The walls were then built with great precision.

Further uphill, there is a copse of larch trees and the way leads down to a grassy bank by the Mosedale Beck, where there are a series of little waterfalls known as Ritson's Force Ⓒ. The damp and shady copse is spongy with cushions of moss in every shade of green, and including sphagnum moss, well-known to gardeners. The trees and the tumbled stones of an old building are covered with lichens, in a mixture of bright and muted colours. Lichens are very responsive to air quality, and thrive here where the air is extremely pure.

Returning downhill, you now cross the picturesque packhorse bridge Ⓓ, to follow the beck towards Burnthwaite Farm. (The farm is National Trust property.) The track from Burnthwaite leads past the church Ⓔ, amongst yew trees.

Climbing first became popular at the beginning of this century and memorials at the church record the names of those who died in mountaineering accidents at that time. On Great Gable, a bronze plaque near the summit marks the gift of the mountain to the National Trust. It was given by the Fell and Rock Climbing Club as a memorial to climbers who died in World War I.

▶*Ritson's Force, on Mosedale Beck, is a series of small, but nonetheless impressive, waterfalls.*

THE BORROWDALE VALLEY

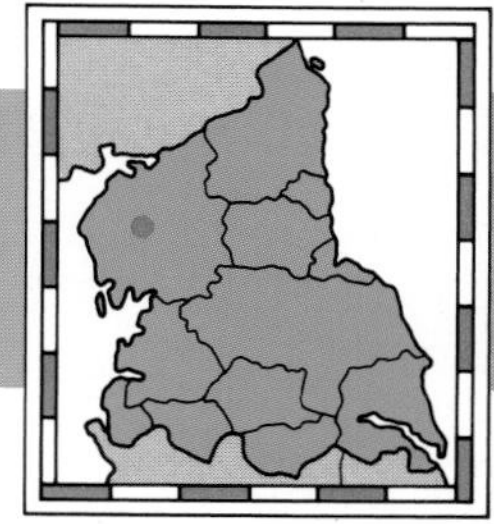

8

CUMBRIA

JOHN WATNEY. INSET: GEOFFREY KINNS/BIOFOTOS

▲*From Lingy End, there is a fine view of the 1,640-foot (500-metre) Eagle Crag. The now-rare red squirrel (left) can be spotted in Borrowdale's woods. Before the 1940s, they were common in Britain.*

A walk with breathtaking views, through wetland

The Borrowdale valley has long enjoyed a reputation as an area of exceptional beauty. Early this century the novelist Hugh Walpole (1884 – 1941) chose it as the setting for much of his four-part Lake District saga *The Herries Chronicle*.

ROGUE HERRIES

Walpole owned Brackenburn, a house overlooking Derwentwater, which is located at Manesty, 3 miles (4.8 km) from Rosthwaite. He lived there from 1923 until his death in 1941. Rogue Herries, the character after whom the first volume of his saga was named, was supposed to have lived for many years with his gypsy wife in a house described as 'on a little hill above the village of Rosthwaite' and 'on the farther side of the little bridge'. The site of this fictional house is thought to have been near where Hazel Bank Hotel **B** now stands. The couple died in the house on the day that their daughter Judith was born.

JOHN GREEN HOUSE

In the second book, *Judith Paris*, Walpole describes the house at Watendlath **D**, where his heroine lived, as 'L-shaped with a double porch... the Tarn in front of the stone wall of the house'. The farmhouse was called 'John Green House'. Today, an L-shaped house beside the Tarn bears a plaque identifying it as the 'Home of Judith Paris'. Its name is now Fold Head Farm. Of the village and its surroundings, he

FACT FILE

- Rosthwaite, 6 miles (9.6 km) south of Keswick on B5289
- Outdoor Leisure map 4 grid reference NY257148

miles 0 1 2 3 4 5 6 7 8 9 10 miles
kms 0 1 2 3 4 5 6 7 8 9 10 11 12 13 14 15 kms

- Allow 3½ to 4 hours
- One steep ascent and one very steep descent (steps at both). Some wet areas. Walking boots or strong shoes recommended
- P At start of walk on edge of Rosthwaite village (arrive early, as usually full by mid-morning)
- T Bus service from Keswick
- Hotels with public bars in Rosthwaite. Small café in Watendlath
- WC At the car park and at Watendlath

THE WALK

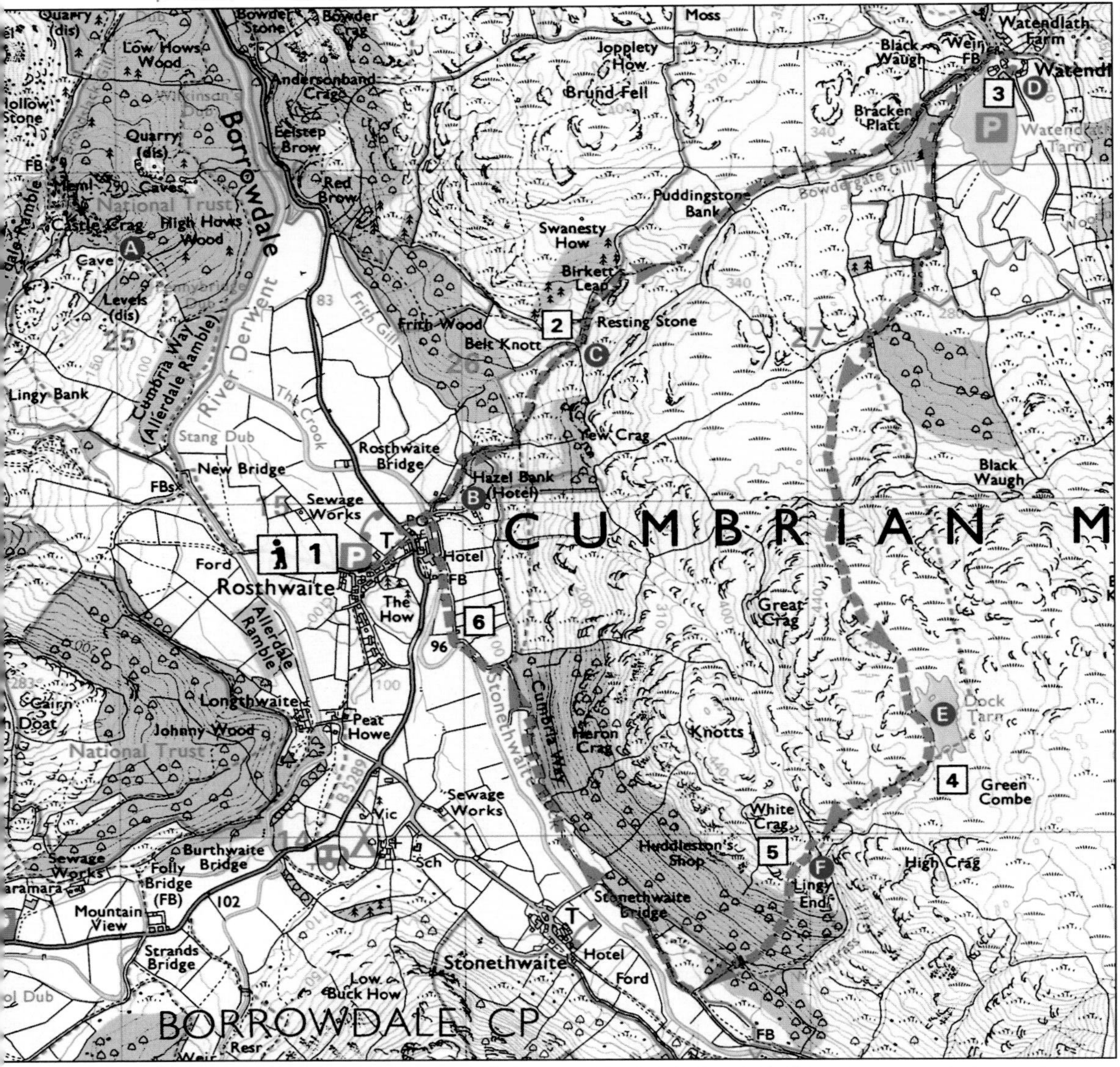

ROSTHWAITE – WATENDLATH

The walk begins at the small car park on the edge of Rosthwaite village.

1 From the car park Castle Crag **A** is visible across the fields. Walk back to the main road, turn left along the road and then right along a metalled track signposted 'Public bridleway Stonethwaite and Watendlath'. Cross the bridge. Where the track divides turn left. Follow a narrow path uphill, passing Hazel Bank Hotel **B** on the right. Pass through a private wood, where the path is raised. After going through a gate the path turns right, then left at a stream on the right, climbing uphill all the time. The land on either side is more open with scattered trees. Pause at the gate — a good viewpoint **C** from which to admire the prospect of the 'Jaws of Borrowdale' to the south-west. The path continues to climb over open ground to another gate.

2 As you pass through the gate, there is a stream on the left. In about

writes: 'Watendlath was an exceedingly remote little valley lying among the higher hills above Borrowdale... with some twenty dwellings, a dark tarn and Watendlath Beck'. It has not changed much since those days.

CASTLE CRAG

In the 1940s, a recluse by the name of Millican Dalton lived in a cavern that was carved out of the hillside by slate quarries in the side of Castle Crag **A**. This is visible from the start of the walk. The remains of the stronghold from which the hill takes its name were destroyed during the slate-quarrying operations.

Stonethwaite Beck, which passes under the bridge at Rosthwaite on its way to join the River Derwent, is typical of many Cumbrian streams. Its crystal-clear waters flow over a bed made up of green and blue stones, against which wild brown trout can often be seen.

From the hillside high above Rosthwaite there are fine views of the 'Jaws of Borrowdale' (the point where the valley splits), with Rosthwaite village below. Beyond are the cottages near the end of the Stonethwaite valley, which branches off to the left. The main valley runs

► *The Hazel Bank Hotel stands near the site where Rogue Herries' house was in Hugh Walpole's* **The Herries Chronicle.**

JOHN WATNEY

300 yards (275 metres) the stream crosses under and continues on the right of the path, which now becomes steep and rocky. Ignore a gate in the wall on the left labelled 'Bowderstone and Keswick' and continue up and through another gate. After this the ground levels out. After about 200 yards (180 metres), with plantations on the right, the path starts to descend and Watendlath and its tarn come into view. At the bottom of the hill go through a gate and keep straight on across the bridge into the hamlet D.

3 Leave Watendlath, crossing the bridge again and going through the gate, but this time do not follow the path back up the hill. Instead fork left and take the walled track beside Watendlath Tarn, passing through two more gates and crossing a small stream that runs across the track. Cross another stream flowing across the path and bear right, following an arrow, keeping the stream and a wall on your right. The path is rocky and goes uphill to a gate, beyond which is a notice asking walkers to keep left in order to preserve an area of wetland. There are good views back to Watendlath. At this point the path is marked by posts with blue or green tops. Where several paths join keep left, following the marker posts, over some stepping stones. After a stretch of gentle uphill climb the ground becomes fairly level but can be wet. Cross a stream that runs across the path and go through a gate. The next section of the path climbs very steeply uphill by a series of steps then levels out again, with rocks on the right, and leads to Dock Tarn E.

4 At the far end of Dock Tarn the path swings away to the right and soon begins to lose height, with a stream on the left. After a short while, Eagle Crag and the Langstrath valley can be seen in front and to the left. Climb a stile over a wall and views of Greenup Gill appear on the left. Pause at a small ruined stone building F to admire the view.

5 The path now falls very steeply downhill, by means of a series of stone steps, through woodland into the Stonethwaite valley. Soon after a stream is seen on the left, cross a stile. Not far beyond this the woodland ends and the ground slopes away gently. There is a wall to the right. When a broad track is reached, turn right onto it, with a wall on the left. Go through a gate and keep straight on (avoiding a left turn through another gate, across a bridge and into Stonethwaite). The track here is part of the Cumbria Way long-distance footpath. It passes fields and woods, and there are often high stone walls on both sides. Nearly ½ mile (800 metres) from Stonethwaite, after many twists and turns, the path meets a bend in Stonethwaite Beck, where it forms a broad pool.

6 After another turn or two, the path straightens out and follows the beck back to the junction of paths below Hazel Bank Hotel. Turn left across the bridge, left along the road, then right just before the post office to return to the car park.

JOHN WATNEY

► *The fence across the corner of Watendlath Tarn prevents the trout escaping or the pike from entering.*

on past Longthwaite to Seatoller and the Honister Pass. The rugged heights of Glaramara stand between the Stonethwaite and Seatoller valleys, which were carved by glaciers during the last ice age. One of the gates across the path is a good place from which to admire this view C and also to study two insectivorous plants, butterwort and round-leaved sundew, both of which grow in wet ground here. The soil in which they grow is lacking in nutrients, so they supplement their diet by attracting insects which become stuck to their leaves and are then digested.

LONELY SPOT

By the section of the path marked by green-topped posts, before it climbs steeply uphill to Dock Tarn, the wet ground supports hundreds of plants of bog myrtle. If you pinch its leaves you will be rewarded with an unforgettable tangy fragrance. In springtime, the shrub is covered with little orange catkins.

Dock Tarn E is a lonely spot. In late spring and summer, sandpipers and pied wagtails can often be seen standing on rocks at the water's edge, and later on in the year the tarn is visited by ducks, including a number of goosanders.

JOHN WATNEY

▲*The section of path that leads from Watendlath to Dock Tarn is steep and strewn with rocks and boulders.*

From the stone ruin **F**, a superb view presents itself. To the left, Greenup Gill runs down from Greenup Edge over which a track passes to Grasmere. Between the valleys of Greenup and Langstrath is the mighty form of Eagle Crag. Langstrath Beck and valley, with the Langdales beyond, as well as Stonethwaite valley beneath the slopes of Glaramara, are also visible here. To the right is Seatoller, on Honister Pass, with the remains of its slate quarries. There is an old tramway appearing as a straight line up the hillside. Farther right you can see the peaks of Fleetwith Pike, Hay Stacks and Hindscarth.

Borrowdale's Ferns

Like most of Britain's flowering plants, ferns have roots to draw nutrients from the soil, a system of veins through which these nutrients are distributed and leafy shoots of new growth. However, they do not produce fruits or flowers. Instead, they use spores as their means of reproduction.

The damp climate around Borrowdale — the village of Seathwaite, 2 miles (3.2 km) away, is the wettest inhabited place in England with 126 inches (320 cm) of rain a year — suits ferns perfectly. At least twelve different species can be seen on the walk.

Maidenhair spleenwort grows in Rosthwaite on a wall by the car park and also on the sides of the bridge. Wall rue and rustyback can be seen on the garden walls of the house beside Rosthwaite post office. Golden-scaled male fern is abundant high on the hillside behind Hazel Bank Hotel and grows beside the path in many places, as do hard fern and lemon-scented fern.

Perhaps the best part of the walk for ferns is the enclosed track by Watendlath Tarn and beyond — polypody, male fern, lady fern, lemon-scented fern and beech fern all grow here. There is also bracken, which is widespread on the route, as well as the delicate parsley fern, so typical of Lakeland rocks and walls.

HEATHER ANGEL

The parsley fern, seen here in its spring growth, originates from the Alps and the far North. It is often used in garden rockeries.

C & H.S PELLANT

◀*The woodland high above the path from Stonethwaite to Rosthwaite is comprised mostly of sessile oak.*

SILKEN THREADS

The woods clothing the steep slopes above the Stonethwaite valley are predominantly of sessile oak. Early in the year the young leaves are reduced to lacework by 'looper' caterpillars, which hang from the branches on long silken threads. Holly, downy birch and rowan are all common on the walk. At Watendlath Tarn ash trees grow beside the path. These are hollow and have been pollarded — the branches cut back to the top of the trunk to provide a plentiful supply of useful sticks for making sheep hurdles and so on. Hazels by the track between Stonethwaite and Rosthwaite are coppiced — cut down to ground level — for the same purpose. Borrowdale is famous for its ancient yew trees, and some good examples can be seen at Yew Crag, which is to be found above Hazel Bank Hotel, and near the bridge at Rosthwaite.

Please note: Walk 2, page 13
Levens Bridge – Sedgwick walk (Elizabethan Topiary Garden): readers who wish to visit the gunpowder mill in Stage 6 of the walk must first gain permission from the warden of the Caravan Club site in Low Park Wood. The lane is not a right-of-way; it is important to keep to the specified route and not wander through the site.

A Quiet Port

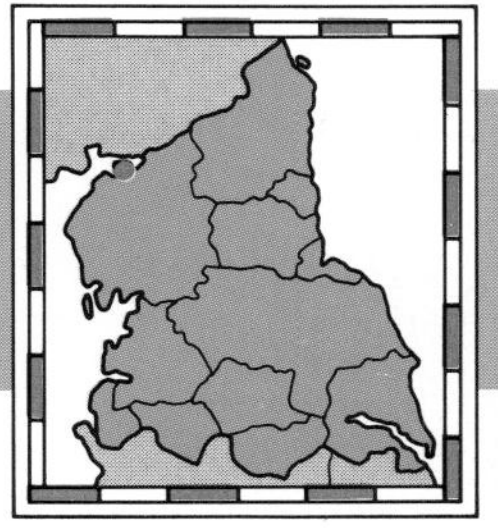

JOHN WATNEY. INSET: L CAMPBELL/NHPA

Wildfowl and waders in an historical seaside setting

The walk starts at Port Carlisle Ⓑ, formerly called Fisher's Cross. Early in the last century, the place became a bustling port with a canal link to Carlisle. President Woodrow Wilson's mother set off for America from here. It is now a sleepy village and a site of industrial archaeology. Its deep water dock Ⓒ, built offshore, was reached by a tramway over the water. The remains of the wooden piles can be seen at low tide when it is easy to walk out to the dock, which is now overgrown and provides a pleasant island picnic site.

The Customs House and the pink sandstone blocks of the quayside are still in place, as is the stonework of the silted-up sea lock Ⓓ into the canal. The first section of canal is overgrown but still holds some water after high tides or heavy rain. The canal opened in 1823 and closed in 1853, when it was drained and a railway built along its bed. The station platform still exists opposite Solway House, an elegant creeper-covered building that was the port hotel. The main street fronting the water is lined with pleasant Georgian houses, quite unexpected in such a small village where the Post Office is situated in the bar of the Hope & Anchor Ⓐ.

The 1-mile (1.6-km) walk from here to Bowness-on-Solway Ⓕ can be made along the road, or over Bowness Marsh except when there are high tides. There are many salt marsh plants here, such as sea aster, sea lavender, thrift, sea blight, scurvy and samphire. Always beautifully green, the marsh is most colourful in early summer. Halfway along the road at the end of the marsh is a lay-by Ⓔ – a fine place from which to spot ringed plover, dunlin and occasional rarities.

ROMAN FORT

Bowness-on-Solway is largely built of sandstone and grew up around five farms, which face into the main street — two are still working. A street plan on a wall shows how the village fits into the area of the second largest Roman fort on Hadrian's

◀*The salt marshes of the Solway Firth are at their most colourful in early summer, when plants such as scurvygrass are in bloom. The pink-footed goose (right) has a musical cry.*

FACT FILE

- Port Carlisle, 12 miles (19.2 km) west of Carlisle
- Pathfinder 544 (NY 26/36), grid reference NY 240621
- miles 0 1 2 3 4 5 6 7 8 9 10 miles / kms 0 1 2 3 4 5 6 7 8 9 10 11 12 13 14 15 kms
- Allow 2½ hours
- Very easy, flat going. Wellington boots recommended in wet weather and periods of high tides
- P Opposite pub in Port Carlisle
- Hope & Anchor in Port Carlisle; Kings Arms in Bowness-on-Solway
- T Regular bus service from Carlisle to Port Carlisle and Bowness-on-Solway

THE WALK

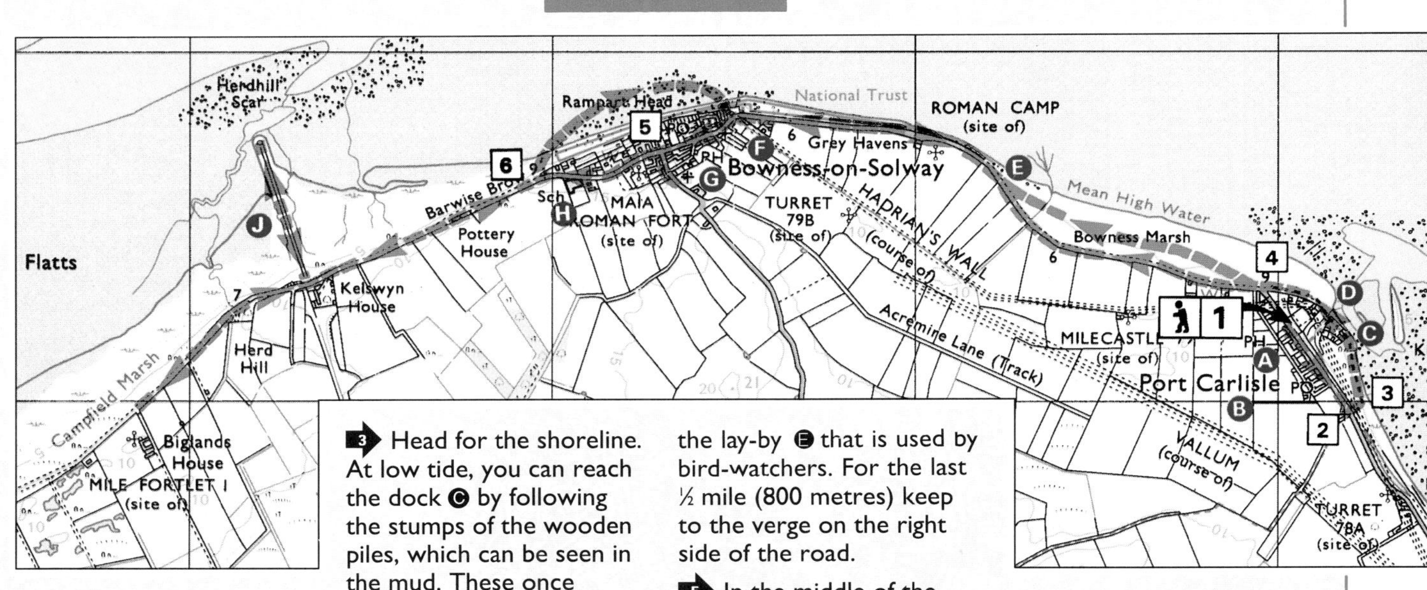

PORT CARLISLE – BOWNESS-ON-SOLWAY

Start at the car park opposite the Hope & Anchor Ⓐ in Port Carlisle Ⓑ.

1 Walk south-eastwards back through the village until just past the chapel on the right. Go through the kissing gate on the left of the road.

2 Turn left; walk for 50 yards (46 metres) to reach the last remaining section of canal, which still fills with water at high tides.

3 Head for the shoreline. At low tide, you can reach the dock Ⓒ by following the stumps of the wooden piles, which can be seen in the mud. These once supported the tramway to the dock. Continue on the grass path through three gates along the top of the old quarry. Go over a footbridge that spans the remains of the sea lock Ⓓ. Follow the path behind the bowling green and past the old Customs House onto the road to Bowness-on-Solway Ⓕ.

4 From the end of the village walk either along the road or over Bowness Marsh (according to your preference) to where it meets the road again by the lay-by Ⓔ that is used by bird-watchers. For the last ½ mile (800 metres) keep to the verge on the right side of the road.

5 In the middle of the village, take the road to the left signposted 'Kirkbride'. Continue for 200 yards (183 metres) to the church Ⓖ. Return to the signpost and turn left. Walk past the school on the left and the little Victorian school Ⓗ by the water's edge on the right, then go downhill to the start of Campfield Marsh. Turn right along the viaduct Ⓙ — at low tide you can walk to its end. Return to the road and turn right to reach a lay-by just before Biglands House. This is a good vantage point in winter to watch roosting birds at high tide. Retrace your steps back along the road, with the viaduct on your left.

6 Leave the road at the bottom of the hill just before the school. Walk along the shore below the village. Near the end of the village, climb the steps in the sea wall, then go along The Banks, a landscaped zigzag path with seats. This leads into the main street. Turn left and retrace your steps back to Port Carlisle.

Wall which, around AD 250, had a garrison of 1,000 men. Many of the buildings include parts of the Roman fort in their construction. The west wall of St Michael's Church Ⓖ, which stands on the site of a Roman temple, is a particularly fine example.

RUSTLING AND THIEVING

In the porch are two bells, stolen in 1626 from churches over the water to replace those carried off by Scots during the days of the Rievers, when rustling cattle and abducting women across the border were commonplace. The oldest artefact in the church is an 800-year-old font.

At the west end of the village, by the shore, is a small stone building with a flight of stairs on the outside to an upper storey. It was the Victorian village school Ⓗ, long since superseded by a modern, functional building. Beyond is Campfield Marsh, a 200-acre (81-hectare) RSPB reserve where more than 10,000 pink-footed geese feed in winter, together with oyster-catchers, bar-tailed godwits, curlews, dunlins, knots, grey plovers and shelducks. In summer it is host to breeding redshank and lapwing. In the middle of the marsh the truncated end of the old railway viaduct Ⓙ, which once crossed the Solway Firth, can be reached at low water. It provides a good viewing platform from which to see skua in late April and into May.

▼*Built in Victorian times, this tiny, two-storey building was once Bowness-on-Solway's schoolhouse.*

JOHN WATNEY

SANDS OF TIME

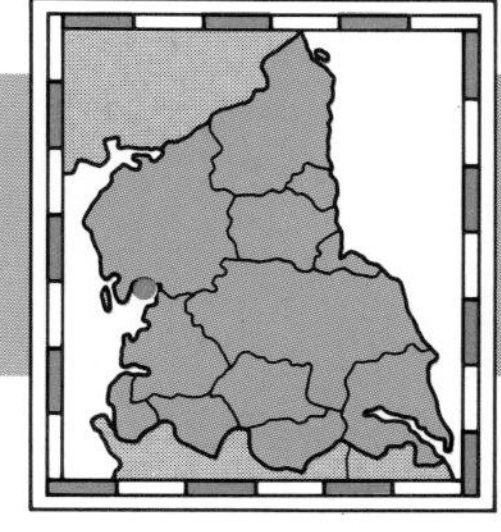

10

CUMBRIA

ED GELDARD. INSET: ANDY PURCELL/BRUCE COLEMAN LTD

A promontory with historic buildings in Morecambe Bay

Cartmel is on the southern fringes of the Lake District, between the mountains and the sea. Cartmel Racecourse, which holds meetings at spring and summer bank holidays, is the starting point for the walk. The route goes along quiet tracks and lanes, through traditional farmland and passes the entrance to the grand country house of Holker Hall Ⓑ. A grassy path leads up Hampsfield Fell Ⓒ, 727 feet (222 metres) high. The return route passes Cartmel's monastic priory Ⓕ.

Cartmel stands on a peninsula jutting into Morecambe Bay Ⓐ. The sands of the bay are notorious for the dangerous incoming tide which sweeps up in a bore, faster than a galloping horse, surrounding sand-banks and softening them into quicksands before covering them.

At low tide there is safe passage along certain routes. Before the days of rail and car there were recognized highways across the sands, saving the long journey around the bay.

FACT FILE

- Cartmel, Cumbria, 12 miles (20 km) south-west of Kendal
- Pathfinder 636 SD 37/47 grid reference SD375 786
- miles 0 1 2 3 4 5 6 7 8 9 10 miles / kms 0 1 2 3 4 5 6 7 8 9 10 11 12 13 14 15 kms
- Allow 4 hours
- Good paths and tracks. Numerous stiles. Steady ascent to Hampsfield Fell
- Train service from Lancaster to Grange-over-Sands. Ribble Bus Services
- At Cartmel Racecourse
- Cartmel: Royal Oak, King's Arms, Pig and Whistle, Larch Tree tea-rooms
- Signposted in village centre
- Holker Hall, Cark, Tel. (015395) 58328. Open April to end October, 10.30 am – 4.30 pm last admission (closed on Saturdays)

▲*Looking east across the sands of Morecambe Bay from near Grange-over-Sands. The wood tiger moth (inset) is found on heathland and downland in summer.*

SHIFTING SANDS

However, the channels and quick-sands frequently changed position, so the monks of Cartmel Priory provided a guide service for travellers. These days, the service is for the benefit of tourists. In the summer, visitors gather in the village of Cartmel before following the guide along a safe 7-mile (11-km) route across the sands to Ulverston.

This walk begins along a broad track, passing through woodland,

THE WALK

CARTMEL PRIORY

The walk starts at Cartmel Racecourse.

1 Leave the car park by the gate at the far end. Walk along the track, passing through three gates and into woodland. Leave the wood by a gate, and continue uphill to the top for views of Morecambe Bay **A**. Where the tracks fork, take the right-hand one uphill. When you reach a tarmac track, follow this down to the B5278.

2 Turn left, passing the entrance to Holker Hall **B** just down the road on the right. Where the main road bends right, take the minor road to the left, signed 'Cartmel and Newby Bridge'. At the end of the houses on the left, go through the metal gate and follow the tarmac lane uphill. Go through a gate and follow the track to a farm. There are views to Hampsfield Fell **C**.

3 At the farm, turn right

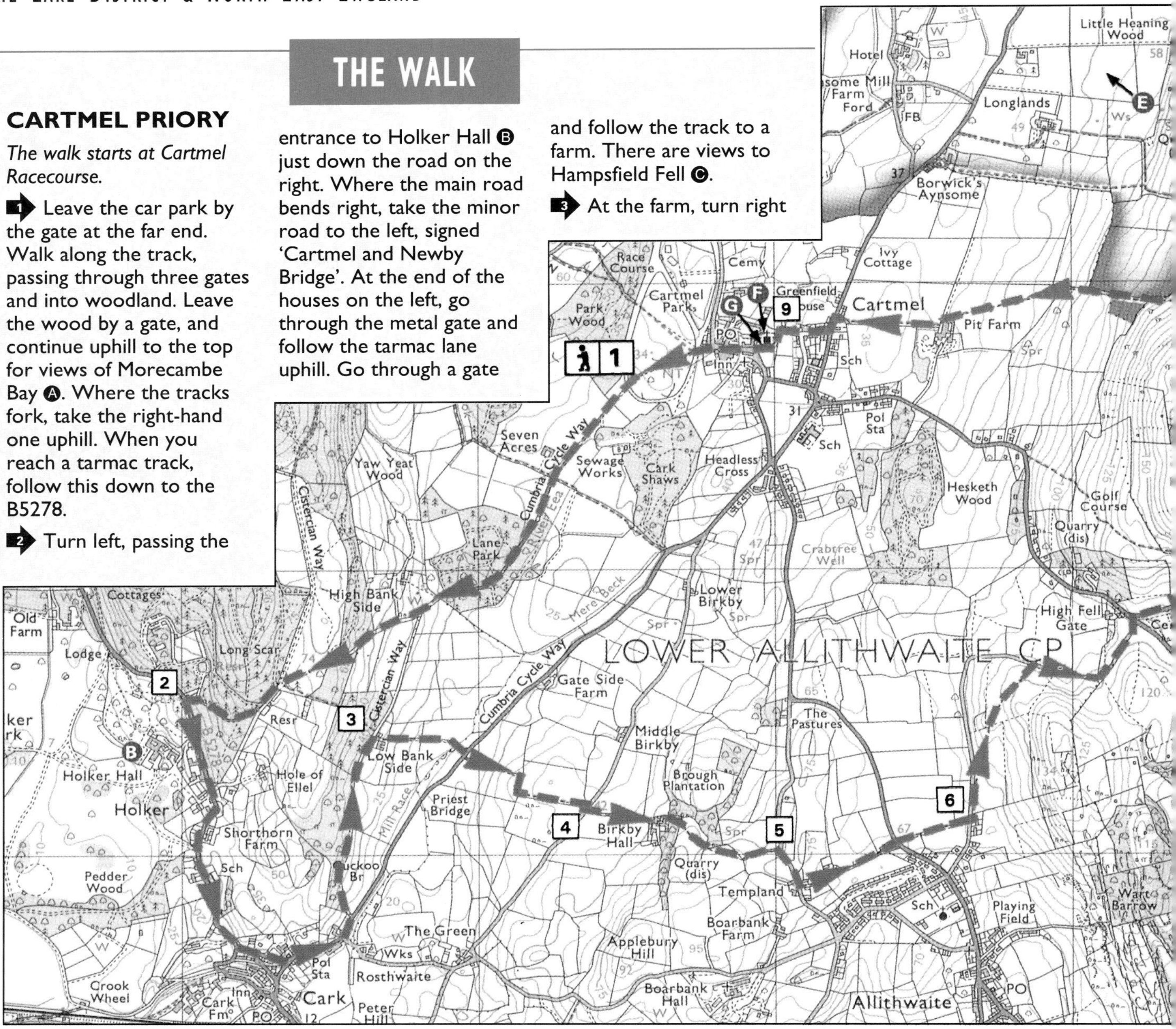

ED GELDARD

▲*The Hospice — an observation tower providing good views of Morecambe Bay and the Lakeland peaks.*

which in spring is full of bluebells. As this path rises, Morecambe Bay comes into view. In the woods alongside the downhill lane, rosebay willowherb grows tall between oak and sweet chestnut trees, and rhododendrons run wild.

The next stage of the walk passes the entrance to Holker Hall, then follows tracks through rolling farmland. Cattle graze the lower pastures, with sheep on the higher ground. Small fields bounded by stone walls support cereal crops. The paths are edged by wayside flowers beneath hazel and hawthorn trees. There are elegant foxgloves and tiny herb-robert, plus creeping purple vetch and tall grasses.

There are a number of links between Holker Hall and Cartmel Priory. Before the dissolution of the monasteries, Holker was part of the monastic estate. In return, owners of Holker Hall have made themselves responsible for carrying out restorations of the priory church.

LIMESTONE PAVEMENT

George Preston built the original house in the early 17th century. He also restored the priory church, which had been in a derelict state for fifty years. The estate passed to the Cavendish family, the Dukes of Devonshire, in 1756.

The route up Hampsfield Fell is along a grassy track. Near the

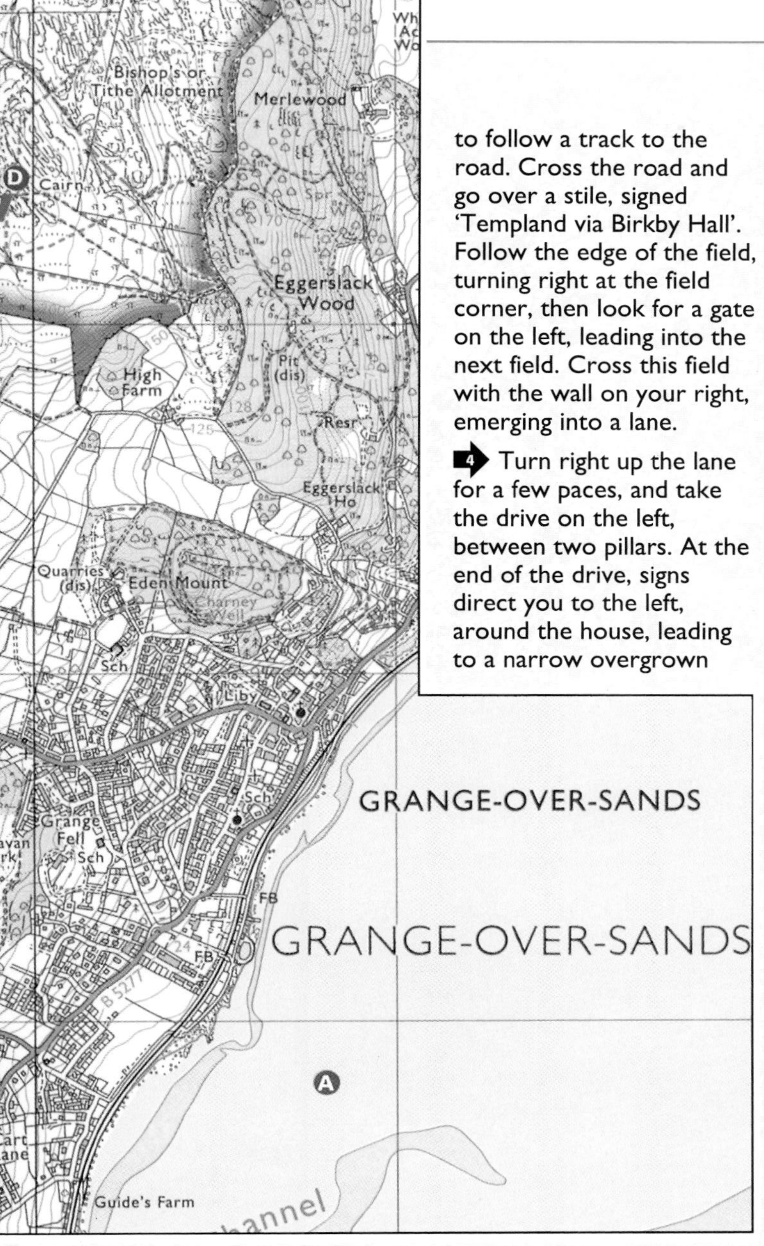

to follow a track to the road. Cross the road and go over a stile, signed 'Templand via Birkby Hall'. Follow the edge of the field, turning right at the field corner, then look for a gate on the left, leading into the next field. Cross this field with the wall on your right, emerging into a lane.

4 Turn right up the lane for a few paces, and take the drive on the left, between two pillars. At the end of the drive, signs direct you to the left, around the house, leading to a narrow overgrown path to the right of the garden. The path leads uphill through trees. Go up the steps into a field. Head straight over the field and cross a stile at the top of the bank, between the end of the wall and some trees. Cross the next field towards farm buildings, and look out for a stile on the left. Cross this, and go along the field edge to the lane.

5 Turn right and after about 100 paces turn left along a tarmac lane, signed to Grange and Lindale. At the end of this lane, cross over the road and climb the steps in the wall a few paces to the left into a field. Follow the wall on the left and squeeze through a gap to continue through the next field to another lane.

6 Turn left here. Just after reaching a public bench, cross a stile on the right. Cross the rough pasture uphill, bearing slightly right, away from the lane. Walk downhill to rejoin the lane via some steps in the wall. Turn right and follow the lane to a crossroads. Go across and take the road to the right, signposted to Grange-over-Sands.

7 After the golf club, turn left up a lane. Continue steeply uphill and, at a public footpath signposted to Ashmount Road and Charney Road to the right, turn left through a gate. Follow the grassy path to the right and continue parallel to a wall on the right. Look out for a stile in the wall near a blue metal gate. Cross the stile and carry on to a crosstracks near a telegraph pole. Here, a left turn takes you to Cartmel; but, to continue to the top of Hampsfield Fell carry straight along the grassy track, crossing two stone stiles, until you reach the stone hut and observation platform known as The Hospice (D), from where there are good views of Morecambe Bay and the Lakeland fells (E). Retrace your steps to the crosstracks.

8 Turn right and follow the path downhill. Pass through a metal gate and cross the field, bearing slightly left to pass through another gate. Cross the next field, bearing left to another gate adjacent to the farm buildings. In the next field, follow the left hand edge and, at the field corner, go through the wooden gate and along a short path which comes out on the lane. Turn left and then right into Cartmel.

9 Take the gate on the left into the grounds of Cartmel Priory (F). Leave by the main gate, entering the village. Continue through Cartmel, passing the gatehouse (G) at the market square, and continue on to the car park.

ED GELDARD

◄*Cartmel, dominated by its priory, seen on the descent from Hampsfield Fell. In the background is Cartmel Racecourse.*

summit are rocky outcrops of water-worn limestone, similar to those found in the Yorkshire Dales. This is the geological feature known as a limestone pavement.

Here are tiny, bright yellow mountain pansies, pale blue hare-bells and purple heather among the grass. Ferns find a sheltered home in rocky cracks and crevices. Dotted

ED GELDARD

▲*A footpath across rolling countryside signposted to Grange and Lindale, encountered in Stage 5 of the walk.*

around are stunted hawthorn trees, blown into odd shapes by the wind.

From the summit of Hampsfield Fell there are panoramic views in all directions. The sea and sands surround the peninsula, tipped by the promontory of Humphrey Head.

Across the sands to the east lies the hilltop of Arnside Knott, the town of Silverdale and the Pennines. Looking northwards from the stone hut and observation platform known as The Hospice **D** the Lakeland mountains **E** can be seen.

MONASTIC RUINS

On the return down the fellside, Cartmel Priory is in view all the way. The priory church was part of a monastery founded in 1188 by William Marshal, Earl of Pembroke. When the monasteries were dissolved by Henry VIII in 1536–1540, the priory was saved because it doubled as the parish church.

The rest of the monastic buildings fell into ruins, except for the gatehouse **G** which now forms an attractive entrance to the village square. It was built at about 1330 as a fortified tower for the Priory. At the Dissolution it was being used as a courthouse; from 1625 to 1790 it was used a school.

The priory's most unusual feature is the tower. For some reason, when the tower was heightened in the 15th century it was built on a diagonal, giving the church a distinctive appearance. Inside, there are intricate carvings dating from 1450 on the tip-up seats of the choir stalls. In 1618, the church was re-roofed and the screen carved. The archway of the north door has elaborate dog-toothed moulding.

In 1643, at the time of the Civil War, Roundhead soldiers billeted themselves and their horses in the church. There is a story that local men expressed their displeasure by firing muskets at the south-west door, now known as Cromwell's door. The bullet holes are still visible today and some embedded fragments of lead have been found.

Holker Hall

Holker Hall is the magnificent former ancestral home of the Prestons, the Lowthers, the Dukes of Devonshire and now the Cavendish family. The Hall was built in the early 16th century and parts of the original structure are incorporated in the Old Wing.

After an extensive fire in 1871 the seventh Duke of Devonshire repaired and extended the Hall, using timber from the estate and local stone. This is the New Wing of the Hall, which is open to the public. The workmanship of the interior woodcarving is a special feature, and the collection of furniture, paintings and silver traces back through many centuries.

There are 25 acres (10 hectares) of gardens and parkland, extending from the Hall down to the shores of Morecambe Bay. All the owners of Holker have improved the land. The Cavendish family planted many trees, including larches, monkey puzzle trees and cedars of Lebanon. One giant monkey puzzle tree was blown over in a gale in the 19th century, but was pulled upright again by a team of horses.

There is something of interest in each season. Bluebells and spring bulbs in the woods are followed by rhododendrons and azaleas. In summer there are roses, clematis, honeysuckle and herbaceous borders. In autumn, the woodland trees come into their own.

Holker Hall has gardens that extend to the shores of Morecambe Bay.

ED GELDARD

AA PICTURE LIBRARY

▶*Cartmel Priory is an imposing building that once formed part of an Augustinian monastery.*

UNDERLAID WOOD

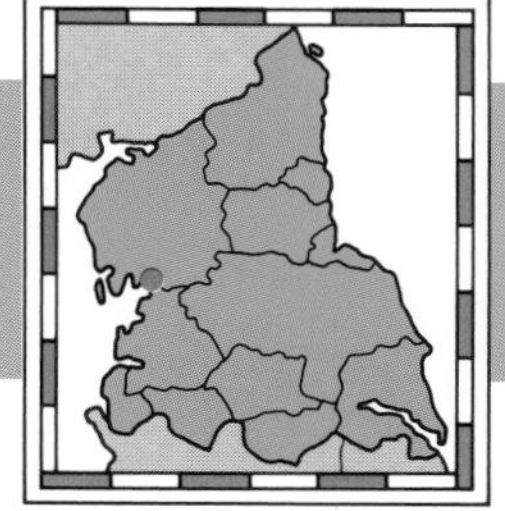

11

CUMBRIA

Through parkland and woodland to an historic church

The walk leads to Underlaid Wood, which lies in a corner of Cumbria near the Lancashire border. In spring, primroses and bluebells carpet the woodland floor before sycamore, beech, ash, hazel, rowan and wych elm come into leaf. Holly and yew grow here, too, in the weathered limestone pavement. In the wood are the Fairy Steps — narrow steps between limestone walls. The wood overshadows the village of Beetham, with its lovely old church of St Michael and All Angels. Further north stands Dallam Tower, and its park grazed by deer.

OLD PEEL TOWERS

The three peel towers (fortified houses) of Hazelslack Ⓐ, Arnside and Beetham were supposedly built by three sisters of a knight who was distantly related to Robert the Bruce. Beetham Hall, a 14th-century peel tower, was once a powerful fortress but it was besieged and captured in the Civil War by the same troops who badly damaged St Michael's Church. All the towers have now become part of farm buildings.

In Underlaid Wood Ⓑ look for yew, which has needles of a dark-green hue, spirally arranged. In autumn, its red succulent berries attract blackbirds and thrushes.

A good path through the beech, yew and hazel comes to the base of a huge limestone wall and the Fairy Steps Ⓒ. These lead to a gentle slope and an even narrower stepped fissure. From the top of each rock stairway are magnificent views of Milnthorpe Sands and the Kent Viaduct strung out across the water.

Legend has it that fairies used the steps to escape from a witches' cauldron set up in Underlaid Wood. The steps are on an old coffin route; the people of Arnside had no church until 1866, and had to carry their dead to Beetham for burial.

In Beetham is the church of St Michael and All Angels Ⓓ. It stands close to the River Bela and still has Saxon stones within its fabric, as well as Norman arches and others from the English Gothic period. In 1834 silver coins that dated from the reign of William the Conqueror

JASON SMALLEY. INSET: HANS REINHARD/BRUCE COLEMAN LTD

▲*The Fairy Steps in Underlaid Wood formed part of a burial route but can be a tight squeeze. The yew (inset) is the longest-living tree in Europe. Its poisonous fruits have hollow ends.*

FACT FILE

- Milnthorpe, 7 miles (11 km) north of Carnforth
- Pathfinders 636 (SD 37/47) and 627 (SD 48/58), grid reference SD 494814
- miles 0 1 2 3 4 5 6 7 8 9 10 miles / kms 0 1 2 3 4 5 6 7 8 9 10 11 12 13 14 15 kms
- Allow 3 hours
- Good walking all the way. Some muddy sections. Take care on limestone after rain, as it can become slippery. Walking boots are advisable
- P Public car park in Park Road
- All facilities in Milnthorpe
- WC In village square, Milnthorpe

THE WALK

MILNTHORPE – HAZELSLACK – BEETHAM

The walk starts by the car park on Park Road in Milnthorpe.

1 Turn left out of the car park and walk along Park Road in the direction of Storth. Take the second footpath on the left, signposted 'Beetham', to cross the River Bela by the double-arched footbridge. Continue ahead, through the deer park, keeping to the right of a hill, the site of an earlier manor house. Dallam Tower lies to your right. Bear right beyond the hill. Pass through a line of lime trees to a kissing gate.

2 Beyond the gate, cross the road and pass through another kissing gate, following the signpost to Haverbrack. Climb the slope ahead to a gated stile. Cross the narrow lane and walk ahead, following the signposted directions for Cockshot Lane. Walk along the tarmac lane, then continue ahead through beech woodland, where the lane continues as a track. At a three-armed signpost, follow the track left to Cockshot Lane.

3 Turn right and walk the narrow lane through deciduous woodland. Take the third signposted way on the left, for Hazelslack. (Ignore the first two, signposted 'Fairy Steps' and 'Hazelslack'.) Walk ahead over open pasture, surrounded on three sides by trees, to a gap stile in the far right corner. Take this path and after the third stile, just before a cross wall, look for a gap stile in the wall on the right. A short path leads to a stile and the road.

4 Cross the road and pass through another stile. Walk across the pasture to a gap stile between two dwellings. Beyond it lies Hazelslack Tower **A**. Turn left beyond the stile and walk to the road. Turn left and walk ahead to cross the road to a stone stile, signposted 'Fairy Steps'.

5 Walk ahead, passing through two more stepped stiles, to enter the high deer gate into Underlaid Wood **B**. Climb the wide path through the woodland. At the first limestone wall, bear to the left to climb the Fairy Steps **C**. Enjoy the view from the top. Continue upwards, following the waymark to the next wall of limestone. Bear to the right and up even narrower steps.

6 From the top follow the waymarked path. At the four-armed signpost, turn right for Slackhead. Walk the path through deciduous woodland. Turn left at the road and take the next footpath on the right, signposted 'Hale'. Walk ahead until Beetham Tower comes into view. Turn acute left to walk diagonally across the pastures to a kissing gate that gives access to a footpath, behind houses, to Beetham.

7 Where the footpath reaches the road, turn left then right to go downhill through Beetham, past a rose pergola and past St Michael and All Angels Church **D**.

8 On passing the church, turn left along the road that leads onto a track to pass a paper-making mill and then Heron Corn Mill. Climb the stile, signposted 'Milnthorpe'. Climb the second stile (a ladder stile) and walk right to a stile over a ha-ha (a ditch to keep stock in or out without spoiling the view with a fence). Cross the park to the footbridge over the Bela River. Turn right when you reach Park Road to return to the car park.

(1027-1087) were found here.

Inside, look for two badly damaged effigies. These were probably of Sir Robert Middleton of Leighton Hall and his wife, Ann, daughter of Roger Beetham. The effigies were defaced by a local mob and Cromwellian soldiers during the Civil War in the 17th century. The troops also damaged some of the priceless stained-glass windows and stabled their horses in the church.

The Dallam Tower deer park, which dates back to medieval times, is still managed for fallow deer. Built two centuries ago, a deer house, with its roof supported by pillars, provides shelter for the herd.

WHERE WORDSWORTH WROTE

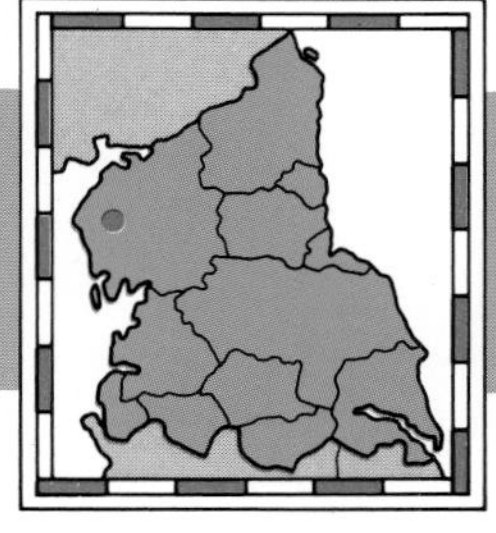

12

CUMBRIA

DEREK FORSS, INSET: NATURE PHOTOGRAPHERS LTD

◀*It is easy to see how Rydal Water, shrouded in mist, would conjure poetic imagery. Daffodils (below left), which abound near here in spring, inspired one of Wordsworth's best known works.*

Along an old coffin road between two of Wordsworth's homes

The old stone arch of Pelter Bridge provides an elegant start to the walk. Leaving the road, you come to the Church of St Mary Ⓐ on your left. The site was selected by Wordsworth and the building of the church was organized by Lady Le Fleming of Rydal Hall (the hall and grounds themselves lie just up the hill on the right), who laid the foundation stone in July 1823.

Wordsworth was unhappy with the design of the church, but the view along the nave towards the stained-glass east window above the altar is most rewarding.

FACT FILE

- Rydal, between Ambleside and Grasmere in the Lake District
- Outdoor Leisure Map 7, grid reference NY 365059

miles 0 1 2 3 4 5 6 7 8 9 10 miles
kms 0 1 2 3 4 5 6 7 8 9 10 11 12 13 14 15 kms

- Allow 3 hours
- The path can be wet and muddy after rain, but casual footwear is usually sufficient. Suitable for all seasons and all ages
- P In Rydal
- Badger Bar, Rydal
- WC White Moss Common
- Rydal Mount, Tel. (015394) 33002 for details. Dove Cottage, Tel. (015394) 35544 for details

DORA'S FIELD

Opposite the entrance to the church, an iron kissing gate leads to Dora's Field Ⓑ, which Wordsworth planted with daffodils for his favourite daughter. Though now somewhat overgrown and unkempt, it is still delightful in spring and provides a quiet haven. Wordsworth's best known poem, of course, is *Daffodils* ('I wandered lonely as a cloud...'), written in 1804.

Just up the road is Rydal Mount Ⓒ, where Wordsworth spent the last 37 years of his life. If the house is closed to visitors you can still admire the fine garden, which was designed by Wordsworth.

The next section of the walk is on the 'coffin road', along which bodies were carried in funeral procession

▼*The drawing room of Rydal Mount contains Wordsworth's own furniture, and some of his most cherished possessions and family portraits.*

JOHN WATNEY

THE WALK

RYDAL – DOVE COTTAGE

Heading north on the A591, turn sharp left, just before the first buildings of the hamlet of Rydal, over the stone arch of Pelter Bridge. Turn right, cross a cattle grid and within a 100 yards (90m) there is a car park. This is the starting point.

1 Retrace your route and turn left over Pelter Bridge. Follow the pavement and, when a pavement appears on the opposite side, cross and continue until you reach a lane on the right, signposted 'Rydal Mount'. Go up past the church Ⓐ and entrance to Dora's field Ⓑ on the left. A steep section of the lane passes Rydal Mount Ⓒ on the left. Just above this, a lane branches off left, signposted 'Public Bridleway Grasmere'.

2 Follow this lane (the 'coffin road') through two wooden gates before emerging from between the stone walls onto an open fellside. Continue on the track, passing through a stone wall via a wooden gate and then a gap in the next wall (no gate). Keep on past a rectangular block of stone (the Coffin Rest Stone Ⓓ) on your right then through a wooden gate. The track now splits. Take the lower path, dipping down slightly, then rising up to follow the stone wall on your left. The lane dips again to cross a small stream. Soon, you pass a small, wooden gate and an overgrown lane to the left. On your right is Brockstone House.

3 Continue along the coffin road, which crosses a beck then becomes a narrow, surfaced road. Once past White Moss Pond Ⓔ on the right, the road begins to descend steeply to a junction.

4 Bear right down the lane for a few hundred paces to reach Dove Cottage Ⓕ. Retrace your steps to the junction and turn right. Follow the road towards Rydal Water,

from Ambleside to be buried in consecrated ground at Grasmere. Magnificent trees, particularly oaks, grace the earlier part of the way.

GRAVE BUSINESS

Rydal Water sparkles down below to the left, and to the right an open, bracken-covered fellside sweeps up to a high planting of Scots pine. Further on, a loaf-shaped block of stone by the wall on the right provides a welcome seat with a splendid view. It was once used for a very different purpose; this is the Coffin Rest Stone Ⓓ. The pallbearers customarily took regular liquid refreshment and by this point were usually in need of a sobering rest.

Soon, you enter a wood, where a mighty oak leans through a gap in the stone wall on the left. Among the healthy trees are the white, skeletal trunks of once magnificent elms which have succumbed to Dutch Elm disease. The ground now rises steeply to the right; steep scree tumbles from the rocky buttresses of Nab Scar. Ravens nest here, and only a few years ago a would-be egg thief fell to his death.

When the track splits, take the lower path. The upper path is a false line leading along the top of the retaining wall of the Victorian aqueduct from Thirlmere to Manchester, and there is a dangerous drop.

WITCH TREE

The tree-lined path leads down to Brockstone House. Just beyond an overgrown lane on the left is a thorn tree growing out of an ash. This is an example of a 'witch tree', revered by the Celts as magical because it

BILL BIRKETT

◀*The lovely Pelter Bridge, a single-arched, stone structure spanning the sparkling River Rothay, is a feature at the start of the walk.*

joining the A591 main road just by White Moss Common G.

5 Bear left through the large car park to emerge at its main entrance. Cross the main road and go through a break in the wall, where steps lead down to the flat area by the River Rothay.

6 Bear right on the track (the river lies directly in front) and cross the footbridge over the river. Continue straight on through the woods until the track begins to steepen and then emerges through a kissing gate onto a lane and open fellside.

7 Take the path opposite, which leads up across the flanks of the fell, until you reach a larger path, which runs horizontally along the fellside (Loughrigg Terrace). Bear left along this, with fine views across Rydal Water to Nab Cottage H. The path rises slightly to the top of a rocky knoll, then dips again to cross a levelled embankment. The huge cavern in the hillside on the right is Rydal Cave J.

8 The track twists down and passes another quarry on the right, then levels off and reaches open ground directly above the lake.

9 Descend to the left, following a short, steep path that cuts across the lake-side track that rises from the shore. Pass through an iron kissing gate at the edge of Jobson Close. Follow the path through the woods to another iron kissing gate marking their end. The path now leads through an open field to a wooden gate or stile. Cross the narrow wooden footbridge over the River Rothay and turn right along the pavement by the A591. The Badger Bar is on the opposite side of the road.

10 Follow the pavement through Rydal, back to Pelter Bridge and the car park where the walk started.

JOHN WATNEY

▲*A huntsman leads his pack past the Coffin Rest Stone, on the coffin road between Rydal and Grasmere. Wordsworth wrote some of his finest poetry while living at Dove Cottage (right), which was later the home of De Quincey.*

has no root in the earth, no place in the sky and therefore occupies a kind of middle world. Rowan trees are more commonly found growing in this way, and it was from such trees that Druids would cut their magic wands.

Just after the stone track becomes surfaced, where rhododendrons

BILL BIRKETT

hide the wall opposite, a gate on the left leads to a fine viewpoint overlooking the end of Rydal Water.

Return to the road and continue for a short way until you come to a wet area on the right, choked with an invading rat-tail-like reed. Though today it looks little more than a mire, this is White Moss Pond E. In Wordsworth's day, the

DEREK FORSS

◀*Rydal Water, seen from White Moss Common. To the left is Nab Scar, and, away to the right, Loughrigg Terrace.*

pond froze over more quickly than any of the neighbouring lakes or tarns and was, therefore, popular with skaters.

When you reach a road junction, Dove Cottage **F** lies a short distance to your right. Wordsworth lived here from 1799 to 1808, during which time he wrote much of his most admired poetry.

LANDSCAPED QUARRY

The walk heads left, taking the path down toward Rydal Water and White Moss Common **G**. The area was once an extensive slate quarry, but has now been landscaped to provide a large car park.

A narrow footbridge takes you across the River Rothay, which runs through Grasmere to Rydal Water and then Windermere to the south. As you walk through the deciduous woods, you may be lucky enough to spot a red squirrel. Loughrigg Terrace, the path that hugs the edge of the hillside here, is famed for its breathtaking views stretching across Rydal Water to Nab Cottage **H** and up to Nab Scar.

JOHN WATNEY

▲*Nab Cottage, a pretty whitewashed cottage to the west of Rydal, was built at the beginning of the 18th century.*

HAPPY MARRIAGE

The writer Thomas De Quincey lodged for a time at Nab Cottage, and married the landlord's daughter. Wordsworth disapproved, but the union proved to be a long and happy one nevertheless.

At the other end of the terrace is the great cavern of Rydal Cave **J**. It is safe to enter, the floor being flat and without danger. The cathedral-like scale of this old slate quarry is quite awesome. Part of the floor is flooded, and shoals of minnows can be seen swimming in the pools.

A walk through woodlands leads you back to the River Rothay. Look out for the dark brown, white-chested dipper here. As this bird hops from stone to stone, it appears quite ordinary, but from the bridge you can sometimes see it walking underwater on the bed of the river. This extraordinary bird (common in these parts) does this with ease, even against a swift current. A short walk through Rydal brings you back to the starting point of the walk.

JOHN WATNEY

▲*From the dark recesses of Rydal Cave, at the east end of Loughrigg Terrace, there is a spectacular vista.*

William Wordsworth

Inspired by the Lake District, Wordsworth's poems broke with the strict, conventional structure and stylized imagery of his day, and eloquently described the wild, natural beauty of the Lakes. From his relatively simple, and therefore unforgettable, *Daffodils* to the masterly *Ode on Intimations of Immortality*, he explored the worlds of nature and of human emotion in new poetic language.

Wordsworth was born in Cockermouth, on the edge of the Lake District, on 7th April 1770, the son of an attorney. He was educated at Hawkshead Grammar School, where he first wrote poetry, and at St John's College, Cambridge.

For a while, he lived in the West Country, and, with the help of a legacy, set up home together with his sister. It was here that he met Samuel Taylor Coleridge.

In 1799, after a period of travel, he and his sister, Dorothy, moved into Dove Cottage, Grasmere. He married Mary Hutchinson in 1802. In 1808, with a fourth child on the way, he decided that Dove Cottage was too small, and five less happy years in rented accommodation in Grasmere followed. In 1813, the family moved to Rydal Mount, where Wordsworth spent his last years. He was made Poet Laureate in 1843 and died, at the age of 80, on 23rd April 1850.

Wordsworth dearly loved the Lake District, and his *Guide to the Lakes*, written in 1810, was a much-acclaimed tourist guidebook to the region. Remarkably, it still remains a bestseller today.

MARY EVANS PICTURE LIBRARY

Across the years, Wordsworth has meant different things to different people. This caricature is by Sir Max Beerbohm.

THE CASTLE AND THE HALL

13

CUMBRIA

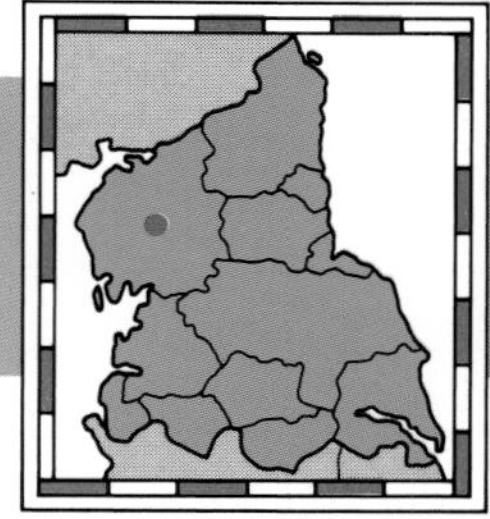

JOHN WATNEY. INSET: W.COSTER/AQUILA

▲*Once a great stately home, Lowther Castle is still imposing even though it is now a mere shell. The oak hook-tip moth (inset) may be spotted in the oak-lined avenue in front of the castle.*

A pleasant ramble around Cumbria's largest private park

This walk explores the parkland surrounding Lowther Castle, the former seat of the Earls of Lonsdale. It begins in the nearby village of Askham Ⓐ, where immaculate 18th- and 19th-century cottages line the high grass banks beside a road that leads down to the River Lowther. This picture-postcard village, which includes two very good pubs, has often been praised as the prettiest in Westmorland. In fact, though, it looks less like a Lakeland village than one from the North Riding of Yorkshire.

GRAND MANOR

You begin by walking past the cottages on the northern side of the village street, towards Askham Hall Ⓑ. This castellated manor house, with its 14th-century peel tower, is just visible if you peer over the stone wall on the way down to the bridge.

Askham Hall is the current residence of the Earls of Lonsdale, who have long been associated with the village. Perhaps the most famous member of the family was the 5th Earl, known as the Yellow Earl from the colour of his livery. He gave his name to the Lonsdale belts that are awarded to Britain's boxing champions and also founded the Automobile Association, which adopted his yellow as its corporate colour.

FACT FILE

- Askham, 4 miles (6.4km) south of Penrith
- Outdoor Leisure 5, The English Lakes, North Eastern area, grid reference NY 512237
- miles 0 1 2 3 4 5 6 7 8 9 10 miles / kms 0 1 2 3 4 5 6 7 8 9 10 11 12 13 14 15 kms
- Allow 2½ hours
- Firm and easy going with one steep downhill path
- P By swimming pool at top end of village, or small space off the road by the bridge
- T Buses to and from Penrith on Saturdays
- Punch Bowl and Queen's Head pubs, café by swimming pool and village store in Askham

RHODODENDRONS

A lane and a bridleway lead you out of the village, past Askham Hall, into woodlands high above the River Lowther. There is a wide variety of trees here, with oak, ash, beech and silver birch, as well as several varieties of conifer. Elderberries, blackberries and wild raspberries can all be picked here in late August. At one stage the path passes between massive rhododendron bushes that produce a stunning floral display in May.

On the northern side of Lowther Park you cross Low Gardens Bridge over the river and turn into the park itself. The road runs uphill by a field beside the river which is the site of

THE WALK

ASKHAM – LOWTHER CASTLE

The walk begins in the car park beside the swimming pool in Askham.

1 Walk south into the village **A**, taking the first left turn. There are cottages on your left and Lowther Castle rises from a belt of trees ahead. At the foot of the road, almost opposite the Punch Bowl pub, turn left up a lane beside the grounds of Askham Hall **B**.

2 Pass through a gate across the lane and continue for about 400 yards (360m) to reach a gate on your right.

3 Go through this gate and make for the opposite corner of the field, where a ladder stile takes you over a dry-stone wall. Turn half right and take a narrow footpath leading through bramble and elder into Heining Wood and onto a forest track.

4 Turn left along the forest track and follow it as it runs slightly up and down hill through a variety of woodland. You will first hear and then see the River Lowther, as it tumbles along some 50 feet (15m) below to your right. Soon the track descends to a metalled estate road.

5 Turn right and go over Low Gardens Bridge into Lowther Park. Carry on uphill along the estate road through an avenue of stately oaks, with views of Lowther Castle **C** ahead, to a T-junction.

6 Turn right along this public road to the gate into St Michael's churchyard to visit the church and the mausoleum **D**.

7 Retrace your steps to the T-junction and continue along the road for another 400 yards (360m) as it bears right, then left. As the road leaves the park take a right turn into Newtown **E**.

8 In the centre of Newtown, which is a one-street village, there are two stone pillars on the grass verge on your right. Go between them and then over a ladder stile back into the park. Follow a line of oaks to the castle gatehouse.

9 Follow the curtain wall and go over a cattle grid into the woods. When the wall takes a right-angled turn to the left (there is an overgrown Corinthian-columned doorway at this point), take a smooth grass path straight ahead, which runs downhill through the trees. This is a pretty, but rather steep way down to the river, but there are iron garden seats set among the trees near the top and just before the bottom. The path bends right and runs through to Askham Bridge.

10 Cross Askham Bridge and walk uphill past the village church and the Punch Bowl pub. At the end, turn right for the swimming pool car park.

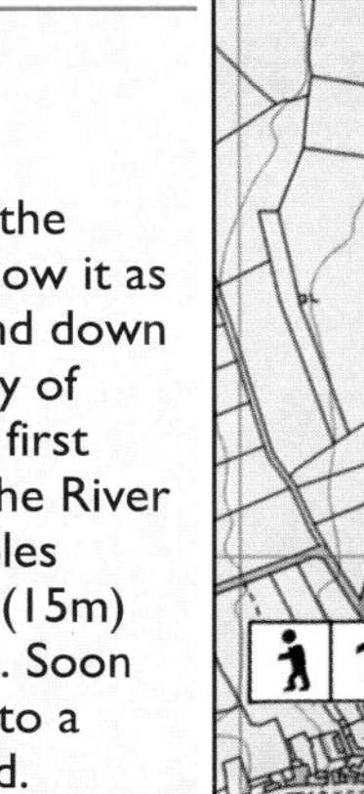

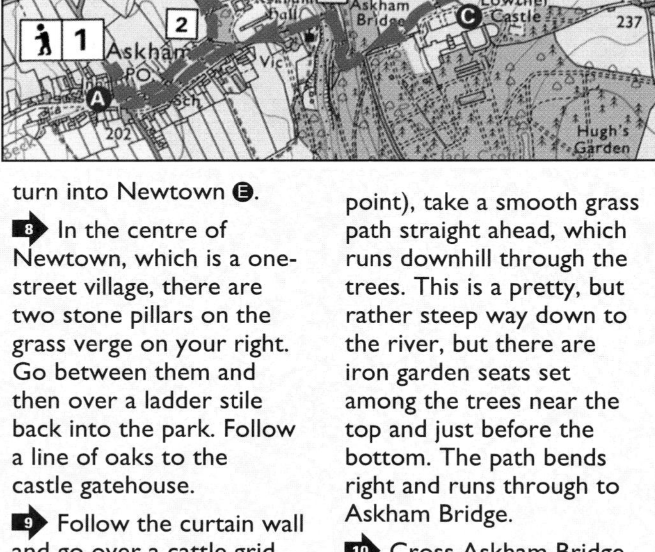

the annual Lowther Show. A steep grass bank here forms a natural grandstand. Beyond this you pass along an avenue of mature oaks.

The magnificent 420-foot (125-m) long facade of Lowther Castle **C** dominates the view ahead. The castle, built of sombre, iron-grey sandstone, is now a shell. It has no roof, and its windows are empty sockets, but a great square tower, like a keep, soars above everything. The formidable curtain wall around its overgrown and abandoned gardens is, however, still intact.

In its time, the castle was one of the great stately homes of England, where royalty and statesmen were regularly entertained, but the Earls of Lonsdale left it in 1936 and two decades later, in 1957, the roof and the interior were demolished. It is, however, still a magnificent sight, albeit a rather sad one.

JOHN WATNEY

◀Avenues of majestic oaks lead to Lowther Castle, which once numbered Mary Queen of Scots among its guests.

RISING BATTLEMENTS

At a T-junction you turn right to visit the Lowther family's church, the Church of St Michael **D**, which was extensively rebuilt in 1686. It is full of family memorials and a Viking tombstone depicting, very faintly, warriors arriving at Valhalla. In the churchyard, atop a mound, is the family mausoleum, a gargoyled extravaganza occupied by a larger-than-life alabaster effigy of William, the 2nd Earl. There is a quite stunning view from here, down along a steep green valley, with the crenellations of Askham Hall rising above the trees at the far end.

From the church you walk through to the eastern end of the park and the model village of Newtown **E**, a street of fine, two-storey, flower-bedecked stone houses. These were built in 1682 by Sir John Lowther, to rehouse his tenants when he destroyed their hovels to improve the view from the castle.

Another avenue leads you across the park to the walled-up gatehouse and along the curtain walls, before you plunge down the wooded slope of the valley to Askham Bridge. Crossing the river, you walk past the parish church and up through the village to return to the car park at the start of the walk.

THE COMMON AND THE SHORE

14

CUMBRIA

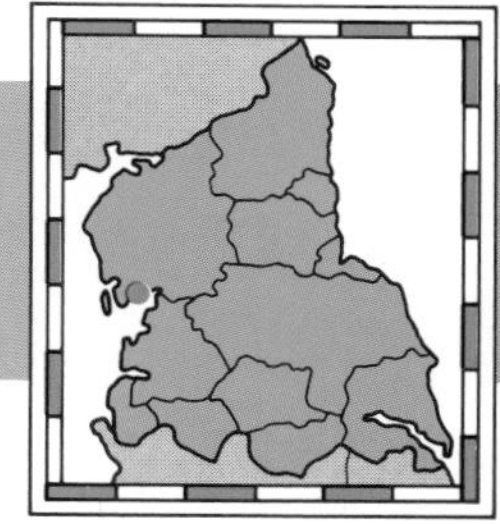

ALAN WILLIAMS/NHPA

◀*The walk follows the Ulverston Canal, passing beneath a bridge that carries the railway south-eastwards. During migration, the greenshank (above) may be seen along the shore.*

JEFFREY BEAZLEY

The fascinating history and wildlife of a corner of Furness

Ulverston is a lively market town just inland from an inlet of Morecambe Bay. This circular walk explores its history, in the form of a Bronze Age stone circle, several associations with the early days of the Quakers, and a rich industrial past. You pass through a variety of wildlife habitats: an abandoned canal; a quiet estuary whose sand-banks are home to many wading birds; and a high limestone common where there is a rich flora.

The route begins with a stroll along the willow-lined Ulverston Canal **A**, a lovely, quiet stretch of water linking the town with the estuary. It was opened in 1796 to bring boats carrying coal, slate, copper and gunpowder to and from the factories that are now hidden by the vegetation on the far side of the cut.

FACT FILE

- Ulverston, 7 miles (11.2km) north-east of Barrow-in-Furness, on the A590
- Pathfinders 635 (SD 17/27) and 636 (SD 37/47), grid reference SD 288783

miles 0 1 2 3 4 5 6 7 8 9 10 miles
kms 0 1 2 3 4 5 6 7 8 9 10 11 12 13 14 15 kms

- Allow 4 to 5 hours
- Some paths may be muddy after rain. One steady climb, steep in parts. Waterproof clothing and walking boots always advisable
- P Brewery car park at the start
- T BR station in Ulverston
- Braddylls Arms pub in Bardsea; several pubs, restaurants and cafés in Ulverston
- wc At the foot of the hill leading to Bardsea

At the other end of the canal — at just over 1½ miles (2.4km), it is the shortest in the country — are the remains of wooden lock gates. This entrance was finally sealed in 1948 by a wall of concrete, and today the only traffic on the canal consists of ducks, coots, moorhens, gulls and swans. It had been in decline since 1846, when the Furness Railway was

▼*To the south-east of Ulverston, near the coast, is the distinctive brick chimney of a former brickworks.*

JEFFREY BEAZLEY

THE WALK

ULVERSTON – BARDSEA – BIRKRIGG COMMON

The walk begins at the brewery car park on the north side of Ulverston, just off the A590.

1 Turn left along the A590. Beyond the Canal Tavern, turn right. Follow the canal **A** to its end, where there is a view of the Leven Viaduct **B** to the north. Cross the canal and turn right down the road.

2 At the end of the factory, fork left to the Sea View Inn. Turn right, then immediately left down the narrow lane on the left of a post box. Cross Carter Beck, then go half left through a kissing-gate along a narrow path through pasture. Follow this path as it bears right and continues due south along a field edge towards a chimney **C**.

3 Just past the chimney, climb a stile and continue ahead on a hedged lane. Conishead Priory **D** is ahead, and the Hermitage **E** is in the trees on the hill to the right. Follow the lane to the beach. Turn right to walk along the shore. Chapel Island **F** is away to your left.

4 After crossing the second of two small car parks, take the right-hand stile of two onto a path through pasture that returns you to the shore. At the next car park, bear left down the A5087, then first right up the hill to Bardsea **G**.

5 Turn left down the lane beyond the Braddylls Arms, then left again down another lane signposted to Wellhouse. Follow the lane, keeping to the right as

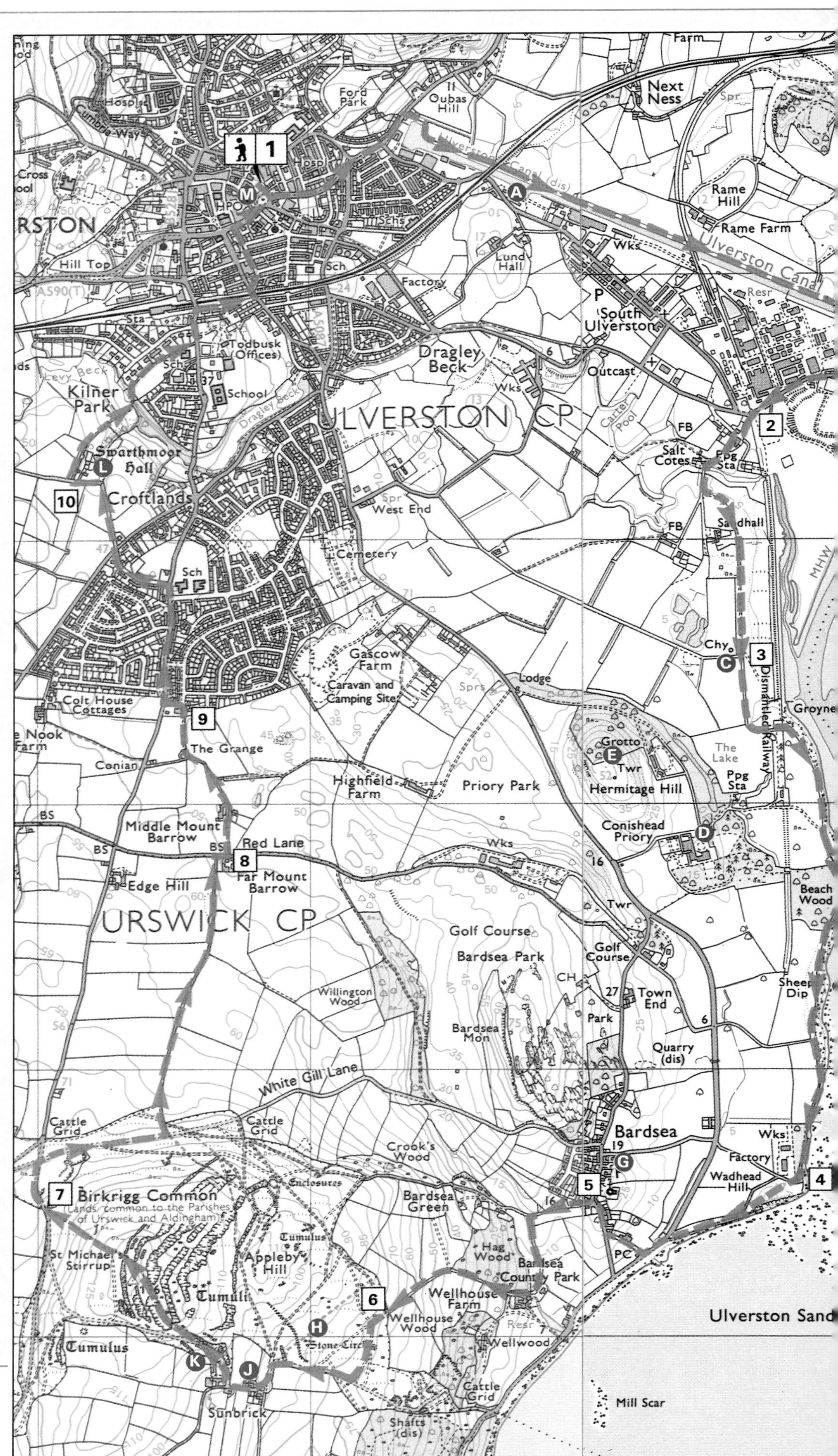

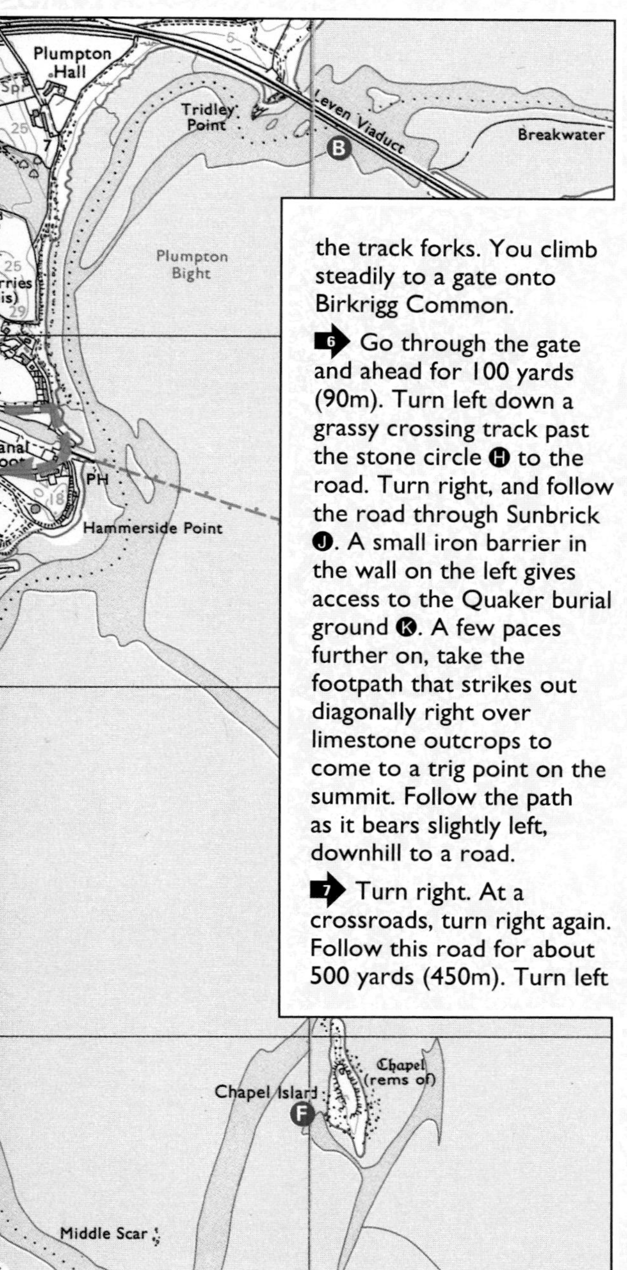

the track forks. You climb steadily to a gate onto Birkrigg Common.

6 Go through the gate and ahead for 100 yards (90m). Turn left down a grassy crossing track past the stone circle **H** to the road. Turn right, and follow the road through Sunbrick **J**. A small iron barrier in the wall on the left gives access to the Quaker burial ground **K**. A few paces further on, take the footpath that strikes out diagonally right over limestone outcrops to come to a trig point on the summit. Follow the path as it bears slightly left, downhill to a road.

7 Turn right. At a crossroads, turn right again. Follow this road for about 500 yards (450m). Turn left through a kissing-gate approached by a grassy track over the verge. Go along the hedged track to a road. Turn right. After about 50 yards (45m) you reach a kissing-gate beside the access track to Middle Mount Barrow Farm.

8 Turn left through the kissing-gate, then pass to the right of the farm to join a road. Just before the first house on the right, go through a gate into an alleyway. Beyond the next gate, cross a pasture to the edge of Croftlands Estate.

9 Bear left in front of the Lancastrian pub then turn right along Mountbarrow Road. Opposite an infants' school, turn left onto Meeting House Lane. Continue over Urswick Road, and follow the lane as it bears left past Swarthmoor Hall **L**.

10 Just after the Hall, take a footpath to your right, signposted to Springfield Road. At the road, turn left, then right into Conishead Road. Turn left to pass under the railway bridge, then turn right into Brogden Street. At its end, turn right onto the A590 and follow it to the roundabout **M**, then back to the start.

ALL PHOTOS: JEFFREY BEAZLEY

▲*The view from Birkrigg Common back to Bardsea and across the waters of the Leven Estuary.*

◀*Chapel Island in Morecambe Bay. The original chapel was built as a refuge for travellers walking over the tidal sands.*

opened. From here, there is a good view northwards to the Leven Viaduct **B**, which carries the railway across the waters of the estuary.

The walk continues past a huge pharmaceutical factory and the Sea View Inn —whose view of the sea is now blocked — onto a path leading past another sign of Ulverston's industrial past; a slag bank, which is now covered with vegetation. To the left, a dismantled railway track is now a grassy highway, while to the right is all that remains of Ulverston's brickworks — a tall chimney **C** built of red bricks banded with yellow, which stands alone, forlorn but magnificent.

RELIGIOUS CENTRE

Ahead, through the trees, is Conishead Priory **D**, a house built on the site of a monastic foundation dissolved by Henry VIII. It was the home of the Braddyll family from the mid-17th century, but has now reverted to religious purposes as a Buddhist centre. On the hill to the right is a hermitage **E**, built by Colonel Braddyll in 1836 to house a hermit, whom he paid to live there.

Across the water from the pebbly beach of the estuary is Chapel Island **F**, whose few trees frame a

▼*The ancient settlement of Sunbrick, with its stone-built houses, stands beneath trees shaped by the wind.*

The Quakers

A charismatic Puritan preacher, George Fox was born in 1624 in Leicestershire. From an early age, he roamed the Midlands and the North, proclaiming his belief that religious knowledge should come from an 'inner light' or God-given inspiration, rather than the teachings and traditions of an established church.

Fox's message was welcomed in the North by, amongst others, a puritan sect called the Seekers. Itinerant men and women preachers known as Publishers of Truth helped him establish local congregations, particularly in Cumbria and Lancashire, and the group eventually became known as the Society of Friends, though from early on they were dubbed the Quakers.

Fox was several times in trouble with the law — he was imprisoned eight times between 1649 and 1673 — and persecution increased when the monarchy was restored in 1660.

When he was in Cumbria, Fox often stayed at Swarthmoor Hall, the home of Judge Fell, a chancellor of the Duchy of Lancaster. Fell always made Fox welcome at the Hall, although he did not fully share the preacher's views. Fell died in 1658. His widow, Margaret, with whom he had eight children, converted to Quakerism and married Fox in 1669.

George Fox died in 1691, less than two years after an Act of Toleration brought the persecution of the Quakers to an end.

THE LIBRARY COMMITTEE OF THE RELIGIOUS SOCIETY OF FRIENDS

'George Fox at Swarthmore' (sic), an etching with watercolour by Robert Spence.

JEFFREY BEAZLEY

▲*The Quaker burial ground, where Margaret Fox lies, is behind this stone wall, just north of Sunbrick.*

Romantic ruin; another folly commissioned by Colonel Braddyll, and built by Conishead monks using stones from an actual chapel.

The shore path skirts the priory woodland, where willow warblers sing in spring. When the tide goes out, rocks and mussel beds are uncovered, and oystercatchers, curlews, dunlins, redshanks and eider ducks feed here and on the newly exposed sands.

LIMESTONE CHURCH

The route heads inland to the village of Bardsea Ⓖ. The splendid church was built on land obtained at auction in 1848 when Colonel Braddyll went bankrupt — perhaps owing to an over-indulgence in architectural conceits. The focus of the village moved uphill around the church. In earlier times, when the village was more vulnerable to attack from the sea, its houses were huddled behind the hill.

From here, you climb steadily to Birkrigg Common, from which there are fine views over Bardsea and the estuary. Grassy tracks through the bracken lead you to a Bronze Age henge Ⓗ consisting of ten standing stones. Just beyond is Sunbrick Ⓙ, a hamlet that was part of Bardsea Manor until about 1586. Lower Sunbrick Farm and Lower Sunbrick Cottage are dated 1655 and 1672 respectively.

Just beyond the settlement, you pass a walled enclosure containing a small Quaker burial ground Ⓚ, the last resting place of Margaret, wife of George Fox, the founder of the Society of Friends (see box).

From the top of Birkrigg Common, the walk continues across country and through a housing estate to Swarthmoor Hall Ⓛ. This substantial, three-storeyed stone building was built by Judge Fell, the first husband of Margaret Fox. Close by, in Meeting Hall Lane, is a 17th-century Quaker Meeting House.

From here, a footpath leads over Levy Beck and back into Ulverston. In the centre of the roundabout, close to the car park where the walk began, is a large stone Ⓜ. This was once used for communal clothes washing and as a podium for auctioneers selling sheep.

JEFFREY BEAZLEY

►*Levy Beck, seen here from the footpath to Springfield Road, is crossed on the outskirts of Ulverston.*

The Tarn and the Water

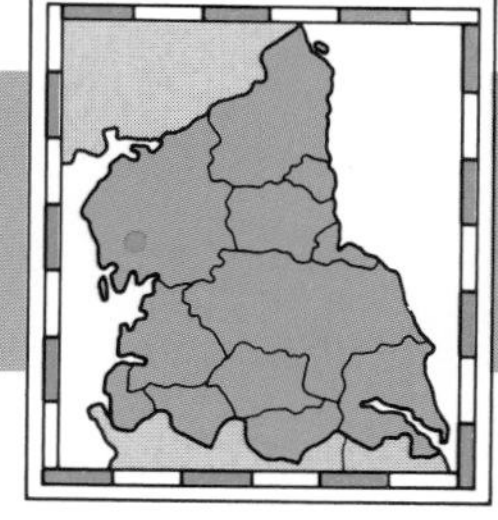

15

Cumbria

JEFFREY BEAZLEY. INSET: NATURE PHOTOGRAPHERS

▲*The jagged Langdale Pikes form a backdrop to the view across Loughrigg Tarn. The green fruits of alder (right), a tree which grows by the waterside, turn brown and woody in autumn.*

FACT FILE

- Elterwater, 3 miles (4.8km) west of Ambleside, on the B5343
- Outdoor Leisure Map 7, grid reference NY 327047
- miles 0 1 2 3 4 5 6 7 8 9 10 miles / kms 0 1 2 3 4 5 6 7 8 9 10 11 12 13 14 15 kms
- Allow 2 hours
- Lanes, stony tracks and woodland paths. Walking boots recommended
- P Free car parks, or off-road parking on and around Elterwater Common
- Britannia Inn, Elterwater
- Café at the slate shop in Skelwith Bridge
- wc In Elterwater

A short Lakeland walk that visits two very different lakes

The village of Elterwater Ⓐ, a cluster of stone houses below the Langdale Pikes, grew up around the bridge over the Great Langdale Beck. This was carefully sited where the solid rock of the gorge upstream gives way to the peaty mud at the fringes of the lake. Just upstream from the bridge are the remnants of a waterwheel. The mill it powered produced gunpowder for use in the Lakeland mines and quarries.

The sheared, slaty rocks that form the rugged scenery in this part of the Lake District were formed from ancient lava and volcanic ash, and are known geologically as the Borrowdale Volcanic Series. The stone is almost as hard as flint, and was used in the same way by Stone Age man to make axes.

Today, it is used everywhere in the roofs and walls of buildings, and in the dry-stone walling that defines the boundaries here. It also offers shelter for the hardy Herdwick sheep that graze the slopes.

The first part of the route leads along quiet lanes towards Loughrigg Tarn Ⓑ. It is as attractive now as it was in 1810, when Wordsworth described it in his *Guide to the Lakes* as 'a most beautiful example of a miniature lake, a small, quiet and fertile domain, with a margin of green firm meadows, surrounded by rocky and barren steeps, overlooked by the solemn pikes of Langdale'.

LONG VIEWS

On the uphill stretch to the lake, it is worth pausing to take in the view to the south-west of the Old Man of Coniston, with Wetherlam nearest, then Swirl How and Grey Friar. The jagged outline of the Langdale Pikes stands out to the west. A lane leads down from the tarn to join the Langdale road at Skelwith Bridge Ⓒ, a two-span structure across the River Brathay. Before the creation of Cumbria, the river formed the

▼*The waters of the River Brathay tumble over the rocks at Skelwith Force on their way to Elter Water.*

JEFFREY BEAZLEY

THE WALK

ELTERWATER – SKELWITH BRIDGE

The walk begins at Elterwater Common.

1 Walk up the lane through Elterwater Ⓐ to the B5343. Turn right. Turn first left by a signposted boulder, and follow the lane past woods and a road joining from the right to a T-junction.

2 Turn right along the lane for almost 200 yards (180m), then turn left over a wooden stile by a wooden gate. Go ahead, then bear right and cross a wooden step stile over the stone wall, with Loughrigg Tarn Ⓑ on your right. Follow the path up a grassy slope to a lane at the top. Go through a wooden gate and turn right along the stony lane.

3 Go through the wooden gate at the end of the lane and turn right down the lane that crosses it. Follow this lane as it bends left down to a road. Turn right.

4 After crossing a little stream, turn left down another lane. Follow it downhill to a main road.

5 Cross the road on your right, and walk past the Skelwith Bridge Hotel towards Skelwith Bridge Ⓒ. Before the bridge, turn right towards the Kirkstone Green Slate Quarry Company, with the river on your left. In front of the slate shop, turn right and then left around the building and through the slate works. Continue ahead, along the woodland path, with the river still on your left. In a short while you pass Skelwith Force Ⓓ. Continue along the lane to its end.

6 Go through a gate into a field. Follow a distinct grassy path the length of the field to the head of Elter Water Ⓔ. Go through a kissing-gate and follow the path through the woodland, then back into Elterwater village.

JEFFREY BEAZLEY

◀*At Elter Water, reeds and sedges are the first to colonize the margins, soon to be followed by willows and alders.*

boundary between Westmorland and Lancashire.

Just before the bridge are the shop and workshop of the Kirkstone Slate Company. The attractive local green slate-stone is made from volcanic ash laid down in thin layers that split easily, like slate. It has been sent all over the world for making fireplaces and ornaments, and for facing buildings.

The volcanic rocks are very resistant to erosion by water or ice, and a bar of this rock has formed a waterfall, Skelwith Force Ⓓ, where the River Brathay foams and cascades into deep, greenish pools. The falls are an especially impressive sight after rain, when the river is in spate.

Downstream from here, the Brathay flows gently over sand, silt and clay washed from the upper valleys. It runs into a saucer-shaped hollow scoured out of the softer rock by glaciers, and now filled with the still waters of Elter Water Ⓔ.

The lake is slowly shrinking; at one time, the flat land around the Water was part of the lake. Gradually, reeds have colonized the sediment on its fringes, a process which is still continuing.

BROADLEAF WOODLAND

The path goes through a National Trust woodland, where oak, ash, larch, birch and beech trees can be found. By the Water are willows and alders. Alder is particularly well adapted to a waterside habitat; its nut-like seeds float, ensuring that they are distributed along the banks.

From the lake, the route returns to the village of Elterwater along the Langdale Beck, a clear stream flowing briskly over a bed of pebbles.

EAST AND WEST OF EDEN

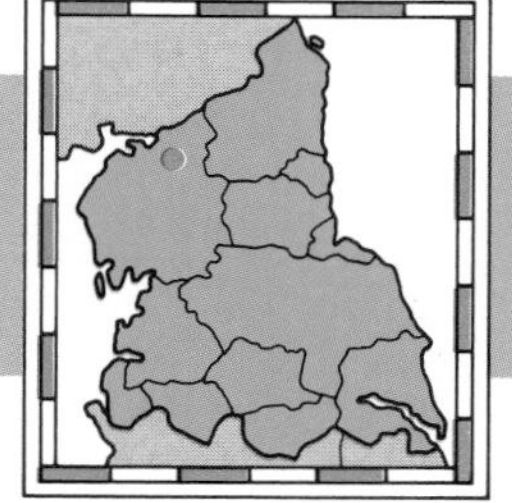

Visit a castle garden on the wooded banks of the Vale of Eden

Corby Castle (A) sits above the River Eden at the top of a 90-foot (27-m) escarpment. Some sections date from the 14th century, but most of it is a Georgian mansion of about 1810. It has been the home of the Howard family since the early part of the 17th century, and is not open to the public.

The grounds were laid out beside the river at the beginning of the 18th century, and it is here that this walk starts. A gently sloping track leads through thick woodland. After about ½ mile (800m), you come to the river-bank by old fish traps and a salmon leap (B) that was built by the medieval monks of Wetheral Priory on the other side of the river.

IMAGINATIVE OVERFLOW

You can, if you wish, stroll further along the river-bank, but the traps mark a turning point back beside the water to view an architectural oddity. A cascade (C) pours out of the fanged mouths of imaginary beasts and down the red sandstone escarpment into a pool. In the middle of the pool stands an incongruous statue of Lord Nelson in full dress.

The cascade's purpose is not purely decorative; it is an elaborate means of allowing rainwater to drain off the estate. In dry weather, it ceases to flow. Beside the cascade is a series of caves carved out of the sandstone, follies for the amusement of the Howard family's guests, who would become trapped in them when water was diverted to form a curtain across the entrances.

A steep path and steps lead back up to the castle grounds. Halfway up is a twice life-sized painted figure of Polyphemus. At the top is a stone summerhouse, with a bird and mermaid statuary on its roof.

ACROSS THE VIADUCT

The walk leads out of the grounds and through the village of Great Corby to Corby Bridge (D), a railway viaduct across the Eden. Running alongside the railway line leading to

JOHN WATNEY. INSET: R.ORR/AQUILA

▲*A small statue of Admiral Lord Nelson stands at the foot of the verdant cascade, above steps leading to the River Eden. Tansy (inset) grows by the river, flowering from July to September.*

FACT FILE

- Great Corby, 4 miles (6.4km) east of Carlisle, off the A69
- Pathfinder 558 (NY 45/55), grid reference NY 471542

  miles 0 1 2 3 4 5 6 7 8 9 10 miles
  kms 0 1 2 3 4 5 6 7 8 9 10 11 12 13 14 15 kms
- Allow 2 hours
- Some short, sharp ascents. The woodland paths are likely to be muddy after rain
- P At the start, or in the village streets
- T BR trains between Newcastle and Carlisle stop at Wetheral
- Several pubs and restaurants in Great Corby and Wetheral

THE WALK

GREAT CORBY – WETHERAL

Start from the car park of Corby Castle (A).

1 An arrow by the coin box indicates the start of the walk. Follow the path alongside the front lawn and into the woods above the river. Continue ahead, downhill to the river-bank by the fish traps and salmon leap (B).

2 Turn right along the green walk beside the river to the cascade (C) and caves.

3 Retrace your steps about 100 yards (90m) back along the river-bank, then take the steep path on your left to the top of the cascade. At the grass above the summerhouse, turn sharp right and rejoin the path from the car park. Bear right to reach the lodge gate.

4 Turn left down the road through the village and continue ahead over a level crossing.

5 Turn left to cross the viaduct (D) by the footway beside the railway line. At Wetheral Station, cross to the opposite platform by a footbridge.

6 Go through the station yard, then down the steep path and steps, which turn under the viaduct. Turn right along Low Road, to walk with the river on your left. At the end of the road, turn left and go down some steps that lead to the water's edge.

7 Turn right along the river-bank to follow a well trodden footpath to a kissing-gate at the entrance to Wetheral Woods (E). Continue ahead, always bearing left at forks, to St Constantine's Cells (F). Retrace your steps a short distance to where there are some steps on your left. At the top of six steps is a higher path.

8 Turn right along it and make for a stile into a field. Follow a line of oak trees to a gate onto a lane.

9 Turn right and follow the lane past the Priory Gatehouse (G) towards the village. At a T-junction, turn right then soon left to visit the church (H).

10 Retrace your steps uphill. Follow the road along the side of the green, exiting at the far right-hand corner. Turn right down a lane, past the Crown Hotel to the station. Cross the footbridge and viaduct to Great Corby, and retrace your earlier steps to return to the start.

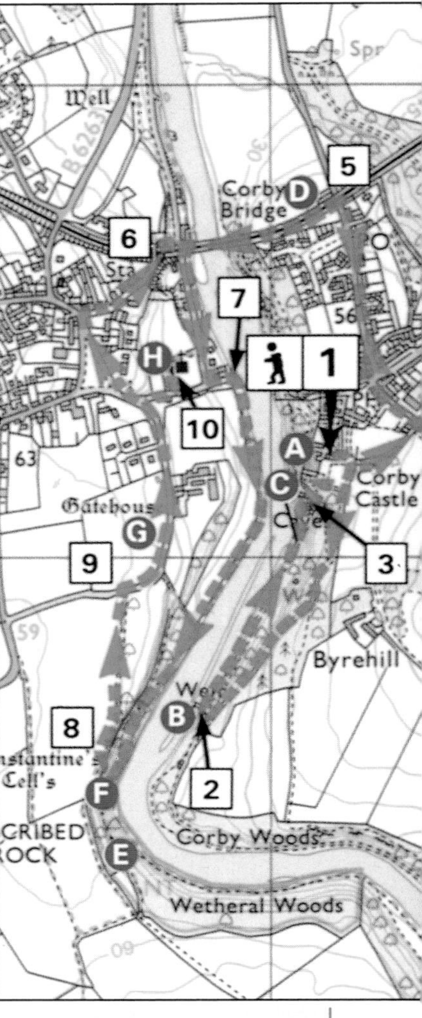

Wetheral station and village is a wooden footpath, which affords a good view downstream. From the station yard, there are steep steps, made from old stone sleepers, that lead down to the river.

As you follow the west bank of the Eden south from the village, the river runs fast and shallow over flat rocks. If you step out (carefully) from the shore onto some of the stone slabs, you get long views of Corby Castle crowning a bend in the river, and the five arches of the viaduct, which were built of local sandstone in 1830.

The route passes through a kissing-gate and enters Wetheral Woods (E), which belong to the National Trust. Near the far end of the woods stands a coast redwood. This species contains the tallest trees in the world. Pied flycatchers and wood warblers inhabit this ancient forest, and water voles and mink have made their homes in the banks. By the path are Himalayan balsam and wild tansy, while willow and alder grow by the water.

The path leads to a series of square-cut caves, hanging high in the sandstone cliff above the river and heavily incised with old graffiti. They are known as St Constantine's Cells (F) or Wetheral's Safeguards. The saint's connection with them is dubious. Little is known of his life; he may have been either a 6th-century prince or a 10th-century king. The caves' alternative name refers to the habit of Wetheral monks of using them to store valuables.

NORMAN PRIORY

The way back leaves the riverside for open fields and a lane to the gatehouse (G) of Wetheral Priory, which was founded in 1088. The gatehouse is all that remains, apart from a few bits of wall now incorporated into Wetheral Priory Farm.

The lane runs into Wetheral near the Church of the Holy Trinity, St Constantine and St Mary (H).

Although many churches in Scotland are dedicated to Constantine, this is the only one in England. It is built in the simple Early English style, with the addition of a Victorian tower. In the Howard Chapel is a superb marble monument by Nollekens, the renowned neoclassical sculptor, to Maria Archer, the wife of Henry Howard, who died in childbirth in 1789.

Wetheral, a dormitory village for Carlisle, is a sophisticated place with a gourmet restaurant and two first class hotels, but the village's finest features are its great triangular green and the river, which you recross to return to the start.

JOHN WATNEY

▶ ***Close by the cascade there are caves hollowed out of the red sandstone cliff above the River Eden.***

THE FALCONS OF MALLERSTANG

17

CUMBRIA

JOHN WATNEY. INSET: L.H. NEWMAN/NHPA

Steam trains, falls and birds of prey in a valley among the fells

Mallerstang Valley runs deep between Wild Boar Fell, rising to 2,322 feet (708m) in the west and the equally high, sheer escarpment of Mallerstang Edge to the east. Through it flows the infant River Eden, and clinging to the fellside above is the Settle-Carlisle railway line, where steam trains can sometimes be seen puffing up the steep gradients at the highest point of the British Rail system.

RAILWAY COTTAGES

This exploration of the valley begins at Aisgill, on the border between Cumbria and North Yorkshire. It should begin early in the morning, so the sun is over your shoulder on the way north, lighting up the valley ahead and the western fells. On the return, the eastern fells will be lit.

Aisgill Moor Cottages Ⓐ, just inside Cumbria, were originally built to house the track maintenance staff of the Midland Railway. The last house is now Aisgill Crafts. Here, among the genuine local craft work, paintings and photos of steam locomotives and timetables for the steam trains may be found. Backpackers may pitch their tents in the garden or book B & B, making an early start feasible.

The outward leg of the walk climbs alongside Hell Gill Beck, the source of the Eden, which pours through a deep gorge whose sides have been worn concave by the winter torrents. This leads to The Highway Ⓑ, a flat grass road along

FACT FILE

- Aisgill Moor Cottages, 9 miles (14.4km) east of Sedbergh, on the B6259
- Pathfinders 607 (NY 60/70) & 617 (SD 69/79), grid reference SD 778962
- miles 0 1 2 3 4 5 6 7 8 9 10 miles / kms 0 1 2 3 4 5 6 7 8 9 10 11 12 13 14 15 kms
- Allow 6 hours
- One steep ascent and some boggy and rocky ground. Waterproof clothing and good boots essential at all seasons
- Along road at start. Roadside car park by Aisgill Crafts should not be used except with permission or by bona fide clients
- None on route; Moorcock Inn, Garsdale Head, is 2½ miles (4km) south of start
- Tea-room at The Thrang is often closed except in August, but may open on request to walkers: Tel. (017683) 71889. Tea at Aisgill Crafts and Ing Hill Lodge
- Falconry Centre open daily, 10am-dusk

▲*The view westward from The Highway to Wild Boar Fell. The saker falcon (inset), a native of eastern Europe and Asia, can be seen at the Falconry Centre (below). Beyond the centre is a trotting ring.*

JOHN WATNEY

THE WALK

AISGILL – OUTHGILL – PENDRAGON CASTLE

The walk begins at Aisgill Moor Cottages Ⓐ.

1 Walk down the short lane to the right of the buildings and cross the railway bridge. Turn left, then right, uphill, going past Hellgill farmhouse to Hell Gill Bridge.

2 Turn left and go up onto the open fell along The Highway Ⓑ, keeping the stone wall to your left. In about a mile (1.6km), the wall veers away from The Highway. Continue ahead on the old track. Go over four small fords; after these the track becomes deeply rutted and very slippery in wet weather.

3 At the bottom go through the gate onto the B6259. Turn right towards The Thrang Ⓒ. Go through a gate on the left by a footpath signed to Deepgill. This farm road curves down and round to a bridge over the Eden. Cross and turn sharp right along the bank to a wall. Climb the stile and continue along the river to Mallerstang Farm, bearing left by the covered stock pens. Ignore the gate on the left leading uphill. Continue on the farm drive for about 50 paces, then head left across the field to a wall stile. Cross and continue beside the Eden on a rough path through woodland to a wooden bridge over the river.

4 Cross the bridge and follow the gravel road ahead back to the B6259.

5 Turn left to Mallerstang church (St Mary's) Ⓓ and go through the village of Outhgill Ⓔ. The Faraday house is a stone cottage on the corner of the second lane on the right. Continue past Ing Hill Lodge on the right, and a row of cottages on the left. Turn right over a stile on a signposted footpath to the right of a stone barn. Follow the wall on the left through a field gate to a white house. Go through a smaller gate on the far side of the house to Castlethwaite Gill Waterfall Ⓕ.

6 Walk up a steep grass bank beside the falls, round the top of them and down a walled lane to Castlethwaite Farm. Cross a stone slab over a tiny beck and turn left through a gate down a farm track. Where it curves tightly to the left, go through a wooden gate on the right, and cross diagonally right to a gate in the far corner of the field, aiming for Pendragon Castle Ⓖ.

7 From the castle, walk up the lane signposted to Ravenstonedale. Immediately after crossing a stone bridge, climb the breeze block stile signed to Shoregill and walk along the river-bank. After 100 yards (90m) follow a Right of Way sign pointing up a slope away from the river. At the top, bear left to keep parallel with the Eden (which is often out of sight) to Shoregill Ⓗ. You may have to leap over Riggs Gill and Moss Gill if they are in spate. On the outskirts of Shoregill, go through one of two adjacent field gates, past a 'bank barn' to another gate. Bear left past the holiday cottages and down the drive to the wooden bridge. Do not cross but retrace your outward steps to Mallerstang Farm. At the entrance, go through the

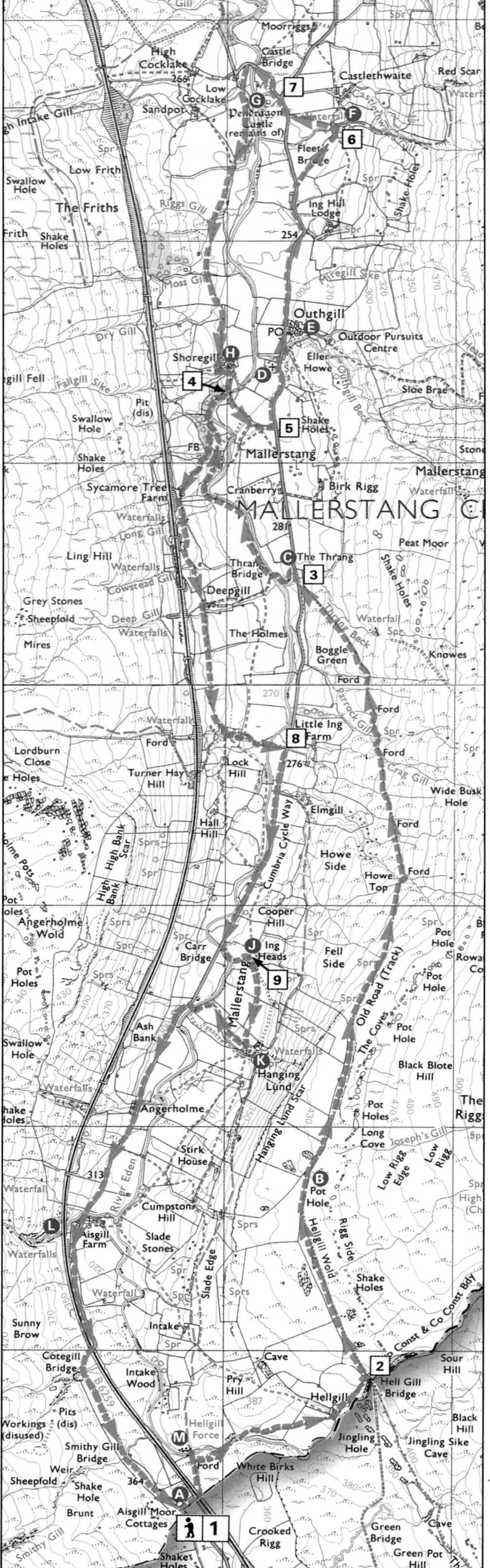

ALL PHOTOS: JOHN WATNEY

◀ *The ruined Pendragon Castle was reputedly built by Uther Pendragon, who failed to divert the Eden to fill his moat. It was twice burned by the Scots.*

the hillside. Originally a Roman road, it was used by Lady Anne Clifford (see box on page 60) in the 1660s as she went to and fro between her various castles.

The Highway is flanked by limestone outcrops or pavements and numerous shake holes and pot holes. At first the valley bottom is not visible, but after a while the way meets the edge of the valley and you can look 475 feet (145m) straight down to the North of England Falconry Centre at Ing Heads. When their birds are being flown they may come up to meet you! A pale yellow circle on the other side of the road to the Centre is a trotting ring.

THE THRANG

The way down is a long slope, in parts rough going and steep. After heavy rain, four streams have to be forded; at other times, there is just a scramble over wet boulders.

On the road at the bottom is The Thrang Ⓒ, a Victorian rectory turned country hotel. There is usually a prominent notice which declares 'Tearoom Closed', but in a window a smaller notice says 'Walkers in urgent need of refreshments, ring and we will serve you if we can'.

There is a short detour through a pleasant wood to Mallerstang's church Ⓓ, restored by Lady Anne Clifford in 1663. Her coat of arms is inside. By the door are shelves from which bread has been distributed since the 18th century, in accordance with a charitable bequest.

ARTHURIAN CASTLE

To the north is the only village in the valley, Outhgill Ⓔ. It has no shop or pub, but some very pretty houses. One of these was the home of the blacksmith, who was the father of Michael Faraday, the scientist.

A little further up the road, a field-path leads to a waterfall Ⓕ in a grotto below Castlethwaite Farm. The water appears from a hole in the rockface and cascades down about 20 feet (6m) of stone stairway. It is hardly dramatic, but very hidden away, dark and curious.

The turning point of the walk is Pendragon Castle Ⓖ, a small, picturesque ruin surrounded by a deep, dry moat. It was supposedly the home of Uther Pendragon, father of King Arthur, but the existing building is only 12th-century.

It was the seat of the lords of the manor, the most notable being Hugh de Morville, one of the three knights who murdered Thomas à Becket. The castle was restored by Lady Anne Clifford in 1660. It stands on

▼ *The route crosses Thrang Bridge on the way to Outhgill. There it passes a cottage (above) where Michael Faraday's family once lived. The great scientist was born in Surrey in 1791.*

gate on the right and follow the drive up to Sycamore Tree Farm. The path continues behind the farmhouse, parallel to the railway. At the derelict barn, go ahead through a decrepit gate and continue along the contours, where the remains of an ancient path can be seen in places. Pass Deepgill Farm and cross three fields. Turn left at the next group of buildings and go down the drive to the B6259.

8 Turn right for over ½ mile (800m), then left on the well signed drive to the Falconry Centre Ⓙ.

9 Leave the Centre by crossing the field on the right of the house to a gate. Cross the next two fields, first to a V-gap stile, then to a stone stile marked by a yellow disc, towards Hanging Lund Ⓚ. The falls, if in water, are large and easy to see without intruding on the farm. Take the farm road back down to the road. Turn left and walk past the viaduct Ⓛ to Aisgill Moor Cottages. To reach Hellgill Force Ⓜ, go over the railway bridge by Aisgill Crafts and continue to a shallow ford which crosses the top of the Force. The best view is to be had from the grass slopes below.

▶*The Blue Peter locomotive crosses Aisgill Viaduct. It took 6,000 navvies six years to build the railway line.*

private ground, but access is permitted through the roadside gate.

There is a gentle stroll along the foot of the fells on the west bank of the river, with long vistas up and down the wider end of the valley to Shoregill Ⓗ, a farm which, along with its outbuildings, has been converted into holiday homes.

FALCONRY CENTRE

You then return to Mallerstang Farm and climb the fellside to walk alongside the railway, with splendid views across the valley, before dropping down again to visit the Falconry Centre Ⓙ at Ing Heads. Here, flying demonstrations are given several times a day, if the weather permits. Visitors, appropriately gloved, may handle the birds, which include various species of hawk, owl, falcon and eagle.

From here it is a few minutes' walk across fields to view Hanging Lund Ⓚ, a fellside waterfall behind some farmhouses. It is not worth the detour after a spell of dry weather, in which case you should continue along the road to Aisgill Viaduct Ⓛ.

This elegant structure spans a deep cleft in the hillside down which three gills pour. There are paths leading up on either side to the high ground above the viaduct, a favourite perch for steam buffs.

It is less than a mile (1.6km) back to Aisgill Crafts, and there is one more sight to see near there. A three minute walk round the back of the cottages takes you to Hellgill Force Ⓜ, where the Eden proper starts. The water plunges in a white torrent after heavy rain, or makes a delicate, tinkling tracery in dry spells. It is either impressive or charming, and either way makes a good place to sit and relax after a long walk.

▼*Hell Gill Beck tumbles over Hellgill Force and becomes known as the River Eden from this point onwards.*

ALL PHOTOS: JOHN WATNEY

Lady Anne

Lady Anne Clifford was born in Skipton Castle in January 1590, during the reign of Elizabeth I, and was the only child of the 3rd Earl of Cumberland to survive beyond infancy. She was brought up around the royal court in London and was a good student, knowing her poetry, classics and history.

Above all she was a girl of great determination, a fact which her father seemed not to notice. He died when she was 15, and she was dismayed to learn that he had left his vast estates in Cumberland, Westmorland and Yorkshire to his brother, judging his daughter incapable of managing them.

From that moment she fought for what she saw as her rightful inheritance. She was opposed by James I, the church and both her two husbands. Eventually, in 1643, her cousin Henry died childless and she inherited the property.

At the age of 60, and twice widowed, she went north to spend her remaining 26 years supervising the rebuilding of her legacy of castles and churches. She travelled constantly by horse litter. The Highway of this walk was the rough, and often bitterly cold and wet, road along which the old lady was borne between her Yorkshire estates and her more northerly properties.

Lady Anne not only restored churches, but built new ones, as well as constructing almshouses at Appleby. She died, at the age of 86, at Brougham Castle, in the room in which her father had been born.

Lady Anne Clifford, depicted here in a triptych at Appleby Castle, also owned castles at Skipton, Brough, Brougham and Castlethwaite.

TAKING THE NATURE TRAIL

18

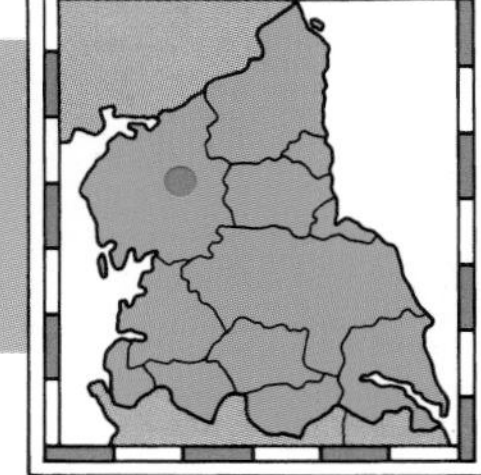

DURHAM

Through a nature reserve to one of Durham's finest waterfalls

Cauldron Snout, one of several beautiful waterfalls in Upper Teesdale, is in a nature reserve. The walk is on a Nature Trail to the falls and crosses Widdybank Fell, an area of rich botanical interest. Apart from the descent beside the waterfall, the route is also accessible to disabled people.

The walk starts by Cow Green Reservoir Ⓐ, which was formed in 1970 by the building of a dam across the River Tees under Cross Fell, at 2930 feet (879 metres), the highest point in the Pennines. The dam was built after fierce opposition since the reservoir flooded a large area of botanical importance.

SIMON WARNER. INSET: J. HAYWARD/NHPA

▲ *Cauldron Snout gushes over sedimentary rocks which have eroded more quickly than the hard Whin Sill at its base. (inset) The rare spring gentian can be seen on close inspection of the grassy areas of the Trail. (below) The weather station on Widdybank Fell.*

FACT FILE

- Upper Teesdale National Nature Reserve
- Outdoor Leisure Map 31, grid reference NY 810309
- Allow up to 2 hours
- Mostly on tarmac road to the top of the waterfall (wheelchair access along road). Rocky path beside the falls. Can be slippery in the gorge
- P By Cow Green Reservoir, reached by a minor road from Langdon Beck, off the B6277 Barnard Castle to Alston road
- T Bus service from Barnard Castle to Forest-in-Teesdale, 2 miles (3.2 km) from start of walk
- Hotels, pubs and cafés at Middleton-in-Teesdale, 10 miles (16 km) away, and Alston, 18 miles (28.8 km) away
- WC Toilets at car park

The Nature Trail leads for a mile (1.6 km) to Cow Green Dam Ⓑ, where the Tees emerges again from the dam wall and starts its descent to Cauldron Snout Ⓒ. The river now plunges in a foaming cataract and a series of steep cascades to the peaceful meadows 200 feet (60 metres) below. The best view of the waterfall is from these meadows, where the Tees quietly flows past the crags of Falcon Clints Ⓓ. Another fine view is from the ridge between the Tees and Maizebeck on the other side of the river.

ALPINE PLANTS

The high altitude of the region means that the average temperature is cool, similar to that of Reykjavik in Iceland. This is one of the factors which have made Upper Teesdale a nature reserve of world importance. A range of arctic and alpine plants

JOHN WATNEY

THE WALK

COW GREEN-CAULDRON SNOUT

The walk begins at the car park which is by Cow Green Reservoir **A**.

1 Leave the car park by Cow Green Reservoir and walk up the road for a short way to a sign by a gravel path across the moorland. Follow the gravel path until it joins a track. Turn left along the track and follow it for 150 yards (135 metres) to a gate across a metalled road which leads to Cow Green Dam **B**. There is a gate for pedestrians and for wheelchairs beside the locked gate.

2 Continue to the dam. Points of interest along the Nature Trail are marked by numbers painted on rocks beside the road. Halfway along, the road passes beside a weather station. After passing the dam, the road descends to a bridge across the river.

3 Do not cross the bridge but follow a path beside the river, initially on

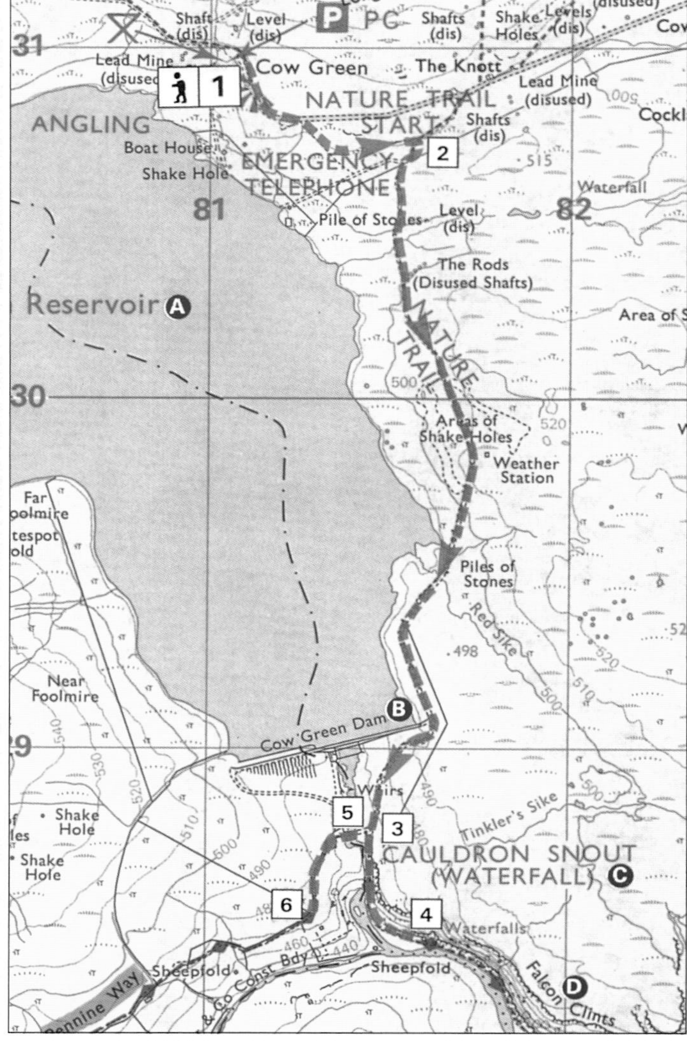

large stones set in the peaty ground, and then on a natural rocky staircase that descends the gorge. Care is needed here, especially in wet weather and good walking shoes or boots should be worn. There are some steep sections, but the route eventually reaches the level ground at the bottom of the falls **C**.

4 Return to the car park, retracing your steps along the same route.

5 A short diversion gives a good view of Cauldron Snout, and the view downstream past Falcon Clints **D**. Cross the bridge at the top of the falls and follow the track for 1/4 mile (400 metres) to a bend. From a little way below the barn on the left, there is a good view over the falls and the route of the Pennine Way along the banks of the Tees below Falcon Clints.

6 Retrace your steps and return to **5.** Then return along the same route to the car park.

◀ *The River Tees meanders past Falcon Clints and the Pennine Way.*

▼ *Part of the walk follows the route of an old mine railway.*

BOTH PHOTOS JOHN WATNEY

has remained here since the ice sheets of the last glaciation receded, some 15–20,000 years ago.

There are many rare plants which are very fragile, so visitors must keep to the paths. The small, hardy Swaledale sheep play an essential part in maintaining the botanical balance by grazing, which prevents coarser grasses from spreading over the rarer species.

The grassy limestone areas contain many different plants and grasses. There are common varieties such as harebell, wild thyme and rock rose and many rare species such as the spring gentian which is only found in this spot and in south-west Ireland.

The limestone grasslands are separated by heather and cotton-grass areas which grow on peat. Many upland birds nest here, such as red grouse, golden plover, redshank, lapwing, curlew, wheatear, skylark and meadow pipit.

THE TEES VALLEY

G.T. CAMBRIDGE/NHPA

AA PICTURE LIBRARY

▲ *The ruins of Barnard Castle tower above the River Tees. The red berries of the cuckoo pint (inset) appear in late summer and provide food for birds, but are poisonous to humans.*

A riverside route from a market town to Egglestone Abbey

This walk leads through the historic town of Barnard Castle Ⓐ along the banks of the River Tees to the majestic ruins of Egglestone Abbey Ⓔ. Woodlands and pastures give way to high, windswept moors, which reach far beyond the crumbling walls of the town's castle.

The town of Barnard Castle lies in the Tees Valley. Not only is it surrounded by spectacular scenery, but it also boasts architecture of historic significance. Along Galgate are fine examples of Georgian architecture, including some of the pubs. The King's Head Hotel is where Charles Dickens stayed while researching *Nicholas Nickleby*.

ANCIENT CASTLE

Behind Trinity Methodist Chapel lie the ruins of Barnard Castle Ⓑ, high above the foaming River Tees. The castle dates from the 12th century and the oldest standing section is Balliol Tower, built from sandstone 700 years ago. Its name comes from its founder, Guy de Balliol, Lord of Bailleul in France. His successor Bernard gave the town its current name. A later Balliol, John, founded Balliol College, Oxford.

The castle itself, once one of the largest castles in England, has a long and turbulent history. For a time, it was home to Warwick the Kingmaker, who met his death at the Battle of Bosworth Field in 1485. During the Middle Ages, servants from the castle were allowed to graze their animals on common ground called the Desmesnes.

Abbey Bridge Ⓕ, with its magnificent balustrade, was built in 1773. County Bridge spans the River Tees below the castle. A bridge has forded the river here for nearly 700 years. A small chapel used to stand in the middle of the bridge where eloping couples were married.

Downstream there used to be woollen mills and carpet factories, as well as the workshops of glove makers, tanners, stocking makers

FACT FILE

- Barnard Castle in the Tees Valley, about 16 miles (25.6km) west of Darlington
- Pathfinder 599 (NZ 01/11) grid reference NZ 051166

- Allow 2 hours
- Fairly easy, though parts can be muddy in wet weather; wear stout shoes or wellington boots
- Free parking in the centre of Barnard Castle
- Bus service from Darlington to town centre
- Pubs and cafés in Barnard Castle. Tea rooms at Bowes Museum open most of the year

▶ *This magnificent stone tower stands in the market place in the centre of Barnard Castle.*

AA PICTURE LIBRARY

THE WALK

BARNARD CASTLE – EGGLESTONE ABBEY

The walk begins at the free car park in the centre of the town of Barnard Castle (A).

1 Leave the car park and walk to the Tourist Information Centre which is clearly signposted on King Street. Turn left into Galgate, cross the road and walk down to the bottom of the hill until facing Trinity Methodist Chapel. Cross road and follow path down the right-hand side of the chapel. Directly behind is the entrance to the ruins of Barnard Castle (B). After leaving the castle rejoin the path and turn left. Continue until the path meets the road.

2 Turn right to go over County Bridge (C), then left at The White Swan Inn. Continue along the road for about 1/4 mile (400 metres). Turn left on to a footpath following the River Tees. When the path divides, take the right fork between houses and bungalows, then turn right again up the hill to a road.

3 Turn left along the road and continue to the end to go through a gate in a narrow stone gap in the wall. Bear right along the road through caravan park and up the steep hill to a row of poplar trees.

4 Just before the first tree is a stile into a field. Cross here and walk to the gate directly opposite. Go through this field and the next, keeping to the hedge on your left. Leave the field through a narrow gap in the wall and continue left along a leafy lane, almost to Bow Bridge. Turn right and cross Thorsgill Beck by this packhorse bridge (D), returning to the lane via a kissing gate. Turn right and right again, opposite a cottage, to the ruins of Egglestone Abbey (E).

5 Leave the abbey, return to lane opposite cottage and turn right. At road junction, turn left over Abbey Bridge (F). Once across turn immediately left through a narrow gap in the wall into some woods; follow path to stile at end of woods. Cross into field and, keeping close to the river, pass through three fields. At the end of the third field, follow narrow path between river and fence to enter field at the end.

6 Head for the barn. Just before reaching it turn right between a hawthorn tree and an oak tree. Continue up centre of field making for a gate with a stile next to it. Cross stile and follow diagonal path left through two fields, coming out at a kissing gate. Turn right down Parsons Lonnen and right again at the end into Westwick Road.

7 Continue for a short distance, cross road and enter ground of Bowes Museum (G). Leave the museum, turn right into Westwick Road and continue along Newgate, which brings you out at Market Cross (H).

8 Turn left at Market Cross, by St Mary's Church and go to the bottom of the hill, passing Blagraves House (J) on your left. Continue along Thorngate to cross footbridge and turn right. Return to the town centre and the start of the walk.

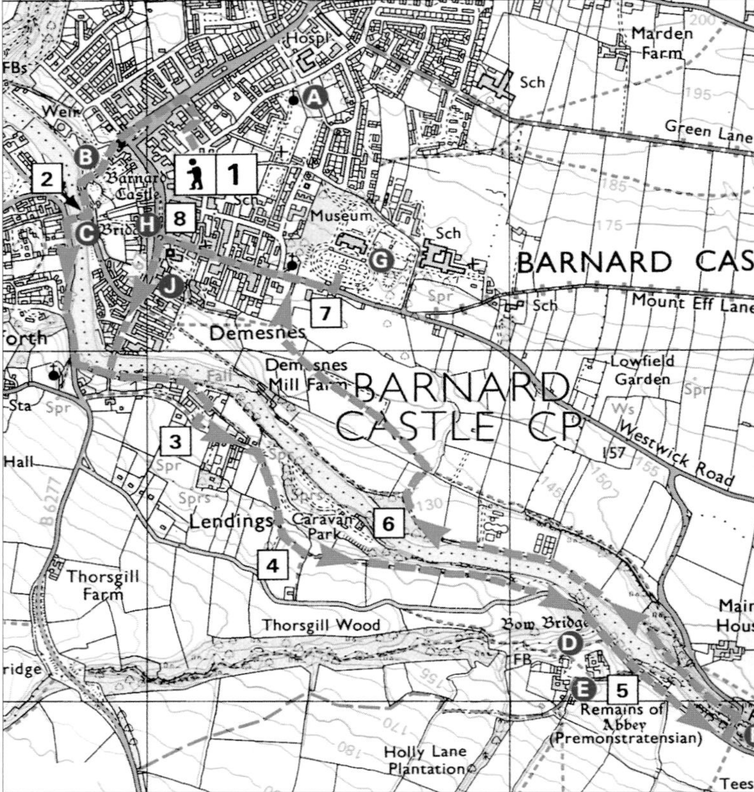

NORTH-HUMBRIA TOURIST BOARD

◀ *The ruins of Egglestone Abbey, where much of the original 12th-century building can still be seen.*

and dyers along the river banks. During the 19th century these were all very successful industries and many fine Georgian buildings testify to the prosperity of the area.

Beyond the river stands the Bowes Museum (G), which was opened by John and Josephine Bowes in 1892 to house fine art objects. The museum is still open to the public and contains paintings, costumes, toys and furniture.

Egglestone Abbey is reached after crossing Thorsgill Beck by Bow Bridge (D), a cobbled 17th-century packhorse bridge. The abbey, now in ruins, was founded in 1190. Henry VIII dissolved the monastery in 1536, though the original and later buildings are all still visible

Near the Bowes Museum is the Market Cross (H). This octagonal building has been a town hall and a gaol. Nearby is Blagraves House (J), one of the oldest buildings in the town.

THE PROUD TOWERS

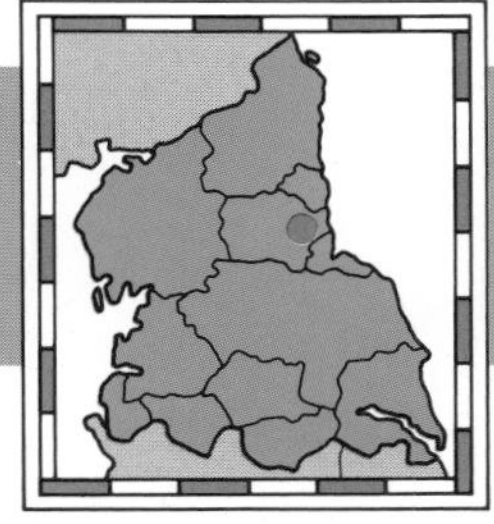

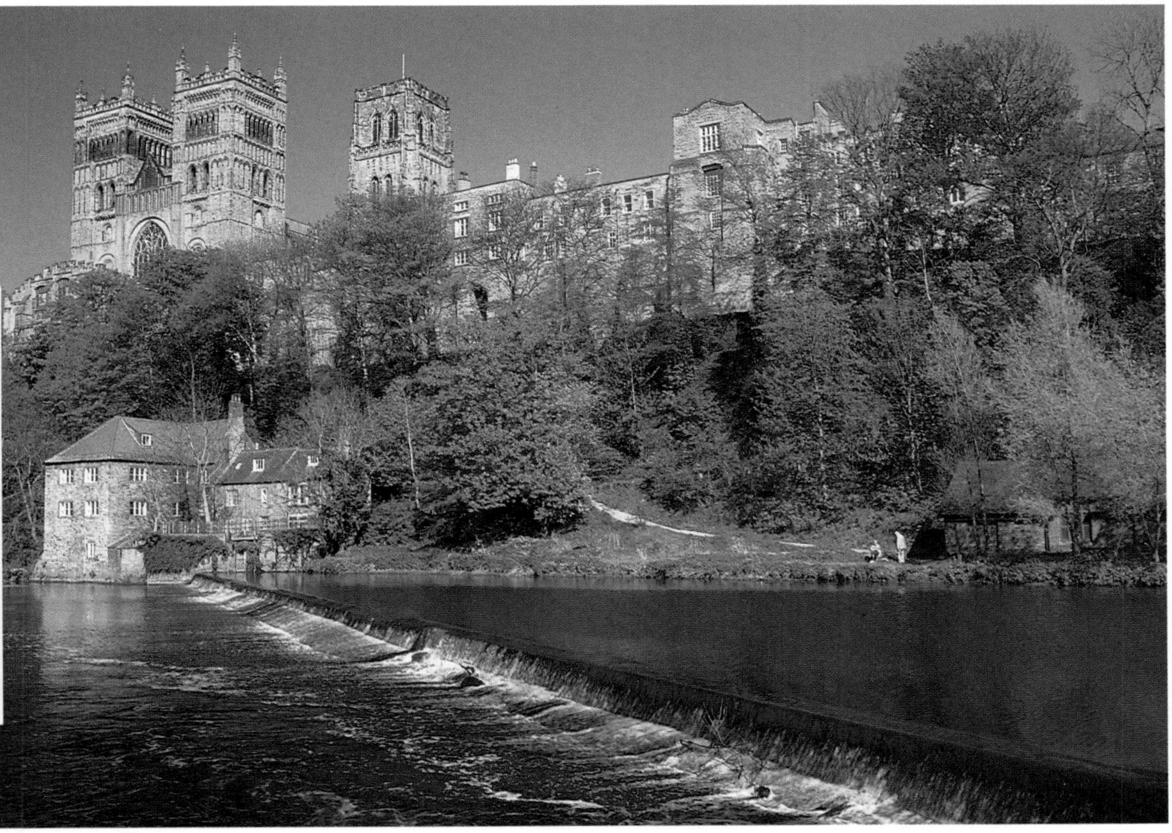

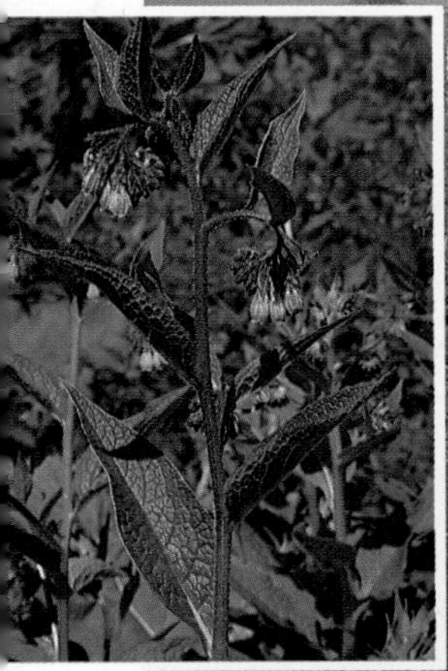

20

DURHAM

AA PICTURE LIBRARY. INSET: J & M BAIN/NHPA

A northern cathedral city on the banks of the River Wear

It is a strange anomaly that, in a country which is flattest to the east, England's three most visually dominant cathedrals — Ely, Lincoln, and Durham ⓓ — stand proudly raised against eastern skies. To appreciate the cathedral fully it is necessary to view the city initially from a distance, and on foot.

This walk avoids any parking and traffic problems in Durham, and threads its way along the lightly wooded banks of the River Wear into the very heart of the city.

ST CUTHBERT

From the river bank under Pelaw Wood ⓐ a grand, complete outline of Durham Cathedral comes into view. Further along the route its twin pinnacled towers can be seen to the right; they are balanced beautifully on the left by smaller turrets. Nearby is Durham Castle, sharing this near-island site.

Durham has several bridges. New Elvet Bridge ⓑ was built in the 12th century as a second river crossing. Of its 14 arches only 12 are now visible, while its chapel and medieval houses have disappeared. The cathedral was built as a shrine for the body of St Cuthbert, replacing an earlier Saxon Church on this site. St Cuthbert died in 687AD, but apparently, 11 years later his body was found to be undecayed.

FACT FILE

- Durham, County Durham
- Pathfinder 572 (NZ 24/34), grid reference NZ 287410
- 5 hours, including visit to cathedral
- A gentle climb to the cathedral. Riverside paths can be muddy
- Adjacent to Shincliffe Bridge in a lane signposted 'Houghall Farm and Gardens'
- Rose Tree Inn across Shincliffe Bridge. Cathedral coffee shop and toilets

▲*Durham Cathedral, on the River Wear, was begun in 1093 and completed 40 years later. Common comfrey (inset) has been used in medicines for centuries and can be eaten when cooked.*

DANISH RAIDS

To escape Danish raids in the 9th century, the monks who were caring for his remains began travelling throughout the north, taking the body of the saint with them. It was over 100 years before they built a church in Durham. Enshrined over a century later, St Cuthbert's body was still well preserved and the fame of this and his great holiness brought vast numbers of pilgrims

THE WALK

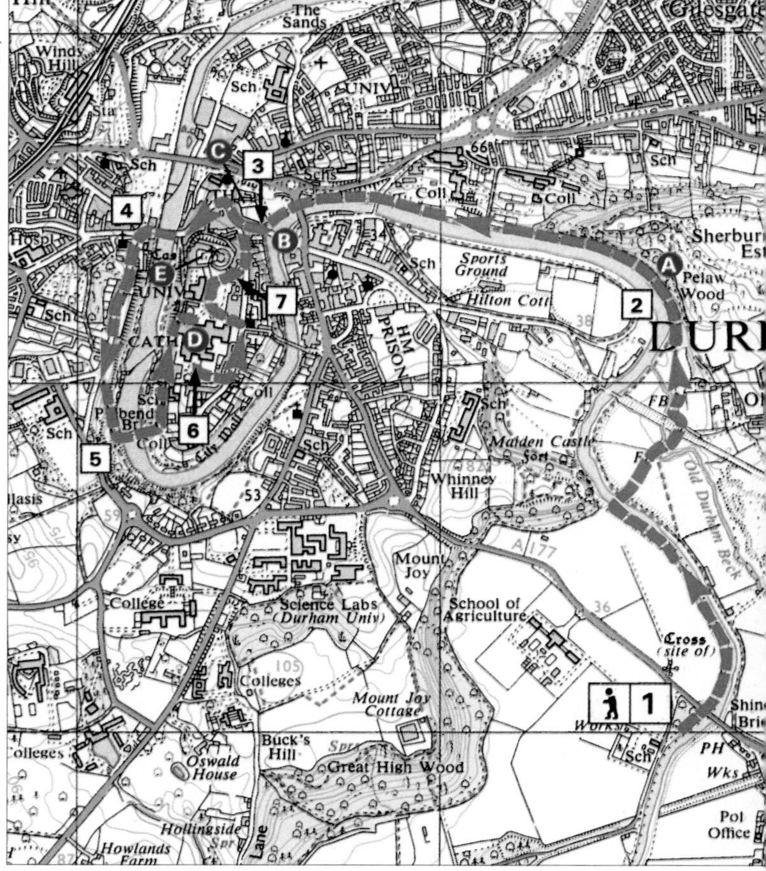

DURHAM

The walk begins next to Shincliffe Bridge in a lane signposted 'Hougall Farm and Gardens'.

1 Cross the road, heading for the river bank. You will see a thread of red hilltop houses ahead. A good path leads to a foot suspension bridge, cross it and continue straight across a playing field to reach another footbridge over a stream. Continue straight on between the red brick cheeks of a derelict railway arch. The path turns left to follow a wooded stream back to the River Wear, which is quite a sizeable river here. There is a better path ahead, following along under Pelaw Wood Ⓐ towards the city.

2 The riverside path continues, flanking the newish buildings of England's third oldest university. Ignore the first two bridges, but at the third take flight of steps up to old Elvet Bridge Ⓑ.

3 Turn right into an attractive stone-clad thoroughfare rising towards Saddler Street and the market place Ⓒ. Now turn left along Silver Street, to cross the River Wear once again at Framwelgate.

4 Go left round two sides of 'The Fighting Cocks', taking the part-cobbled South Street which rises steadily to afford splendid views of the cathedral. Beyond the top of the hill at the junction with South Street turn left through a gap in the stone wall, which gives access to a path through woodland, down to Prebends Bridge.

5 Cross the bridge, then take the upper of the two paths on the left, rising towards the cathedral Ⓓ. At the top, keep to the left-hand path which passes under the west end of the cathedral. Turn right at top of next rise between high walling and come out onto Palace Green. The north door of the cathedral with its sanctuary knocker is on the right. Enter the cathedral.

6 Leave the cathedral Treasury, return through the cloisters and exit at the south-east corner into the College. Turn left through archway at the east turning left into North Bailey. Pass east end of the cathedral and turn left to Palace Green. Ahead is Durham Castle Ⓔ, part of the university and open to the public (restricted during term time).

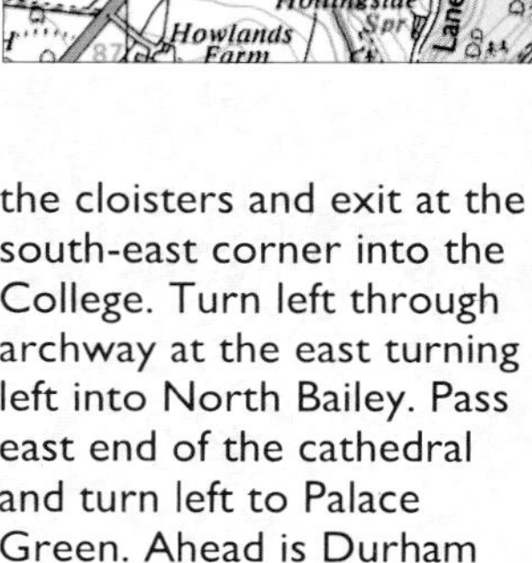

7 Leave the castle and walk into Saddler Street which leads down to Elvet Bridge. From Stage 3 retrace your steps to the start of the walk.

NORTHUMBRIA TOURIST BOARD

▲*Framwelgate Bridge, partly constructed of York stone, has been a pedestrian bridge since 1975.*

►*Prior Castell's clock survived after 3,000 Scots were kept prisoner in the cathedral after the Battle of Dunbar.*

and enormous wealth to his shrine. St Cuthbert's earliest coffin, his pectoral cross and unique embroidered stoles are now on display in the Cathedral Treasury.

LAY RULERS

Durham Castle Ⓔ occupies the second most commanding position in the city. The Crypt Chapel is probably all that remains of the castle built in 1072, while the keep dates from 1840. Between the two is ranged a curve of buildings spanning the centuries when the bishops of Durham were lay rulers as well as religious leaders.

NEIL HOLMES

A Village on the Tees

21

DURHAM

◀*On the gentle, verdant slopes that roll away from the valley of the River Tees sit the buildings of East Barnley Farm. Shrubby cinquefoil (inset) is a typical Teesdale flower found on riverbanks.*

SIMON FRASER. INSET: ROBIN FLETCHER/SWIFT PICTURE LIBRARY

Exploring the slopes above the wooded banks of the River Tees

The green and fertile valley through which the River Tees flows is criss-crossed with dry-stone walls and punctuated by sturdy field barns. This walk along the valley begins at Romaldkirk, a picturesque village with three greens, stocks and a splendid water pump. It stands on a terrace above the river, overlooked by wild fells.

The church Ⓐ, dedicated to St Romald, dates from the 12th century, with later additions. Swifts nest over the Norman doorway. Inside, look for the Devil's Door, behind which Satan was supposed to lurk. It was blocked up in the late Middle Ages to keep him out. There is a 13th-century font and an effigy of the Lord of Bedale, Ravensworth and Cotherstone.

WILD FLOWERS

You walk down a path bordered with forget-me-nots and greater stitchwort, then cut through pastures in which cowslips, primroses and violets flower, to join the Tees Ⓑ. The river rises on the wilderness of Cross Fell, then courses down a narrow valley to thunder, impetuously and magnificently, over the falls of Caldron Snout and High Force. By the time it arrives at Romaldkirk, its progress is serene and stately, as it gathers itself for another surge through the tree-clad gorges by Cotherstone and Barnard Castle.

FACT FILE

- Romaldkirk, 5 miles (8km) north-west of Barnard Castle, on the B6277
- Outdoor Leisure Map 31, grid reference NY 994220
- miles 0 1 2 3 4 5 6 7 8 9 10 miles / kms 0 1 2 3 4 5 6 7 8 9 10 11 12 13 14 15 kms
- Allow 3 hours
- Level or gently sloping paths most of the way. Woodland paths close to the river may be slippery after rain. Some fallen trees across the path. Walking boots advisable
- P At the start
- The Rose and Crown pub, Romaldkirk

▶*The stocks on the green in the centre of the village of Romaldkirk have undergone some recent renovation.*

17TH-CENTURY FARM

You go over the tributary stream, Wilden Beck, on stepping stones, then cross a footbridge to climb through gorse and pasture to High Shipley Farm Ⓒ, which carries a plaque dated 1670.

The original farm is thought to have been built for Richard III, and was given to Miles Forest for his alleged part in the murder of the Princes in the Tower. The theory goes that High Shipley was far enough from London to keep the murderer out of the way, and attractive enough to keep him silent.

You continue on the high ground, where you can often hear curlews call, to Raygill Beck, an unassuming little stream that forms an exuberant waterfall as it plummets into a sheer-sided gill. Descending through pasture, you come to Great Wood Ⓓ, a Site of Special Scientific Interest. Wood anemones, bluebells and red campion grow by the path in this glorious deciduous woodland, where the noise of the river mingles with the wonderfully sweet

SIMON FRASER

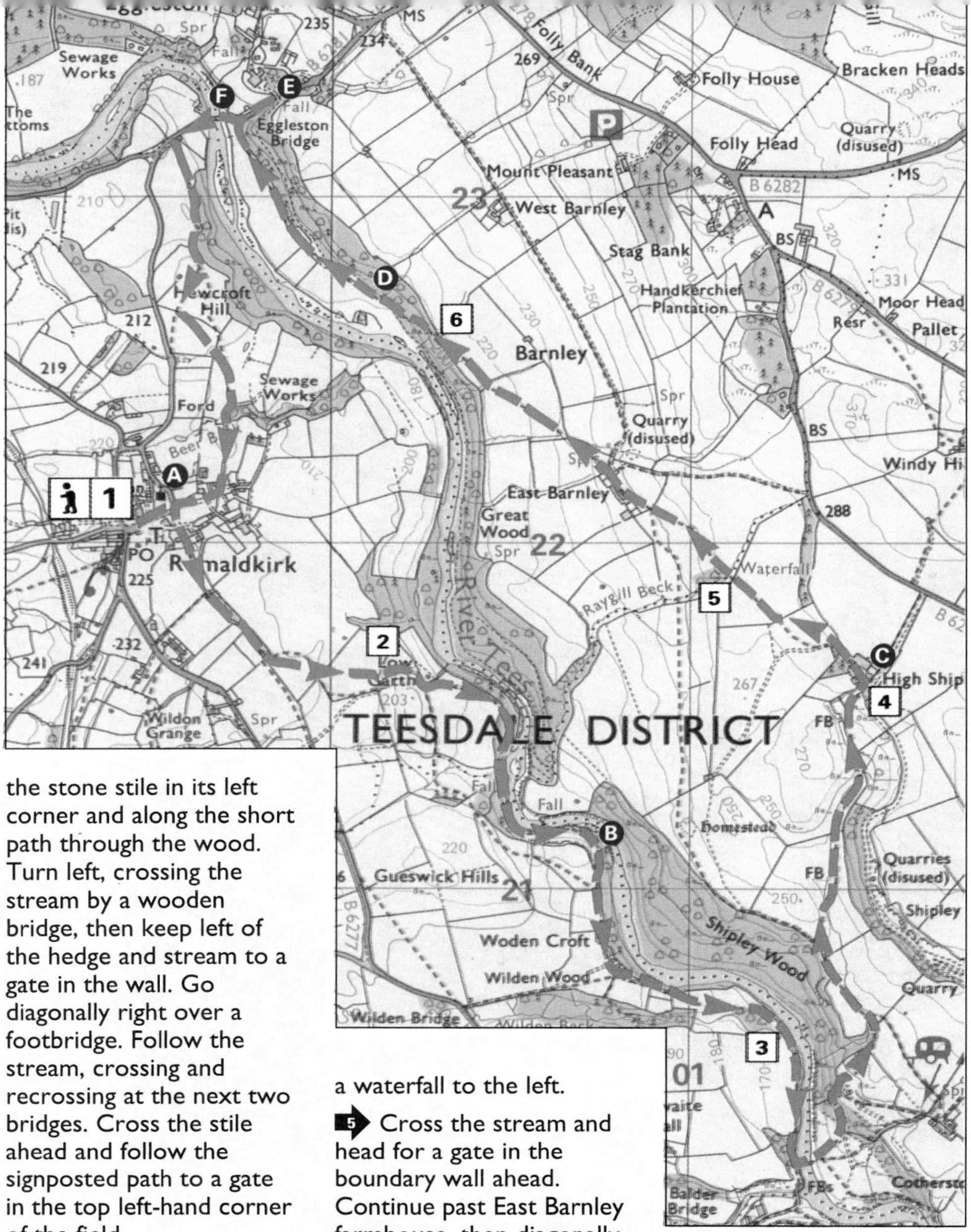

THE WALK

ROMALDKIRK – HIGH SHIPLEY

The walk begins in the car park behind the Rose and Crown pub in the centre of Romaldkirk.

1 Turn left to visit the church Ⓐ. Walk across the green to take a signposted footpath to the left of Rose Stile Cottage. At two gates, go through the left-hand one, and then go half-left across the pasture to another gate.

2 From a waymarked gap-stile, descend to a derelict farm. Cross the stile beyond. At the far left corner of the pasture, go through the waymarked gate into a wood. Follow the path along the Tees Ⓑ and up out of the wood. Walk ahead and join a farm track at a stile. Continue ahead past beech trees and farm buildings and along a cobbled yard to a white gate. Follow a wall round to the left, passing in front of a large house. Go through the next gate and walk across the parkland to a stile in the far left corner.

3 Go across stepping stones and up some sandstone steps. Follow the path close by the river to a footbridge. Cross it and climb through the gorse on the slope ahead. The path joins a cart track. Cross a stile, and walk through the caravan site past a brick building. Take a track through more gorse up a slope to a waymarked gate. Go through the pasture to the stone stile in its left corner and along the short path through the wood. Turn left, crossing the stream by a wooden bridge, then keep left of the hedge and stream to a gate in the wall. Go diagonally right over a footbridge. Follow the stream, crossing and recrossing at the next two bridges. Cross the stile ahead and follow the signposted path to a gate in the top left-hand corner of the field.

4 Turn left on a narrow lane to High Shipley Farm Ⓒ. Go left through the main gate and walk between the farmhouse and outbuildings to a white, waymarked gate. Go through another gate, and follow the field wall as far as a tree beside a gate in the wall ahead. Continue diagonally left to a signposted stile. Cross a field to another stile. Beyond is Raygill Beck with a waterfall to the left.

5 Cross the stream and head for a gate in the boundary wall ahead. Continue past East Barnley farmhouse, then diagonally downhill through a waymarked gate and over a stile into Great Wood Ⓓ.

6 Go down some steps to cross a stream above a waterfall, then up and down a stepped path to a tarmac road. At the junction, turn right to the waterfall below the bridge Ⓔ, then retrace your steps to cross the Tees via Eggleston Bridge Ⓕ. Take a signposted path to the left, keeping to the right of a fence and wall to a waymarked stile. Cross and go ahead and slightly right to another stile in the right corner, then follow a sheep track bearing left around the stone-walled burial ground. Just before Beer Beck, cross a stone stile into a copse on your left. Turn right through the trees to cross a stone bridge over the stream and follow Primrose Lane back into Romaldkirk.

songs of willow warblers, and the rich, clear calls of blackcaps.

At the other side of the wood, it is worth making a short detour up the road to your right towards a two-arched bridge, part of the Eggleton Hall estate, to look over the wall to where a splendid fall Ⓔ tumbles beneath one of the arches. If you continue uphill, you will see another waterfall on the right, in the grounds of the Hall.

Eggleston Bridge Ⓕ takes you back across the Tees. The dressed sandstone bridge has huge, pointed cutwaters cleaving the river. The bridge probably dates originally from some time in the early 15th century, but was rebuilt in the 17th century and again in 1983-4.

On the other side of the bridge a path and a track, known evocatively as Primrose Lane, return you to Romaldkirk and the start.

VALLEY OF THE PRINCE BISHOPS

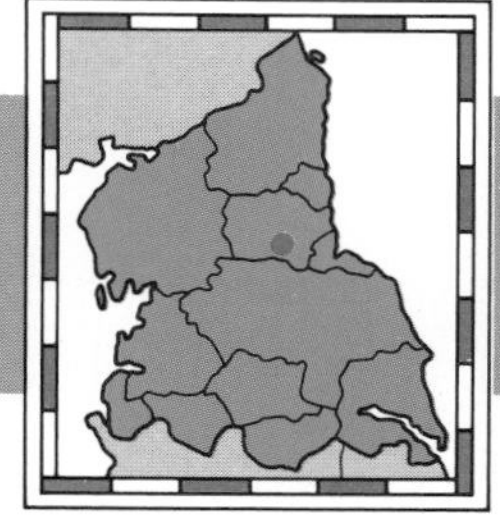

PAUL STERRY/NATURE PHOTOGRAPHERS

FACT FILE

- Bishop Auckland, 10 miles (16km) south of Durham, on the A689
- Pathfinders 580 (NZ 12/13), 581 (NZ 23/33) and 590 (NZ 22/32), grid reference NZ 208301

miles 0 1 2 3 4 5 6 7 8 9 10 miles
kms 0 1 2 3 4 5 6 7 8 9 10 11 12 13 14 15 kms

- Allow at least 4 hours
- Woodland, riverside and open paths. Some steep ascents and descents, which are slippery when wet. Good walking shoes or boots are essential
- Plenty of free parking in the town
- For details of BR train services, Tel. (01325) 355111
- Several pubs in Bishop Auckland, and the Saxon Inn in Escomb
- Shops, restaurants and cafés in Bishop Auckland
- In Bishop Auckland and in Escomb
- Auckland Castle is open May-Sept, Tel. (01388) 601627. Vinovia Roman Baths are open Apr-Sept, Tel. (01388) 663089
- For tourist information, Tel. (01388) 527650

JASON SMALLEY

▲*Auckland Castle, begun in the 12th century, was an elaborate fortified palace for the powerful Prince Bishops of Durham. The water vole (above left) can be seen in the local rivers.*

From a 12th-century palace to an out-of-the-way Saxon church

In the heart of County Durham, just south of where the old Roman Road, Dere Street, crosses the River Wear, is Bishop Auckland, the gateway to Weardale.

In the Middle Ages, the area was an immense hunting ground. An elaborate palace was built here for the Prince Bishops of Durham, who ruled an area stretching from the Tees almost to the Forth. Often more powerful than the monarch, they raised their own armies to quell the Scots, held their own courts and even minted their own coinage.

This walk around the heartland of their domain begins in the Market Place Ⓐ, which has a distinctly Continental air. The large town hall of 1860 is in Franco-Flemish style, while the neighbouring buildings have prominent Germanic facades and elegant Grecian columns.

Victorian St Anne's Church, built in the Early English style, is the fourth place of worship on the site. The first was well established by the end of the 14th century, when it was used to hold services for the overflow from the bishop's own chapel.

THE WALK

BISHOP AUCKLAND – BINCHESTER – ESCOMB

The walk begins in the car park west of Market Place in Bishop Auckland.

1 Turn left along Bondgate to Market Place **A**. Go through the square to join the road through the Bishops' Gate. Beyond Auckland Castle **B**, you enter Auckland Park. Go through a gate and turn left. Bear right at a fork to the Deer Shelter **C**. Proceed on a narrow track to rejoin the main path.

2 Cross Jock's Bridge. Go through a kissing-gate and

bear right onto a narrow uphill path. Bear right at the first fork, then left at the next, and cross a field to a step-stile. Continue on this path around the edge of the golf course. Go straight over the club's entrance road, to reach a path running alongside the perimeter wall.

3 Follow this path over step-stiles to a T-junction and turn left along an old railway line. Pass under the Bishop's Bridge **D** and

The route into town follows Newgate Street, which was built over Dere Street, and retains its straight Roman course beyond the bustling precinct to where the ramshackle tenements of Bishop Auckland's poorhouse once stood.

CASTLE AND CHAPEL

The massive Gothic gatehouse of the castle is flanked by old, cream-washed stone cottages with Dutch gables and red pantile roofs. It is crowned by a turreted clock and weather vane, built for Bishop Richard Trevor in the 1760s. The upper floor of the three-storied porter's lodge on the right is a fake.

A battlemented screen wall, built by James Wyatt in 1796, separates the magnificent Auckland Castle **B** from the park. The building is a rugged mix of architectural styles. It was begun by Bishop Hugh Pudsey in the 12th century as a Norman manor house, and has been embellished by several of the 57 bishops who succeeded him.

Adjoining the castle is St Peter's Chapel, an architectural treasure. Once the great banqueting hall of the manor house, it was converted into a place of worship in 1665. Its tall, wide arcades and handsome marble arches complement some baroque 17th-century screens and a richly ornamented ceiling.

Undulating parkland leads to the

JASON SMALLEY

◀Auckland Castle's Gothic gatehouse. Last century, herds of Highland cattle passed here on the way to London.

another bridge. Over the crest of the hill, branch off left, opposite a seat, onto a narrow path to a step-stile. Cross and turn immediately left over another stile into Bellburn Wood. Follow the path through the woods, bearing right at each fork.

4 At the end of the woods, go over a step-stile and turn immediately left over another stile. Cross a field, keeping the fence to your left. At the top corner, go over a step-stile and turn left around the edge of the field and over another step-stile, the fence to your left. Another stile will lead you immediately onto a narrow path, then down a steep incline to a road.

5 Turn right. Where the road bends left, bear right uphill onto a driveway, past Binchester Nursing Home to the Roman fort of Vinovia **E**. Retrace your steps to the road and continue uphill into Bishop Auckland. Turn right into The Batts. Beyond the houses, cross a field and go under the viaduct

6 At the river bridge, go up onto the road and turn left. Turn first right along a road. Follow the riverside. After about ¾ mile (1.2km), the path swings left, uphill, away from the river. At a fork by a seat, bear right. Continue ahead on this path. Cross the fields and two step-stiles.

7 Join a tarmac footpath between houses. Continue ahead to visit Escomb's church **F**. Retrace your steps to the second step-stile, recross and turn right, uphill across fields, with hedgerows to your right. Continue ahead beyond the railway, across fields and step-stiles, with hedgerows to your right. Follow a track to the main road.

8 Turn left. Opposite the Masons Arms, turn left onto a rough track. Continue across the railway line and turn right onto a narrow path to the riverside path. Follow the riverside path, then turn right on the main road, back to the car park.

▲*The lazy River Gaunless wanders through the parkland where deer once roamed. In 1760, Bishop Richard Trevor built the Gothic Deer Shelter (below right) for the animals.*

◀*Bishop's Bridge, screened with trees, crosses the line of an old railway.*

Deer Shelter **C**, a large, grassy quadrangle with crenellated cloisters, in which fallow deer once sheltered and were fed. The 18th-century building has an impressive tower; the upper floor was used by the bishop and his guests for a rest or a meal during hunting expeditions. Deer have not been seen in the park since 1856, but the shelter remains an eye-catching feature.

SPECIMEN TREES

The castle grounds cover 800 acres (320ha) and contain several magnificent specimen trees. Their natural silhouettes have developed fully away from the competition for space found in a natural woodland habitat. The park is full of birds, including tits, wagtails, finches and the handsome nuthatch, which may be heard hammering relentlessly on an acorn jammed into a bark crevice.

The River Gaunless meanders through the trees, its banks festooned with link frond, a seaweed that has spread inland. With luck, you may see a brilliant flash of colour as a kingfisher flies past.

You skirt the golf course to join Auckland Walk, a disused railway line whose banks are overgrown

◀*The shingle banks of the River Wear are a good place to see waders such as oystercatchers and common sandpipers.*

ALL PHOTOS: JASON SMALLEY

with brambles, rosebay willowherb and clumps of ox-eye daisies. Spanning the old line is the Bishop's Bridge **D**, which is lined by trees. They were planted at the request of the bishop, so that his guests, arriving by carriage along the Palace Drive, would not have their delicate sensibilities upset by having to gaze upon the unsightly railway.

You pass through Bellburn Wood, a dense broadleaved woodland, to visit the Roman fort of Vinovia **E** at Binchester. Built around AD80 to guard the main thoroughfare between York and Hadrian's Wall, Vinovia was a large fortification, covering 10 acres (4ha) in all, and with a garrison of 500.

Only a small section has been excavated. On display, inside a large timber structure, are the remains of the commandant's house and the heated baths, the most complete Roman bathhouse in Britain.

A series of connecting rooms was heated by hypocaust — hot air from furnaces was ducted through a labyrinth of underfloor tunnels to provide temperatures ranging from comfortably warm to sauna-hot. The ingenious underfloor structure is remarkably well preserved. Stacks of tiles were set close together, the top tile larger than the rest, and overlaid with concrete.

From here, the route leads to the River Wear, whose banks are a profusion of yellow loosestrife, monkey flower, Himalayan balsam and viper's bugloss. Dippers, oystercatchers and sandpipers can all be seen along the river, and the banks are honeycombed with the tunnels of water voles.

WHISKERED BATS

The path goes under the elegant, 13-arch Newton Cap Viaduct, which was built in 1857 to carry the railway over the Wear. Eventually, you come to Escomb, a former pit village sheltered by a steep hill. At its heart are a circular churchyard, and the smoke-blackened stones of one of the most complete Anglo-Saxon churches that can be found anywhere (see box).

Escomb's church **F** supports a number of whiskered bats, which are less than two inches (5cm) long and weigh less than ⅕ ounce (5.6g). The females gather here in a large breeding colony, hiding in the ancient roof space. The bats emerge to hunt for insects as dusk falls across the leafy graveyard and its lichen-covered tombstones.

From here, the walk leads across fields and twice goes over the railway line, before rejoining the path alongside the River Wear. This leads you back towards the start.

Escomb Church

Escomb's church, whose dedication has long been forgotten, was built between AD670 and AD690, and owes its survival in an almost untouched condition to its out-of-the-way location. The neighbouring Prince Bishops were far too preoccupied with their grandiose palace and chapel to pay much attention to the tiny, insignificant church on their doorstep.

All but the upper parts of the walls of this curiously tall, narrow structure contain dressed stone taken from the deserted fort at Binchester by Saxon settlers. Embedded in the north wall is a small, raised rosette, thought to be from a Roman altar, while beneath a ledge is an upside-down stone inscribed 'LEG VI' — sixth legion.

On the south wall of the nave is the oldest sundial in the country still on its original site. It bears a snake and the head of a beast, and is said to represent a stag (Christ) stamping on a serpent (the Devil).

Inside, the church's simplistic charm is enhanced by white-washed walls and plain glass windows. A small grave cover in the chancel marks the burial place of a long forgotten Christian. It is made from black marble, flecked with white fossilized coral, and was quarried in Frosterley on Wearside.

Perhaps the most attractive and evocative feature, though, is the elegant, round-headed chancel arch, with the broken outlines of a 12th-century painting still visible on its underside. It seems certain that this arch is Roman, and was transported stone by stone from Binchester to be carefully reconstructed at the core of a Saxon church.

A solid building with narrow windows, Escomb Church has neither tower nor spire.

▼*In spring and summer, the country path to the village of Escomb is lined with attractive wild flowers.*

IN SEARCH OF THE CHESHIRE CAT

JASON SMALLEY. INSET: STEPHEN DALTON/NHPA

▲*Croft Bridge, which was built 500 years ago, spans the Tees between North Yorkshire and Durham. The heart and dart moth (left), named after its wing markings, generally flies at night.*

Exploring the countryside in which Lewis Carroll grew up

The tranquil villages of Hurworth and Croft nestle on opposite banks of the River Tees. The former is in Durham and the latter in North Yorkshire. They share a timeless, rural quality best expressed in their quaint country churches, and each of them nurtured men whose mathematical talents, among others, bordered on genius.

The walk begins in Hurworth-on-Tees, which boasts several elegant Georgian houses. Their doorways and windows are hung with roses, wisteria and clematis, and their gardens are awash with colourful perennials. This lovely village was the birthplace and lifelong home of William Emerson (1701-1782).

The son of a local schoolmaster, he began his working life as a mason and thatcher, teaching himself the rudiments of mathematics and mechanics in his spare time. Later, he lived in semi-retirement, and wrote influential books on maths, geometry, navigation and optics. His bedraggled appearance, prodigious knowledge and somewhat peculiar habits led locals to regard him with a mixture of fear and awe.

FACT FILE

- Hurworth-on-Tees, 3 miles (4.8km) south of Darlington, on the A167
- Pathfinders 600 (NZ 21/31) and 610 (NZ 20/30), grid reference NZ 309101

  miles 0 1 2 3 4 5 6 7 8 9 10 miles
  kms 0 1 2 3 4 5 6 7 8 9 10 11 12 13 14 15 kms
- Allow 3 hours
- Narrow country lanes, field and woodland paths. Woodland sections may be muddy. Good walking shoes or boots are recommended
- Free parking areas in Hurworth's main street
- The Emerson Arms in Hurworth; the Spa Hotel and several pubs in Croft
- In Croft, near the bridge

TIMELY REMINDER

As he was a lover of ale, it seems appropriate that his birthplace is now the Emerson Arms Ⓐ. Nearby, above the entrance to the Bay Horse Inn, is a complex sundial, one of many fascinating timepieces the great man devised for the village.

Emerson's altar tomb, together with the grave of his lifelong friend and pupil John Hunter, stands in the churchyard of All Saints' Ⓑ, at the heart of Hurworth. The church, which was founded in the late 12th century, has a fine 15th-century tower, although the rest of the building was restored and rebuilt in the Victorian Gothic style.

Emerson spent his adult life in apartments overlooking the green;

THE WALK

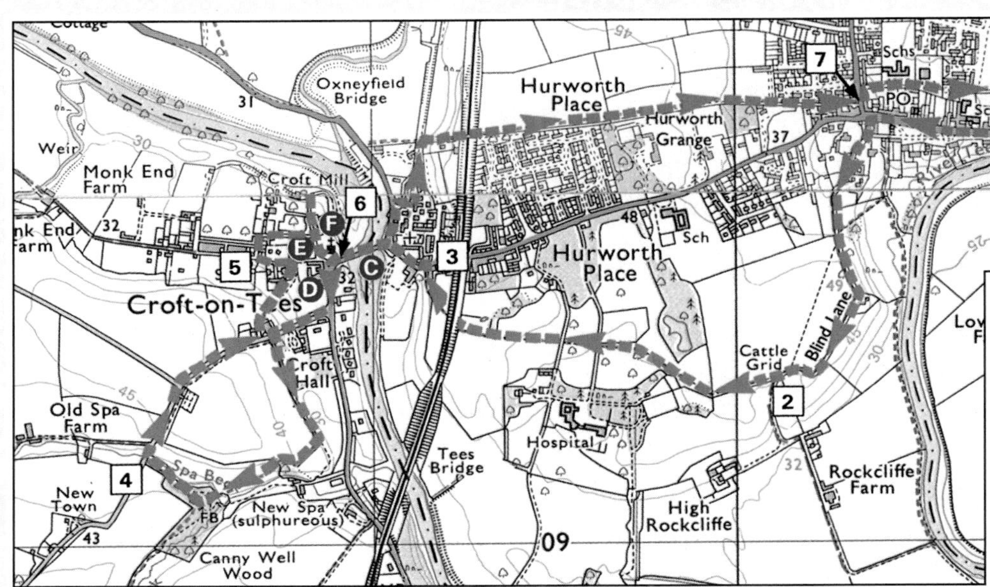

HURWORTH-ON-TEES – CROFT-ON-TEES

The walk begins outside the Emerson Arms Ⓐ, on the main street of Hurworth-on-Tees.

1 Head west along the main street past All Saints' Church Ⓑ. Go past the village green and left behind the monument, down Blind Lane.

2 When the lane bends sharp left, cross a step-stile straight ahead, onto a path between two field fences. Cross a second step-stile and a small field, with the hedge to your left. Cross another stile into a larger field. Head for a stile in the far corner near the cricket pitch. Cross the lane and a stile into a field. Go straight ahead to a kissing-gate then over a second field to another kissing-gate. Beyond the railway line, bear slightly right across the field to a gap in the hedge opposite. Follow a narrow path to the road.

3 Turn left. At a T-junction, go left over Croft Bridge Ⓒ. Follow the main road past the Croft Spa Hotel Ⓓ. Take the right turn, signposted 'Newton Morrell'. Immediately beyond Croft Hall, turn left across a field, with the hedge to your left. Follow the hedge around the field to a wire fence. Turn left over a step-stile. Bear right, downhill, to a small gated entrance into woodland. Go over a footbridge to join a woodland path. After about 40 paces, turn sharp right, uphill. Follow the path to a stile out of the woods. Cross the field and go over a stile into a lane.

4 Turn right. Continue over the hill. Almost at the bottom, turn left onto a tarmac drive between houses. Go through the gate and bear right downhill across a field, towards the church. Cross a step-stile into the road and turn left.

5 Beyond Lewis Close on your left, turn right into a narrow tarmac lane. Bend right at the entrance to Monkend Hall to continue along this narrow lane, passing the Old Rectory Ⓔ on your right. At the junction, turn left along Monk End Terrace to the Old Mill. Return along the lane to Croft's church Ⓕ.

6 Turn left over the bridge. Bear left past the post office, then take the next right. At a T-junction, turn left. About 50 paces beyond the last house on your left, turn right over a step-stile onto a narrow path, uphill across a field. Cross the footbridge and continue walking straight ahead on the narrow path, which eventually becomes a dirt lane.

7 At a T-junction, cross the road to follow the path past Hurworth School onto a road. Where the road bends left, go straight ahead onto a footpath which double bends around a house to a road. Turn right, then right again into Lych Gate. Turn immediately left, alongside the garage of the first house, onto a footpath. Turn right at the junction, and right again along the main street to the start.

JASON SMALLEY

the house that currently occupies the site bears a plaque to this effect.

The village green, surrounded by beeches and sycamores, is an idyllic site, belying the fact that it is the burial site of the entire population of the medieval village, which was wiped out by bubonic plague.

◄*The tomb of William Emerson, mathematician, inventor and eccentric, in All Saints' churchyard, Hurworth.*

▲*St Peter's, Croft, where Reverend Charles Dodgson was vicar, and his son was inspired with the idea for the Cheshire Cat. On the edge of the village is Georgian Monkend Hall (right).*

The route leads over fertile farmland and crosses the Tees into Yorkshire at the red-brick and sandstone Croft Bridge **C**, which dates from the 15th century. A plaque records its restoration following the flood of 1753, in which the turnpike toll-house was swept away. Beneath its seven arches lives a colony of Daubenton's bats; they feed on caddis flies and mayflies taken from just above the water's surface.

HEALING WATERS

Nearby stands Croft Spa Hotel **D**, built in 1835 to accommodate wealthy visitors who came here to take the waters. In 1714, a group of horses with swollen legs had bathed and drunk from springs underlying Spa Wood and were supposedly miraculously cured. The waters were found to have some of the highest concentrations of sulphur, magnesia and iron in Britain.

A lane leads past Croft Hall, an impressive country pile that was once the home of Sir William Chaytor. Despite his beautiful house, he lived in distressed circumstances, and spent the last 20 years of his life as a debtor in Fleet Prison. Croft spa water was sent to him in prison to relieve his many ailments.

The fields are a dazzling sapphire blue on bright summer days when the flax flowers open their petals to the sunshine. Further on, the path leads into the shade of woodland and on to Monkend, where the Hall resembles a huge doll's house. Nearby is the former corn-mill. The mill ran day and night until 1947, when the mill dam burst and the millpond flooded into the Tees, leaving the old mill motionless and mute. It is now a private house.

Back along the lane in Croft is the Old Rectory **E**, a rambling, three-storey house. In the 19th century it had its own laundry, bake-house and brewery, along with enough livestock to make its inhabitants almost self-sufficient. In 1843, this became the home of the Reverend Charles Dodgson and his family of four boys and seven girls. The eldest, Charles, was later to find fame as the author, Lewis Carroll.

▼*The River Tees, which rises in the Pennines, meanders through the area on its way to the sea at Middlesbrough.*

ALL PHOTOS: JASON SMALLEY

Close by is St Peter's F, a long, low church dating from the early 12th century. In the shadowy graveyard, weathered, lichen-encrusted tombstones lean at odd angles, and pipistrelle bats weave darting patterns against the sky at dusk.

LOCAL GENTRY

Inside, the nave is dominated by the enormous 18th-century, two-storied family pew of the Milbankes. This was erected a pretentious 6 feet (1.8m) above the floor, a reflection of a time when the gentry flaunted their privilege in no uncertain terms. Lord Byron married a Milbanke, and the newly-weds used the pew when attending services during their honeymoon at nearby Halnaby Hall in January 1815.

Another feature of the church is a handsome monument of 1490, while a bronze memorial plaque is one of two mementos of Lewis Carroll to be found in the church.

More intriguing, by the wall to the right of the altar, is a 14th-century triple sedilia that is richly carved with figures, flowers and a procession of animals. Low down on the far right is a peculiar animal's head with a leering expression that grows 'curiouser and curiouser' as you walk away — the outlines fade and all that remains is the grin on the face of the Cheshire Cat.

The return route to Hurworth follows a track that passes the grounds of Hurworth Grange.

▶*This sundial, on the wall of the Bay Horse Inn in Hurworth, was one of several designed by William Emerson.*

JASON SMALLEY

Lewis Carroll

THE HULTON PICTURE COMPANY

Charles Lutwidge Dodgson was born on 27 January 1832. Shy and awkward, with a severe stammer, he was academically brilliant, and became a lecturer in mathematics at Oxford. The dean of his college, Christ Church, was one H G Liddell. Dodgson regularly used to entertain Liddell's three young daughters, one of whom, called Alice, was a particular favourite.

One summer's afternoon, he and his friend, Robinson Duckworth, a fellow of Trinity, took the girls out on the Thames. To pass the time, Charles began spinning tales of Alice's fantastic adventures. He later wrote the stories down as a Christmas present to Alice. They were published in 1865, as *Alice's Adventures in Wonderland*, under Dodgson's pen name, Lewis Carroll, created by transposing his Christian names and Latinizing them.

The book was an instant and abiding success, with 180,000 copies sold during his lifetime. Its sequel, *Through the Looking-Glass and What Alice Found There* (1872) was almost as popular. The bizarre characters of these books have an enduring appeal — the White Rabbit, the barbarous Duchess, the Mad Hatter, the somnolent Dormouse and the Do-Do (a caricature of Carroll himself, who, because of his speech impediment, always introduced himself as 'Do-Do-Dodgson'). Dodgson also published several academic works under his own name, but today they are of purely historical interest.

Only ever really at ease in the company of young people, when his stammer frequently abated, Dodgson became one of the 19th century's most highly regarded photographers of children. He died a bachelor in 1898.

Charles Dodgson (above) wrote his two Alice books, Alice's Adventures in Wonderland *and* Through the Looking-Glass, *while he was in his thirties. Both titles were originally illustrated by Sir John Tenniel. The picture here shows Alice's encounter with Tiger Lily in* Through the Looking-Glass.

PRIVATE COLLECTION/THE BRIDGEMAN ART LIBRARY

In Hadrian's Footsteps

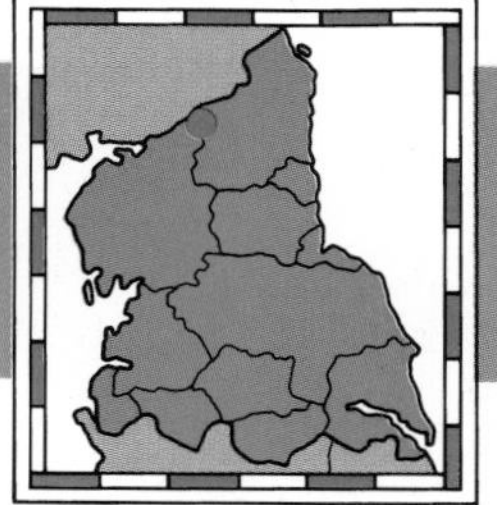

24

NORTHUMBERLAND

SIMON WARNER. INSET: LAURIE CAMPBELL/NHPA

▲ *Hadrian's Wall twists and turns its way across Northumberland. It is almost 2,000 years old. (inset) The goldeneye duck is a winter visitor to northern Britain. (below) The granaries at Housesteads Fort had stone pillars raising the floor to ventilate the grain.*

Exploring Housesteads Fort and Hadrian's Wall

An ancient frontier of the Roman Empire, Hadrian's Wall **A**, although man-made, still has the atmosphere of a natural barrier. The craggy ridge it is built on divides the empty pastures north of the Wall from the gentler country to the south. This walk explores Housesteads Fort **B** and Hadrian's Wall, one of Europe's finest archaeological sites. It also gives a taste of the wide open spaces of Northumberland, the most sparsely populated county in England, and one of the most beautiful.

As the route passes through spacious pastureland, there are some superb views of distant scattered

SIMON FRASER

Housesteads Fort was fully equipped with flush latrines for up to 24 people.

FACT FILE

- Hadrian's Wall, Northumberland National Park
- Pathfinder 546 (NY 66/76), grid reference NY 794684
- miles 0 1 2 3 4 5 6 7 8 9 10 miles / kms 0 1 2 3 4 5 6 7 8 9 10 11 12 13 14 15 kms
- Allow 3½ hours
- Several uphill sections mainly on rough footpaths. Trainers or walking shoes for summer. Boots or wellingtons for winter when it can be cold, wet and windy. Warm, windproof clothing recommended
- P Car park off B6318, by Housesteads Information Centre (open April–October)
- T Buses run from Hexham to Haltwhistle via Hadrian's Wall during school summer holidays
- Hadrian Hotel, at Wall; George Hotel at Chollerford; Twice Brewed Inn, Once Brewed at Visitor Centre

JANET & COLIN BORD

THE WALK

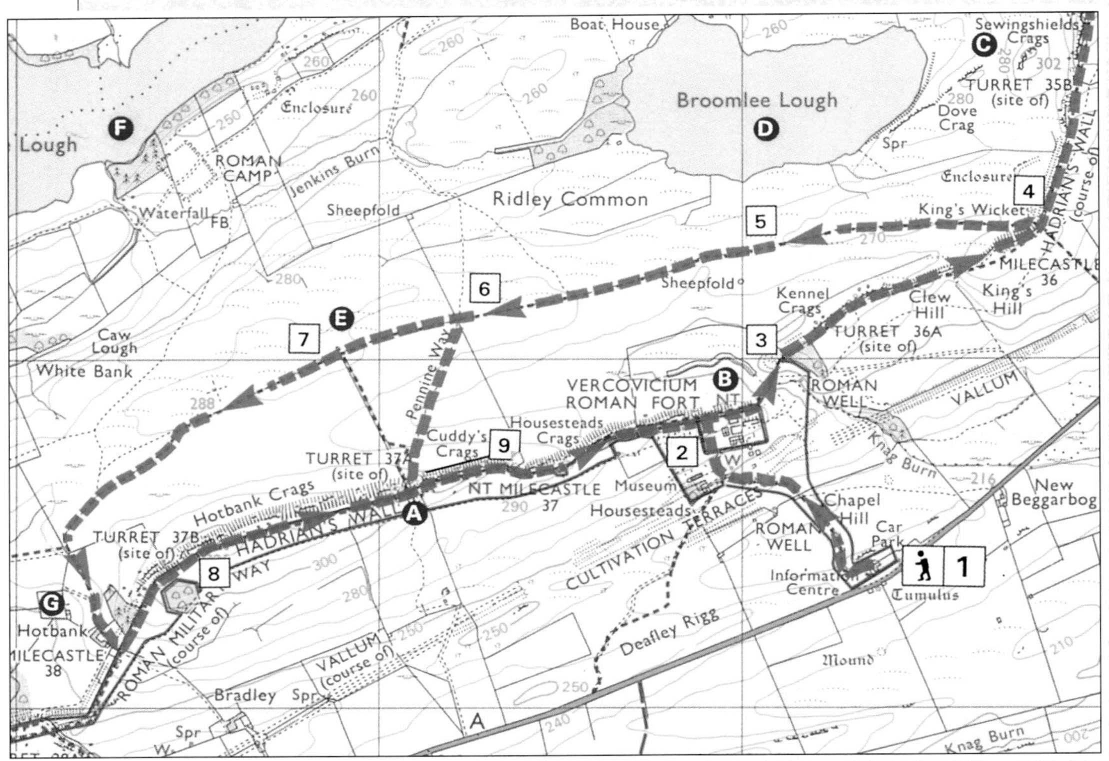

HOUSESTEADS FORT — HADRIAN'S WALL

The walk begins at the car park beside Housesteads Information Centre on the B6318.

1 Follow the well-made path leading to Housesteads Fort **B**. Tickets to enter the Fort are available at the Museum beside the Fort, open all year round.

2 After exploring the Fort, leave by the west gate. Turn right to cross Hadrian's Wall **A** by the wooden steps outside the north-west corner of the Fort, and turn right down the grassy bank running below the north wall of the Fort. Following Hadrian's Wall beyond the fort, descend to Knag Burn Gate, and go through the gate, back to the southern side of the Wall. An alternative way to reach this point is to exit from the Fort by the East Gate (notice the wheel ruts in the stone here), and descend the bank to Knag Burn Gate.

3 Continue in the direction of Sewingshields. The path leads through a small wood before emerging into open country again and undulating over Clew Hill and King's Hill. The Wall here is a field wall, rebuilt from the stones of Hadrian's Wall, which lies hidden underneath. Walk down from King's Hill to King's Wicket which appears on the left as a gate and stile through the field wall about 40 yards (35 metres) before the slope levels out at the bottom of the hill.

4 To reach the top of Sewingshields Crags **C** keep straight on. The round trip from King's Wicket takes about half an hour. The less energetic can miss out this ascent and cross the stile at King's Wicket. Follow the edge of the steep hillside round to the west for about 50 yards (45 metres) to a wooden post with a small yellow arrow pointing out the route across the rough grazing land. Take the narrow footpath through the grass which leads across half a dozen drainage channels to another yellow arrow. Continue along the path to a fenced-in plantation of mixed woodland, opposite Kennel Crags (the plantation is not marked on the map). Enter the plantation over a stile, walk through it and leave over another stile on the other side to the right, where another yellow arrow points the way.

5 Broomlee Lough **D** is now visible to the right, and Housesteads Fort to the left. Opposite Housesteads Crags the path becomes more distinct as a grassy track and soon comes to a stone wall with a gate and a stile, opposite Cuddy's Crags. The area near the gate is extremely wet and muddy in winter, and is churned up by cattle. At this point the route crosses the Pennine Way.

6 To shorten the walk, turn left on to the Pennine Way and follow it until it meets the Wall at Rapishaw Gap. Turn left and follow the instructions from stage **9**.

7 A little further on, the path passes a disused limekiln **E**. Keep to the crest of a very broad grassy ridge, with a small plantation on the left, below Hotbank Crags. Greenlee Lough **F** is now visible on the right. The path here is very indistinct but soon joins an obvious track, which bears left, to Hotbank Farm **G**. Crag Lough also comes into view. Go through the gate to the farm. Pass a water trough on the left to another gate. Immediately after this gate, turn left over a stile and head up the steep hill to the top of Hotbank Crags.

8 At the top of the steep hill, a wooden signpost points out two routes back to Housesteads. Take the higher route which follows the undulating ridge of the Whin Sill, along a very fine section of Hadrian's Wall, with magnificent views in all directions.

9 The steep scramble out of Rapishaw Gap towards Cuddy's Crags can be avoided by turning right, going through the gate, and turning left up the hill to the Wall. Continue over Housesteads Crags, past Milecastle 37 and enter a wood. The path now runs along the top of the Wall itself. Soon the path emerges from the wood by the north-west corner of Housesteads Fort. Walk down the hill, past the museum and follow the route back to the car park.

NATURE WALK

NURSE TREES New plantations of trees like beech may be planted with conifers to shelter them when young.

TRIANGULATION POINT A concrete pillar from which the surrounding landscape is surveyed.

RICHARD PHIPPS

SIMON WARNER INSET JOHN WATNEY

▲ *The waters of Crag Lough (above and inset) are home to several varieties of duck, mute swans and fish. This stretch of water is dominated by the rocky ledge of Whin Sill.*

farmhouses, loughs (lakes) and moors, leading to the edge of huge forests which run to the modern boundary with Scotland. The final section of the walk follows one of the best-preserved sections of the Wall which offers magnificent views in all directions, before returning to Housesteads Fort.

Along Hadrian's Wall, Roman forts housed the defending garrisons. The great fort of Housesteads (Vercovicium) is grandly situated on the vast rocky ridge known as Whin Sill, and is probably the best known. The site, covering 5 acres (2 hectares), has been well excavated and contains the remains of the barracks, the Commanding Officer's house, the granaries, the, latrines and the only remains of a Roman hospital in Britain.

SIMON WARNER

Hotbank Farm in its picturesque setting at the foot of the Wall.

A DRAMATIC LANDSCAPE

The Great Whin Sill is one of the best known geological features of northern England. This scarp extends from the north Northumberland coast to the south-west of the county. 'Whin' is a local term for basalt or dolerite rock, and the Whin Sill, as it is called, is particularly dramatic along the central section of Hadrian's Wall.

The ascent of Sewingshields Crags Ⓒ leads on to the triangulation point — one of the highest points on the Whin Sill, at 1,066 feet (325 metres) above sea level. This is well worth reaching as the views of the Wall stretching in either direction, and of Broomlee Lough Ⓓ below are superb. The highest point is a little further on (just off the top right corner of the map), but is unmistakable to a walker who is approaching from the direction of King's Wicket.

FORESTS AND MEADOWS

Over the wall from King's Wicket the northern horizon is dominated by large tracts of coniferous forest planted by the Forestry Commission to supply sawmills and pulpmills. In summer, the pastures are a mass of buttercups, thistles and grasses, grazed by hardy breeds of sheep and cattle. The air is full of birdsong — meadow pipit, skylark, curlew, lapwing, rook and jackdaw. The beautiful curlew, with its haunting cry, is the symbol of Northumberland National Park.

Here there is a feeling of great space, with distant horizons and a huge sky arching overhead — typical features of the Northumbrian landscape.

The path passes a disused limekiln Ⓔ, built on a limestone outcrop. During the early 19th century, limestone was quarried nearby and alternate layers of coal and limestone were fed into the kilns from above. Quicklime was drawn out from below and spread on the pastures to improve the quality of the grazing for sheep.

TRADITIONAL FARMHOUSE

Approaching Hotbank Farm Ⓖ there are excellent views of Crag Lough. Like all the lakes in this area, it was formed by glaciers carving out softer rocks. The rich vegetation here makes it important for waterfowl and other birds.

Hotbank Farm is a typical example of a Northumbrian hill-farm, with its sturdy stone buildings grouped around a yard, and steeply pitched slate roofs to allow winter snow to slide off easily. From the top of Hotbank Crags there is a small plantation of Scots pine, Sitka spruce, oak, ash, birch and beech. Plantations such as this are established as shelter belts for hill pastures and farms. On a clear day, the views stretch as far as the Lakeland hills to the south-west, the Pennines to the south, and the Cheviots far to the north-east. It is also the only place on the Wall where the four loughs, Crag, Greenlee Ⓕ, Broomlee and Grindon, are all visible. From here the path actually follows the Wall along the airy crest of the Whin Sill to the fine viewpoint of Cuddy's Crags. After passing Housesteads Crags and through a shady wood the path soon reaches Housesteads Fort.

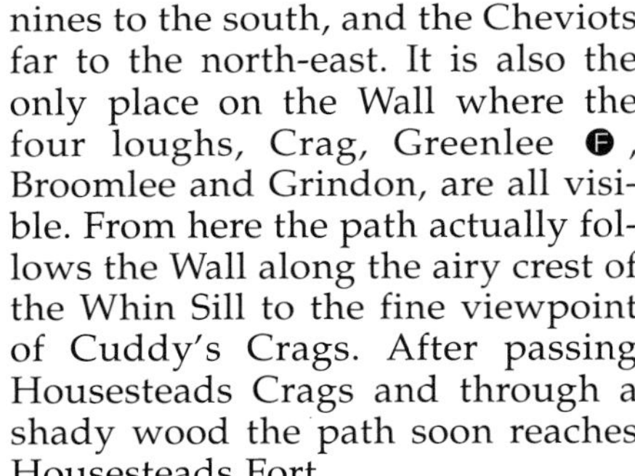

Remains of Roman Might

In AD 122, the Emperor Hadrian came to Britain. The Roman Empire was well established, extending throughout Europe and North Africa. However, northern tribes in Britain were still hostile. Hadrian decided to build a wall in order to subdue attacks on his legions, and to form a northern limit on the Empire.

Hadrian's Wall took five years to complete. One million cubic yards (760,000m^3) of stone were quarried in order to build the wall, its forts, milecastles, and turrets, which formed a massive defence system stretching for about 73 miles (117 kilometres) from sea to sea across the north of England. The Romans had sufficient resources, wealth, manpower and organisational ability to build the Wall and then to man it for more than 250 years. It was a tremendous undertaking and today is a fascinating memorial to Roman military might and skill.

A Roman Legionary in battle dress. Legionaries were foot soldiers and served in the army for 25 years.

Rugged and dramatic, Hadrian's Wall (below and below right) was not a popular posting for Roman soldiers, but now delights thousands of visitors.

JOHN WATNEY

THE CASTLE ON THE ROCK

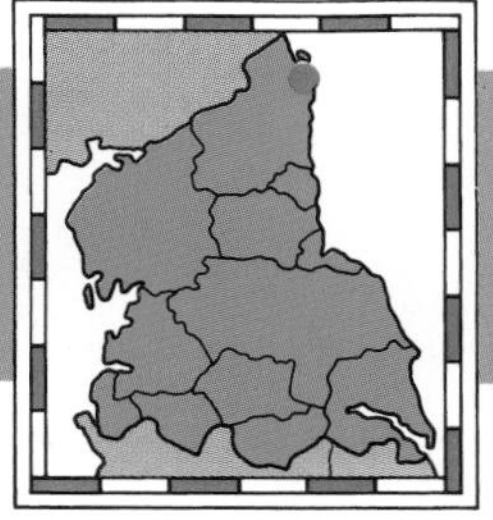

25

NORTHUMBERLAND

SIMONE FRASER INSET: MICHAEL LEACH/NHPA

◄ *This view of Bamburgh Castle has been the inspiration for countless paintings and photographs.*
▼ *Sea birds flock to Stag Rock, while short-eared owls (left) remain inland.*

A coastal and country walk along Northumberland's Heritage Coast

Starting from the spectacular Bamburgh Castle, this walk takes in wide sandy beaches, crags, dunes, gorse-covered hillsides and a hidden valley.

Steeped in the history of the ancient kingdom of Northumbria, Bamburgh is dominated by its castle **A**. A great Norman keep, it has towered above the sea on its basalt crag for nine centuries. There has been a castle on the site as far back as Roman times. It was attacked by the Vikings, and during the Wars of the Roses it was the first English castle to succumb to gunfire. It was largely rebuilt in the early 1900s.

Much of the walk follows the coast, and grey seals, which breed on the nearby Farne Islands, may be seen. There is even the chance of glimpsing a killer whale.

COASTAL LANDSCAPE

Stag Rock **B** is famous for bird watching. In addition to a variety of waders and scores of eider, many sea birds such as gannets fly along this coast. Looking out across Budle Bay from Budle Point **C**, Ross Back Sands stretch towards Holy Island and diving birds hunt for fish in the shallows.

In summer the wild flowers include sea pinks and yellow vetch on the crags; wild thyme, heather and gorse on the heathland, and foxgloves and wild roses amongst the bracken. Butterflies are plentiful, including the coast-loving grayling. Short-eared owls and kestrels hunt over the hillsides and the bracken

FACT FILE

- Bamburgh, where the B1340, B1341 and B1342 meet
- Pathfinder 465 (NU 13/23), grid reference NU 184349

miles 0 1 2 3 4 5 6 7 8 9 10 miles
kms 0 1 2 3 4 5 6 7 8 9 10 11 12 13 14 15 kms

- Allow 2½ hours
- One section may be overgrown in summer with bracken or grass. There are some steep banks, and rocks on the coast can be slippery in wet weather
- P Public car park at the eastern end of Bamburgh village, opposite the castle on the B1340
- Restaurants in the village
- WC Toilets next to Bamburgh village green

SIMON FRASER

THE WALK

BAMBURGH - BUDLE - NEWTOWN HILL

The walk begins at the public car park on the B1340 at the eastern end of Bamburgh, opposite the entrance to Bamburgh Castle **A**.

1 From the car park entrance cross the road and take the stony track opposite up to the castle car park. Go forward on a path descending beside a fence. Continue through the dunes with the castle above, to the far northern corner of the castle crag. Turn left up to the remains of the castle wall, then right to meet a road at Lifeboat Cottage.

Follow the road to the right and, after crossing Mill Burn, turn right at the top of the rise. Cross the wide verge and go down through the dunes to the beach.

2 If the sea permits, walk left along the beach and over Harkess Rock (if not, return to the road) to the lighthouse above Stag Rock **B**. The white stag painted on the rock comes into view on the approach. With the lighthouse on your left, follow the path at the foot of the grassy bank leading to a small sandy bay. Keep along the shore until a lifebuoy is reached then turn left and take the path up to the top of the bank.

Turn right along the green path to the edge of the golf course to reach a stony track going on round Budle Point **C**. Ross Back Sands and Holy Island are in view to the north. The track descends to a wartime gun emplacement standing above the old quay. Follow the path round it to the left, then sharp left up to the golf course. Beware of golf balls. Turn right round the edge of the greens and along a wide green path leading to a metalled road.

3 Keep straight ahead on the road for a few yards, go left through a gate and, keeping to the right, go behind the recently developed dwellings. Take the green track which goes uphill near the fence to a stile which leads back on to the golf course.

Continue ahead over the fairway, keeping to the left of a low gorse and heather ridge, and descend into a valley filled with bracken where a drystone wall encloses a copse on the left. From this point, until the road, the walk is little used and may be overgrown from June to the autumn. The path becomes indistinct but continues alongside the wall on the left to a gate leading into a field.

4 Turn left along the edge of the field to the far corner and right along that side of the field. Cross the stile to meet the road to Bamburgh. Keep left on the verge path, passing Grace Darling's cottage **D** and her memorial **E**, and past the village green to the car park.

and gorse often hide roe deer. On every side there are open views — the Cheviot Hills to the west, great expanses of sand along the coast, rocky headlands jutting out into the waves, the Farne Islands and the open sea beyond.

On the return route to Bamburgh, the first cottage on the right **D** is the birthplace of Grace Darling, who became famous when she and her father, the keeper of Longstone Lighthouse, bravely rescued the survivors of the *Forfarshire* in 1838. She became a national heroine, but died, probably of tuberculosis, four years later at the age of 26. There is a memorial in St Aidan's churchyard **E**, opposite her birthplace, and the Grace Darling Museum is in the same street.

◄ ***Bamburgh is overlooked by the huge castle. (right) Grace Darling, a national heroine, is buried in the churchyard.***

BOTH PHOTOS: EIB/BIAS

HIGH-TIDE ISLAND

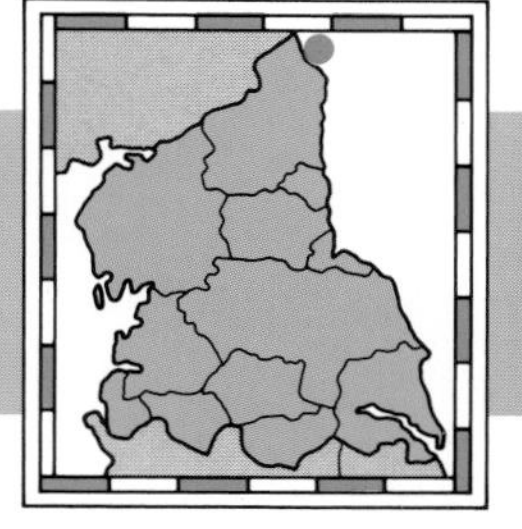

26

NORTHUMBERLAND

NORTHUMBRIA TOURIST BOARD. INSET: LAURIE CAMPBELL/NHPA

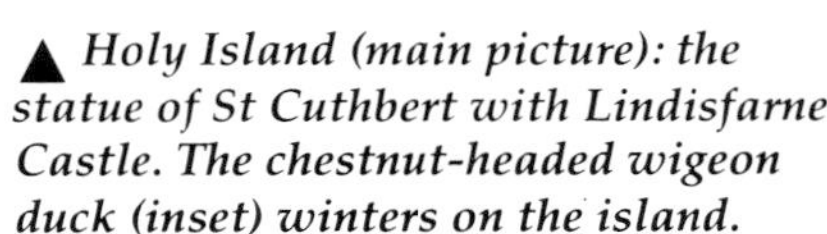

FACT FILE

- Holy Island (Lindisfarne), off the Northumberland coast
- Pathfinder 452 (NU 04/14), grid reference NU 127420
- 3 hours
- Tracks and paths. Castle Point is pebbly. Strong shoes recommended. Main car park, Holy Island. Alternative parking along the Ouse
- T Northumbria Motor Services Limited buses. Note: vehicles can only reach the island at low tide across the causeway, which is impassable at high tide. Essential to check tides in advance from information centres. Tide information boards at each end of causeway
- Toilets in car park and near village centre. Shop, pubs, hotels and cafés. St Aidan's winery produces and sells Lindisfarne Mead (free samples available)

A causeway crossing to a fishing village, castle and priory ruins

Part of the attraction and adventure of visiting Holy Island is that it is cut off from the rest of the world by the sea for much of the time. The mainland can only be reached at low tide.

In the seventh century, monks found this an ideal location, leaving the island occasionally by crossing the sands when the sea had receded.

▼ *Old upturned herring boats are now used as fishermen's stores.*

▲ ***Holy Island (main picture): the statue of St Cuthbert with Lindisfarne Castle. The chestnut-headed wigeon duck (inset) winters on the island.***

Their route became known as the Pilgrims' Causeway and, until recent times, it remained the only way across. It was improved by the position of poles to mark the route in 1860 and the provision of refuge huts on stilts for anyone caught out by the swift inrush of the tide. But it

DEREK FORSS

THE WALK

HOLY ISLAND

The walk begins at the main car park on the island.

1 Leave the car park and turn right. At the end of the road, turn left. After a short way, turn right, then immediately left, towards the market place. There are signs to Lindisfarne Priory **A**. Holy Island museum and church are just ahead.

2 Go round to the tower side of the church, and leave by the gate. Turn left, and go down the track towards St Cuthbert's Island **B**. Bear left, up a steep, stony path to the top of the Heugh **C**. Walk along the top of the Heugh, nearly to the end, then descend the grassy bank on to the concrete jetty below.

3 Turn left, and follow the inner harbour, called the Ouse **D**, past the upturned herring boats, and walk all the way round until you meet the road which leads from the village and runs alongside the sea to Lindisfarne Castle **E**.

4 Bear right towards the castle, passing through a gate. Bear right again to visit the castle, or bear left behind the castle to the large rocky outcrop. To view the walled garden **F**, cross the field behind the castle. Bear to the right of the rocky outcrop, and walk over the grassy area to the fenced square of limekiln chimneys **G**. To the left of these are some stony steps, which take you down to the base of the limekilns. Bear left around the pebbly beach at Castle Point.

5 Pass through a kissing gate to join the old wagon way, heading along a grassy ridge. Follow this northward path, with the sea on your right, until you pass a marshy lake on the left, the Lough **H**, and come to a stile.

6 Cross the stile and, after about 200 yards (180 metres), you reach a wicket gate. Go through the gate, and continue for 100 yards (90 metres) until a wide, grassy path crosses the way. Turn left, then take the path which bears right. Continue along this path, keeping the dunes to your right, until you reach a junction with a wide lane, called the Straight Lonnen.

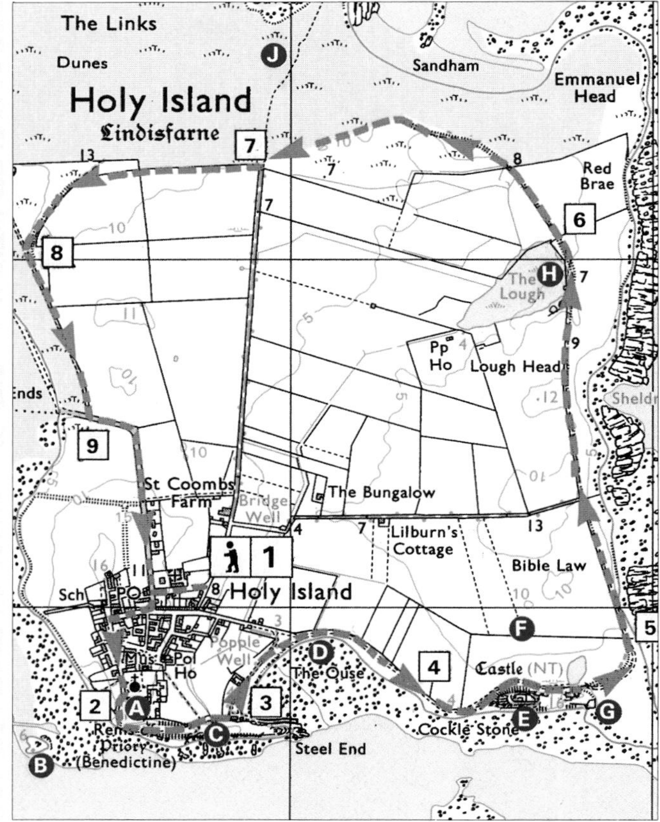

7 To explore the dunes nature reserve **J** and sea shore, turn right here. For a short cut back to the car park, turn left. To continue the walk, cross the track, going in the same direction until you reach a well-defined track which curves away to the left.

8 Follow the track to a gate on to the road near the start of the causeway.

9 Turn left and follow the road into the village. Take the first turn left to return to the car park at the start of the walk.

◀ ***Lindisfarne Castle is a famous landmark; its colourful garden was designed by the renowned Gertrude Jekyll.***

was not until 1954 that the metalled road was opened; and this was extended and improved in 1965. Tide tables at each end of the causeway are still essential when planning a crossing.

From the island's main car park, a short walk brings you into the village centre. Nowadays it caters mainly for visitors, but its heyday was in the 19th century, when fishing, farming and quarrying were the main occupations. Herring were cured and donkeys were used to carry panniers of fish across the sands to be sold by fishwives. Life was hard and rough for much of the time, but there were at least 10 inns to provide some solace.

EARLY CHRISTIANS

The museum, church and priory **A**, are at the south end of the village, beyond the square. In the priory ground stands the impressive statue of St Aidan. In 635 AD, the Northumbrian King Oswald asked the monks of the Irish monastery on Iona to send missionaries to bring Christianity to his kingdom. They sent Aidan, who founded a simple wooden monastery on Holy Island,

SIMON WARNER

◀ *The ruins of the red sandstone priory, with its carved stonework, built in 1093.*

The path from the west gate of the church leads to a grassy shelf and a view of St Cuthbert's Island **B**, which is joined to the mainland at low tide. Cuthbert spent whole days in prayer here, but eventually he chose an even more remote location, on the Farne Islands, further out to sea, now popular for spotting wildlife and sea birds.

A stony path leads on to the Heugh **C**, a hill created by an intrusion of hard volcanic rock. There are some fine views from the promontory. The route comes down the Heugh on to the Ouse **D**, a harbour sheltering fishing boats. Lobster pots line the jetty and there are upturned old herring boats which serve as fishermen's stores.

There is a path from the harbour leading towards Lindisfarne Castle **E**. By Northumbrian standards the castle is modern (16th century) and small, having only 12 rooms. Its original purpose was to guard the harbour. The volcanic outcrop called Beblowe Hill, at the harbour entrance, was the obvious site for the castle. Its history is entirely peaceful; the only exception occurred when two Jacobites took the castle, having discovered that there were only two people left in charge, out of a garrison of seven. They attempted to flee the next day,

which was then called by its Celtic name, Lindisfarne. (The castle and priory are still referred to by the old name). Aidan and his companions spent much time travelling through the north, visiting the people in their huts among the hills. In Aidan's lifetime the Christian faith was firmly established in Northumbria.

ST CUTHBERT

Aidan's sixth successor was Cuthbert, a warm-hearted and practical person according to accounts given to the 'father of English history', the Venerable Bede. Cuthbert became an early folk hero, revered by everyone. It was in honour of God and St Cuthbert that the Lindisfarne Gospels were produced by the monks. These exquisite illuminated manuscripts are now in the British Museum.

The wooden monastery was burnt in Viking raids, and the monks were forced to flee, taking the Gospels with them. But it was rebuilt, in red sandstone, by Benedictine monks from Durham, who dedicated the building to Saint Cuthbert. The ruins of the monastery church remain. It is a favourite spot for visitors and photographers, especially in summer. The history of the island is described in the small museum, where there is a reconstruction of a monk's cell. Next to the priory ruins is St Mary's Church, which was begun in Norman times.

EMBROIDERED GOSPEL

The north porch, now a vestry, doubled as a mortuary for bodies recovered from the sea, and was in use until 1886. The design of the modern altar carpet represents a page from the renowned Lindisfarne Gospels and was made by local needlewomen. There is a copy of the facsimile of the Gospels, presented by Rockford College Community, Illinois, in 1956.

S & O MATHEWS

▲ *Grey seals and sea birds are among the wild inhabitants of the Farne Islands, visited by tourists during the summer.*

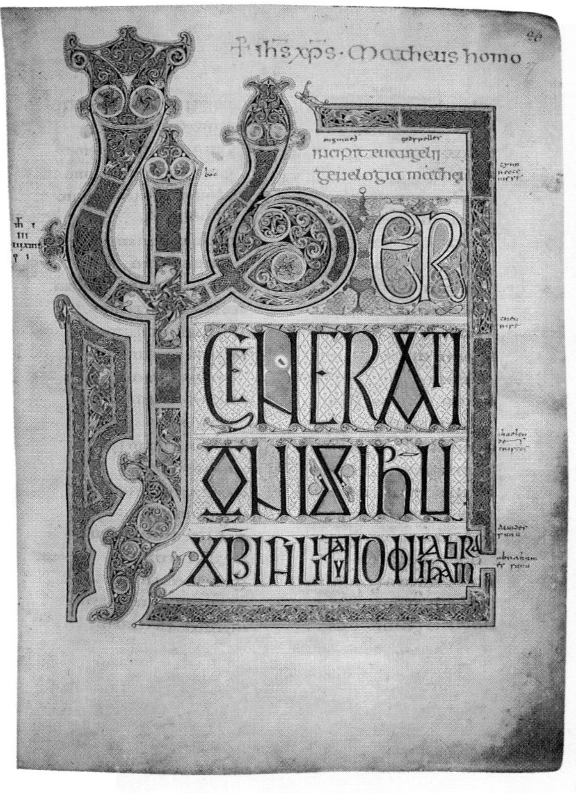

BRITISH LIBRARY, LONDON/BRIDGEMAN ART LIBRARY

The Lindisfarne Gospels

The monks of Lindisfarne are remembered for one of the finest examples of Celtic art — the Lindisfarne Gospels. The monastic community required some form of written scriptures, which the missionaries could carry to their converts and which could be read aloud in the monastery services. The manuscript was written in Latin, but some years later a priest called Aldred added an Anglo-Saxon translation between the lines. It is thanks to Aldred that we know about the three monks who created the manuscript. Eadfrith is said to have written and decorated the entire text, probably before he became Bishop of Lindisfarne in AD 698. He chose a stately, formal script, using a fairly broad nib to create an effect suitable for reading aloud. With a reed pen or quill, he wrote on sheets of vellum, prepared from calfskin.

The main decoration occurs at the beginning of each Gospel. This is where there is an initial page of elaborate design, an interwoven pattern of birds and animals. The first letter of the Gospel text is illuminated in pure Celtic style. There are paintings of Matthew, Mark, Luke and John.

The task of binding the manuscript went to Ethelwald, who, as a young novice, was personal attendant to St Cuthbert. Billfrith, who was a priest within the monastic community, added silver, gold and gems to the binding.

The decorated initial to the Gospel according to St Matthew. The Lindisfarne Gospels are on display in the British Museum, and there is a copy on Holy island.

but were captured when reinforcements arrived.

This century, the castle was restored by Sir Edwin Lutyens, to provide a desirable residence for Edward Hudson, proprietor of *Country Life*. The castle is now open to the public, and is in the care of the National Trust.

Inland from the castle, it comes as a surprise to see a delightful walled garden (F), among the bare fields. It was created by the garden designer, Gertrude Jekyll, early this century. She was well-regarded for her inspired colour themes, which often involved the used of silver foliage. The garden can be viewed over the gate and it is possible to look round when the gardener is present.

LIMEKILNS

Beyond the castle and the coast, there is a well-preserved set of lime-burning kilns (G), in use in the last century. The kilns can be viewed from beneath by going down on to the storm beach at Castle Point, where there is a plaque to explain the process by which the lime was produced. Wagon-loads of limestone were brought from a quarry in the north of the island. The coal used to burn the limestone came from Dundee, in return for lime.

The old wagonway, once used to haul the stone, ran along a grassy embankment. This is now a good footpath for the next part of the walk, which follows the coast northward, towards Emmanuel Head. The path goes by Holy Island Lough (H), a shallow, freshwater lake, fringed by marshes, and home to whooper swans from Iceland in the winter. The large white pyramid on Emmanuel Head is a beacon to guide boats.

WILDLIFE

The route now curves left, and it leads to a junction with a wide lane called the Straight Lonnen. The nature reserve (J) on the right is well worth exploring for its wide variety of wildlife. Beyond the dunes, there are deserted sandy bays, cliffs and caves, and the old quarries.

JOHN PARRY/NATIONAL TRUST PHOTOGRAPHIC LIBRARY

◀ ***When the tide has turned, travellers must leave plenty of time to cross the causeway. As the sea closes in, Holy Island is totally cut off from the mainland and becomes a true island again.***

A MEDIEVAL STRONGHOLD

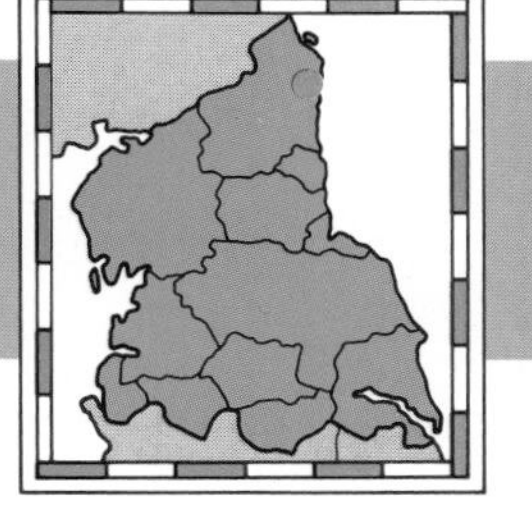

A riverside walk to Warkworth Castle and a hidden hermitage

The small, attractive town of Warkworth, on the eastern side of the county, boasts a fine castle, a hermitage hewn from a sandstone cliff and a medieval bridge. The walk is a riverside ramble along the banks of the River Coquet **A**, overlooked by Warkworth Castle **B** high on its grassy mound.

A QUIET TOWN

Warkworth is situated on the last bend of the river, which slips quietly round the little town in a horseshoe loop. The Coquet begins as a sparkling Cheviot stream, which hurries down between the remote hills of Upper Coquet Dale. At Warkworth, it is broad and placid, on its last meandering stage before entering the sea at Amble.

FACT FILE

- Warkworth, 1¼ miles (2 km) from Amble
- Pathfinder 501 (NU 20), grid reference NU 246062
- 1½ hours
- The riverside path can be muddy and slippery in wet weather. Short, steep climb to Warkworth Castle
- Free riverside parking and in Warkworth (Castle Street and Dial Place)
- The Hermitage Inn, the Jackdaw pub and Castlebridge House tearoom
- Warkworth Castle (English Heritage), open daily 10am-6pm and Warkworth Hermitage. Ferry to hermitage May-September weekends only

AA PICTURE LIBRARY. INSET: STEPHEN DALTON/NHPA

▲*Warkworth, one of Northumberland's great castles, is mainly in ruins but has a well-preserved keep. The large emerald moth (inset) can be spotted between the months of June and August.*

The remains of Warkworth Castle are particularly attractive when viewed from the river. Like most castles, it has been extended and altered over the years. It began as an early Norman motte-and-bailey, although the site itself was probably fortified even earlier, in Saxon times. The later building is in the style of a tower-house, laid out in a square, elaborated with a tower-like projection at the centre of each face. The interiors were also elaborate, with a complex pattern of rooms, passages and staircases, and an unusually large number of windows.

The castle belonged to King Edward III, who gave it to Lord Percy of Alnwick in 1331. The Percy family, who were Earls of Northumberland, kept Warkworth as their home, retaining their fortress at Alnwick. However, when they fell from favour and left Northumberland the castle declined. Part of the family history was dramatised by Shakespeare in 'Henry IV Part Two'. Three scenes

THE WALK

WARKWORTH

The walk begins at the car park by the river.

1 Walk along the riverside footpath, following the River Coquet **A** upstream, passing beneath Warkworth Castle **B**.

2 Below the castle, there is a landing stage for rowing boats, then the path continues alongside woods.

3 Cross a stile. Just ahead is the landing stage for the ferry that, on summer weekends only, crosses the river to Warkworth Hermitage **C**. If visiting the hermitage, return by ferry, then return to the rowing boat landing by the same path. Retrace your steps along the riverside footpath.

4 Take the path to the right, up the steep bank towards the castle. Bear left near the top and leave the castle grounds at the top of Castle Street.

5 Follow Castle Street downhill, into the centre of Warkworth **D** and continue along the main road (Bridge Street) until you reach the two bridges across the river.

6 Just in front of the medieval bridge **E**, turn left to rejoin the riverside footpath. By the path a wooden signpost indicates 'Public Footpath Mill Walk'. Take this path, which passes the church of St Laurence **F**, and return to the car park.

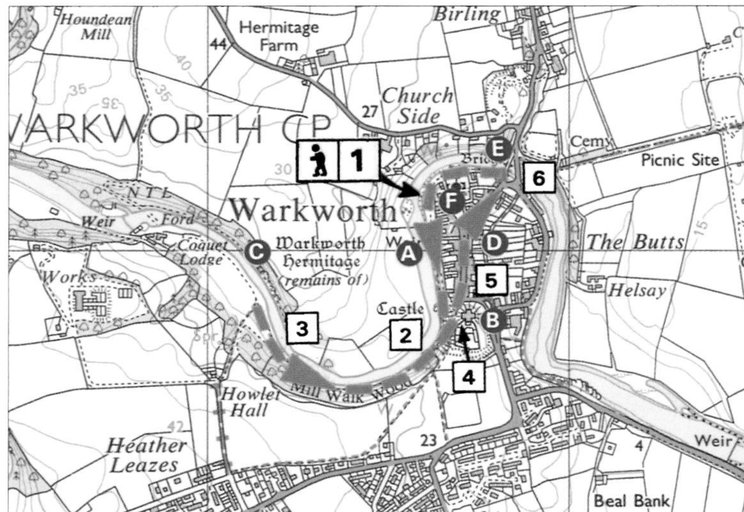

▲*The River Coquet is crossed by three bridges at Warkworth, including this 14th-century bridge with its own tower.*

are set at the castle. In the play, Percy and his son, Harry Hotspur, plot to set Henry Bolingbroke on the throne. However, when Henry became too autocratic after becoming king, Harry Hotspur plotted against him.

The castle is now in ruins, but the keep has been restored and there are still large parts of fine medieval masonry. Today, it is owned by the present Duke of Northumberland, but maintained by English Heritage. In spring, its velvety, green mound is covered with daffodils.

Below the castle's steep banks there is a landing stage where rowing boats can be hired. The path continues along the edge of woods, then emerges into a more open aspect, opposite Warkworth Hermitage **C** on the far bank.

THE LAST HERMIT

Carved into the sandstone cliff is a vaulted chapel, with a stone altar. Next to that is a sacristy — a room for vestments and the sacred vessels. The hermit's life would have been spartan, but there was at least a large fireplace and bread ovens in the living quarters. The last hermit to live at Warkworth was the chaplain to the Sixth Earl of Northumberland, George Lancaster, in the 16th century.

The return route offers glimpses of the castle, framed by trees. From the castle, a wide street slopes steeply down through Warkworth **D**, to the market place. Georgian and Victorian buildings line the way, many with colourful window boxes, tubs and hanging baskets.

At the end of Bridge Street, the river flows under a medieval bridge **E**, and a modern bridge built in the 1960s. The 14th-century bridge, with two bold and graceful arches, replaced an even earlier stone bridge. It has a defensive tower and bears the Percy coat of arms.

The riverside path leads past the Norman church of St Laurence **F**, which stands on a Saxon foundation. Its stained glass depicts the Abbess of Whitby, Saint Hilda.

▲*Little is known about the hermitage at Warkworth, which, even today, is only accessible by a small ferry boat.*

The Coastal Path

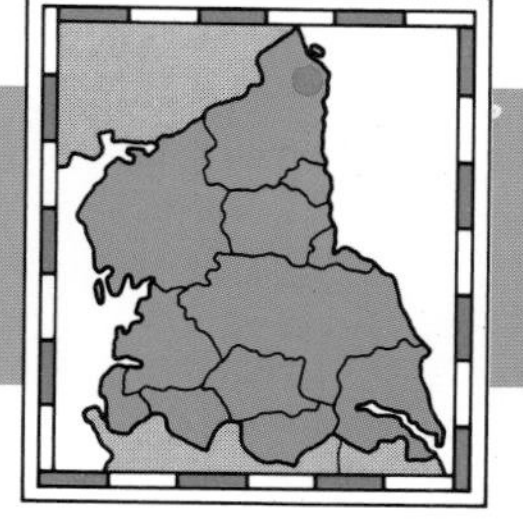

28

NORTHUMBERLAND

From a fishing village to a ruined castle on the Northumberland coast.

A century ago, there were 27 traditional fishing boats or cobles in Craster's fishing fleet. Although there are now only a handful, they still venture out for lobster and herring. Lobster pots are a familiar sight along the harbour wall, built in 1906 in memory of a member of the Craster family that the village Ⓚ is named after.

NEIL HOLMES

DEREK FORSS

Kippers are a Craster speciality. Visitors can look into the smoking sheds, where the herrings are hung above smouldering oak chips. Local salmon is also smoked here.

Along the coast are the ruins of Dunstanburgh Castle. The Earl of Lancaster had it built in 1313, but he was executed a few years later. John of Gaunt prepared the castle for the Border Wars, and built another gateway in 1380. During the Wars of the Roses, the castle was a Lancastrian stronghold. But from the mid-1400s, it was redundant and was, in total, in use for only 140 years. Now all that is left are the dramatic ruins and a number of ghostly legends.

▲Above Embleton Bay stands Dunstanburgh Castle, the largest ruined castle in Northumberland. In Craster (above left) kippers are still smoked as they were at the turn of the century.

An old whinstone quarry Ⓐ is now Craster's car park and the starting point of the walk. At the top end of the car park, the quarry face is now home to hundreds of gulls.

The first part of the walk passes between the Heughs Ⓑ, a line of gorse-covered whinstone hills on

DEREK FORSS

◀Embleton Bay is in a National Trust conservation area. Alongside the sandy beach, bushes of burnet rose compete with wild flowers such as cranesbill.

FACT FILE

- Craster, 6 miles (10 km) north of Alnwick
- Pathfinder 477 (NU 21/22), grid reference NU 255198

miles 0 1 2 3 4 5 6 7 8 9 10 miles
kms 0 1 2 3 4 5 6 7 8 9 10 11 12 13 14 15 kms

- 2½ hours. Extra time for farm tour or castle visit
- Field paths, a concrete track, sandy path through dunes, sandy beach, open grassland
- P In Craster
- T Bus service from Alnwick (Northumbria Motor Services)
- Tearoom and pub in Craster. Restaurant next to kipper-smoking sheds serves traditional kipper teas
- WC
- Dunstanburgh Castle (English Heritage). Open all year, check opening times

THE WALK

CRASTER – EMBLETON BAY

The walk begins by the old quarry Ⓐ, now a car park.

1 Opposite the entrance to the car park, take the footpath marked 'Dunstan Square 1m'. This leads through a thicket, and opens out onto a grassy path. Go through a kissing gate, and continue along the path, with the whinstone crags (the Heughs Ⓑ) on your right.

2 After another kissing gate, turn left, alongside fields, uphill towards Dunstan Square farm. Go through a farm gate, and continue up to the farm.

3 Pass through a metal gate, and turn right along the track. Pass through another gate, onto a concrete track. Follow the track for about 1 mile (1.6 km), passing a World War II pillbox Ⓒ. There are distant views of Dunstanburgh Castle.

4 Go through the farmyard of Dunstan Steads Farm Ⓓ, and turn right, into the lane. Walk to the end of the lane, and through the gate leading to the dunes Ⓔ. Follow the path which leads across the dunes towards Embleton Bay Ⓕ.

5 At the beach turn right and walk along the sand until you reach the boulders at the end of the bay. Climb the grassy bank to join the path heading towards the castle.

6 Follow the coastal path, past Saddle Rock Ⓖ, and Gull Crag Ⓗ. Take the path round to the right of Dunstanburgh Castle Ⓙ. Continue along the grassy clifftop towards Craster.

7 Go through the gate at the end of the path, and at the harbour in Craster Ⓚ turn right to follow the road for a short distance back to the car park.

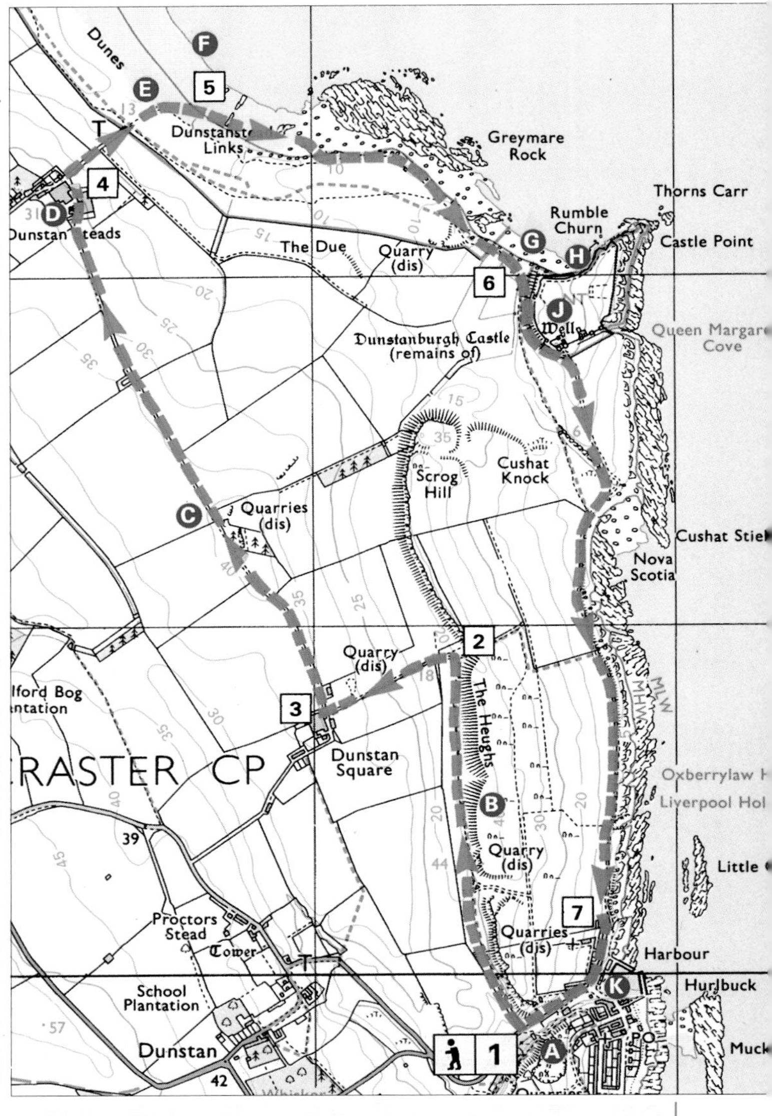

the seaward side, and cornfields inland. After Dunstan Square Farm, the route is along a quiet, open lane between the cornfields. On the left, just after a pine plantation, and looking curiously out of place, is a World War II pillbox Ⓒ, a gun emplacement made from concrete-filled sandbags. From the lane, there are tantalizing glimpses of the sea at Embleton Bay, and the towers of Dunstanburgh Castle.

The route passes through the farmyard of Dunstan Steads Farm Ⓓ, a working farm which provides guided tours at set times. A lane leads to extensive sand dunes Ⓔ behind Embleton Bay Ⓕ. This is a conservation area owned by the National Trust. In summer, bloody cranesbill can be spotted, and the scrambling thorn bushes of burnet rose. The long, sandy beach marks the halfway point of the walk.

At the end of the beach, the sand gives way to rounded boulders of grey dolerite. Here, the coastal path passes Saddle Rock Ⓖ, a distinctive, saddle-shaped hump of limestone.

Above the dunes, the shriek of hundreds of sea birds fills the air. They cover the face of Gull Crag Ⓗ, below the castle. There are kittiwakes, fulmars, guillemots and shag and sometimes puffins. The top half of Gull Crag is dolerite, and below that is sandstone and shale.

NEIL HOLMES

▶ *Crab and lobster pots are a common sight around the tiny harbour at Craster which was built in 1906 as a memorial to a member of the Craster family.*

ABOVE THE LAST BASTIONS

29

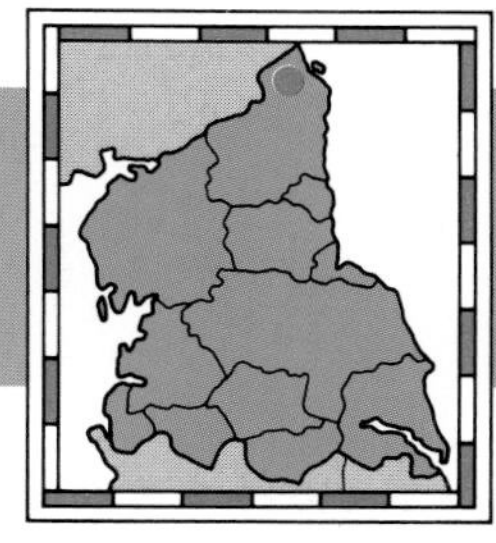

NORTHUMBERLAND

ALAN SPENCE. INSET: MANFRED DANEGGER/NHPA

▲*Royal Border Bridge spans the Tweed estuary — the last link of the London-to-Edinburgh railway. Swans (left) are common here.*

Beside a river estuary and through a fortified Elizabethan town

In 1482, Berwick-upon-Tweed changed its nationality for the last time, from Scottish to English. Its ownership had swayed between the two countries no fewer than 14 times. This almost constant warring had led to a need for strong fortifications. These can still be seen in the medieval walls and the remains of Berwick Castle Ⓑ, where Edward I sat in judgment over the claimants of the Scottish throne. As a punishment for crowning Robert the Bruce at Scone as King of Scotland, Isabella, Countess of Buchan, was imprisoned from 1306 to 1310 in a cage hung from the castle walls.

Today, Berwick railway station occupies the site of the Great Hall of Berwick Castle, which was finally demolished by Victorian engineers using explosives. This completed the work of the town's builders and masons, who, after the castle had fallen into disuse, had partially demolished it by treating the walls as a convenient quarry from which to get ready-dressed stone.

JAMES VI OF SCOTLAND

The Elizabethan walls, with their bastions (Ⓕ and Ⓖ), never saw a shot fired in anger. They became redundant 40 or 50 years after their completion, when James VI of Scotland became James I of England.

Local legend has it that King James ordered the Old Bridge Ⓓ, a 15-arch stone structure, to be founded upon woolsacks, such was the difficulty in obtaining sound foundations. The bridge was built to replace a rickety wooden one that the King is said to have crossed 'in fear of his life'.

With its 28 sandstone arches and

▶*The White Wall, which is also often appropriately known as the 'Breakneck Stairs', descends from Berwick castle.*

FACT FILE

- Berwick-upon-Tweed, border town at north-east extreme of England
- Pathfinder 438 (NT 95/NU 05), grid reference NT 986539
- miles 0 1 2 3 4 5 6 7 8 9 10 miles / kms 0 1 2 3 4 5 6 7 8 9 10 11 12 13 14 15 kms
- 2 hours
- One muddy section, so not suitable for pushchairs
- P In Berwick-upon-Tweed
- T Mainline station with Intercity links, Tel. (01289) 306771. Bus station for local and Newcastle-Edinburgh services (for services to Duns, Tel. (01289) 307461)
- All facilities in Berwick-upon-Tweed
- WC Adjacent to Tourist Information at Old Cattle Market

ALAN SPENCE

THE WALK

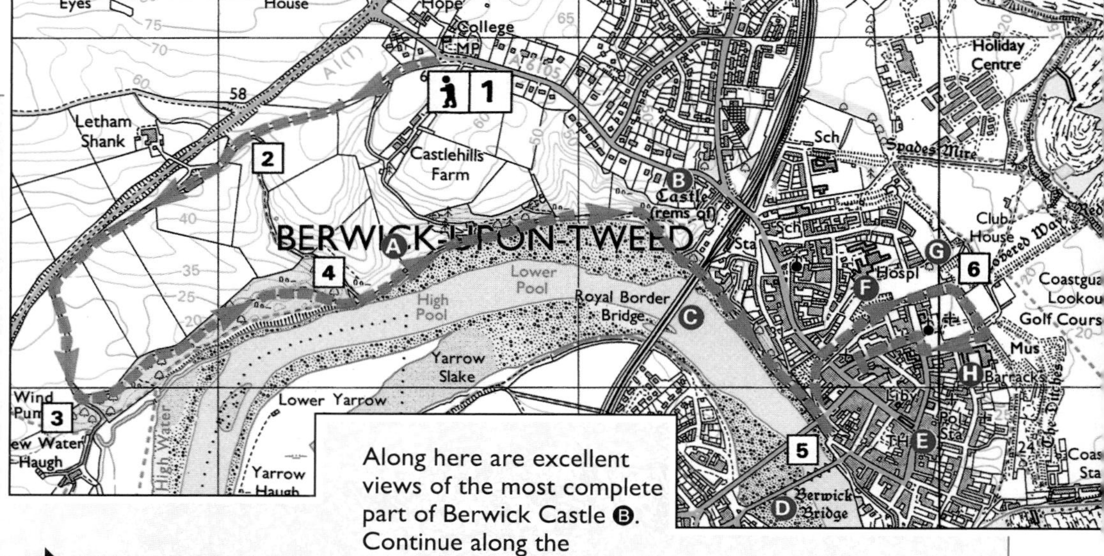

BERWICK-UPON-TWEED

This linear walk begins at the Bible College just outside Berwick-upon-Tweed. This may be reached by walking north-west from the centre of town for about 20 minutes along the Duns Road, or by catching a bus for Duns from the bus station.

1 Head along the road marked 'Letham Shank Farm only'. After about 100 yards (91 metres) you will leave the outskirts of the town where, as the road rises gently, there are fine views around the Tweed Valley.

2 After five minutes' walking, take a path opposite a layby, which leads to the left downhill towards the River Tweed. After a while, you will pass a sign that states 'Private road, no cars, footpath only', then a house advertising Bed and Breakfast. With the A1 close by you on the right-hand side, continue downhill where the paved road changes to a stony track.

3 Where the track enters woodland, leave it and take a path branching left, passing between gateposts to follow a well-defined path through what is known locally as 'The Plantation'. The path is muddy here, especially following rain. You emerge at a stand of magnificent mature beech trees.

4 Turn downhill here, where there are both path and steps, heading for a riverside cottage, which is just visible. Cross a small stream by a concrete bridge to pass between the cottage and the river. The path becomes tarmacked and 50 yards (46 metres) beyond the white-washed building is the Shiel Ⓐ.

Along here are excellent views of the most complete part of Berwick Castle Ⓑ. Continue along the riverside path, below the guntower at the base of the White Walls, then under the Royal Border Bridge Ⓒ which leads to the railway station on the north bank. Keep along the path to pass below the new concrete bridge.

5 Downstream lies the graceful Old Bridge Ⓓ, but beside a gas street lamp turn uphill to pass back under the new bridge. Continue to where a sign identifies this as part of Berwick's Elizabethan walls. To the left is Meg's Mount, from where the view extends upstream alongside the river where you have just walked. Continue for about 50 yards (46 metres) to reach the centre of the town. Stand upon Scotsgate, and look into Marygate with the dominant town hall Ⓔ at its foot. Take the upper of two paths to gain a good view of the next bastion, the Cumberland Ⓕ. Continue along the walls to Brass bastion Ⓖ.

6 Leave the bastion and turn right with the Holy Trinity Church on the right. Continue to drop down a ramp leading to the Parade, opposite the barracks Ⓗ. Keeping the barracks on your left, turn right and walk round the Parade, then turn left into Walkergate. This leads you to Marygate and the bus station where the walk ends.

NEIL POTTS

▲*The Holy Trinity Church is believed to be the only parish church built during Oliver Cromwell's protectorate.*

sweeping curve, the Royal Border Bridge Ⓒ, designed by Robert Stephenson, was a wonder of late-19th-century railway engineering, and was the final link of the London-to-Edinburgh railway. It was opened in 1850 by Queen Victoria, who, much to the chagrin of the local dignitaries, spent only 12 minutes over the task!

GEORGIAN TOWN HALL

At Berwick Barracks Ⓗ, home of the King's Own Scottish Borderers, there are four separate museum exhibitions. Seldom out of sight anywhere in Berwick is the 150-foot (46-metre) spire of the Town Hall Ⓔ, which is one of the most outstanding examples of Georgian town hall architecture in Britain. The building is open to visitors, and contains, amongst other interesting features, old prison cells on its upper floors.

The town sits at the mouth of one of the most famous salmon rivers in Britain. The salmon trade was once the mainstay of the town, and the estuary had netting stations alternating from bank to bank. While many of the fisheries have been bought out by angling interests in the shape of conservation bodies, several (including the White Sands fishery by the Shiel Ⓐ), still survive.

There is some impressive birdlife where the walk leads alongside the estuary, including golden-eye duck and eider duck as well as the resident mallard. There are feral mink here too, as well as a wide range of colourful wild flowers.

By the Banks of the Allen

30

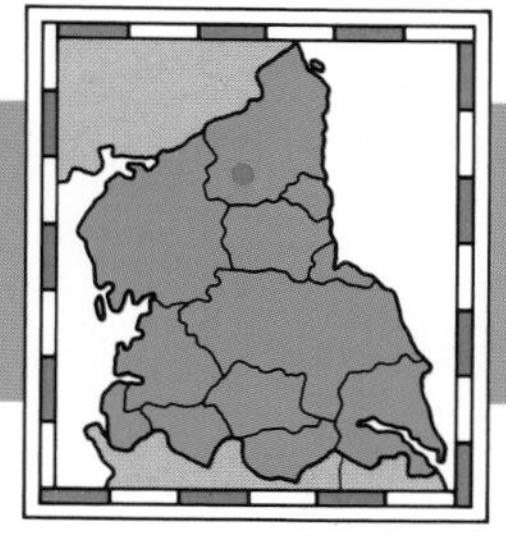

NORTHUMBERLAND

SIMON FRASER

A riverside walk past deciduous woodland to a nature reserve

Allen Banks consists of just over 193 acres (78 hectares) of hill and river scenery, donated to the National Trust by the Bowes-Lyon family. There are many pathways stretching through and around beautiful deciduous woodland beside the River Allen. The best times of year to visit this area are spring and early summer when the trees are bursting out with fresh green leaves and wild flowers carpet the woodland floor, or in the autumn when the woods are a magnificent blaze of gold.

The walk follows a variety of paths to cover the most interesting parts of the nature reserve including Briarwood Banks, which is a Site of Special Scientific Interest of national importance for wildlife.

The walk starts at the car park and follows a path by the river as far as a suspension bridge. From April to June the woods are full of wild garlic with its characteristic, powerful smell. Other common flowers to be seen here include wood sorrel, stitchwort, violet, red campion, forget-me-not, herb-robert, woodruff, bugle and bluebell.

FACT FILE

- Allen Banks, by the River Allen, 1 mile (1.6 km) south of the A69 Hexham to Carlisle road
- Pathfinders 546 (NY 66/76) and 547 (NY 86/96), grid reference NY 797639

miles 0 1 2 3 4 5 6 7 8 9 10 miles
kms 0 1 2 3 4 5 6 7 8 9 10 11 12 13 14 15 kms

- Allow 2½ hours
- Mature, deciduous woodland, rich in wildlife. Good paths, steep in places; wet and muddy in winter. Wear good walking shoes
- P Off the minor road leading from the A69
- Cafés, pubs, restaurants and shops in Haltwhistle, Haydon Bridge and Hexham — all within 10 miles (16 km)

TALL SCOTS PINES

Crossing the suspension bridge **A**, which sways gently over the river, the path leads up into Morralee Wood through beech and oak woodland, with many beautiful ferns. There are also species such as rowan, birch and the exotic rhododendron. The Tarn **B** is a peaceful and scenic place, with some tall Scots pines, larch and oak. In summer, this small lake is covered with white water lilies.

◀The River Allen flows north through a wooded valley, eventually reaching the River South Tyne. The pied flycatcher (below) feeds on a variety of insects which it chases from perch to perch.

FRANK V. BLACKBURN/NATURE PHOTOGRAPHERS LTD

The path continues through rhododendrons and descends again to the river with several good viewpoints over the woodland canopy. Rejoining the riverside path, the route leads into open meadowland where there are sun-loving plants such as crosswort and wild pansy. Reaching Plankey Mill **C**, the path crosses back over to the west bank of the river and soon leads to

THE WALK

ALLEN BANKS – PLANKEY MILL

To reach the car park where the walk starts, turn down a minor road off the A69.

1 From the car park, take the path by the information boards that leads upstream beside the River Allen. After ½ mile (800 metres), cross the river on a suspension bridge **A**. Climb steps ahead of you and join another path. Straight ahead is a stone with 'tarn' carved on it and a small arrow. Turn right here and follow the path, which zigzags up to a larger path below some crags. Turn left and follow the path through Morralee Wood until a fork is reached. Take the right fork. Follow this path past the junction with path on left, then turn left at the next fork. Continue along this path which eventually makes a sharp right bend and ascends by the Tarn **B**, below to your right.

2 Follow the path to the far end of the Tarn. The path now goes uphill for 25 yards (23 metres) and forks right through rhododendrons. After another 25 yards (23 metres) it joins another path ascending from the right. Turn left onto this path and follow it uphill. Soon there is a bench on the left, from where there is a view of Ridley Hall through a clearing in the bushes. The path levels off and descends steps to cross another path. Follow the path straight across and after 20 yards (18 metres) there is another bench and a view over the woods of Allen Banks. The path now descends and the river can be heard below. At a fork in the path, steps lead left and the path leads right. Stay on the path to the right along a level section, then descend steep steps to another path. Turn left and walk on the level path before crossing a small stream (dry in summer) below a crag. Pass under a fallen tree across the path. The river is now visible through the trees below. Descend steep steps past another small crag to join yet another path just below a huge beech tree, which towers overhead. Massive boulders are scattered in the woods here. Turn left and cross a wooden bridge over a stream that flows into the River Allen. Then cross a wooden stile. The path follows a fence and meadow on the left and continues for ½ mile (800 metres), over three more stiles to a road. Turn right and down a hill to Plankey Mill **C**.

3 Cross the suspension bridge. Follow the path to a footbridge over a tributary stream. Cross the bridge to an information board on the left for Briarwood Banks. Go left here and then take a left fork beside the stream.

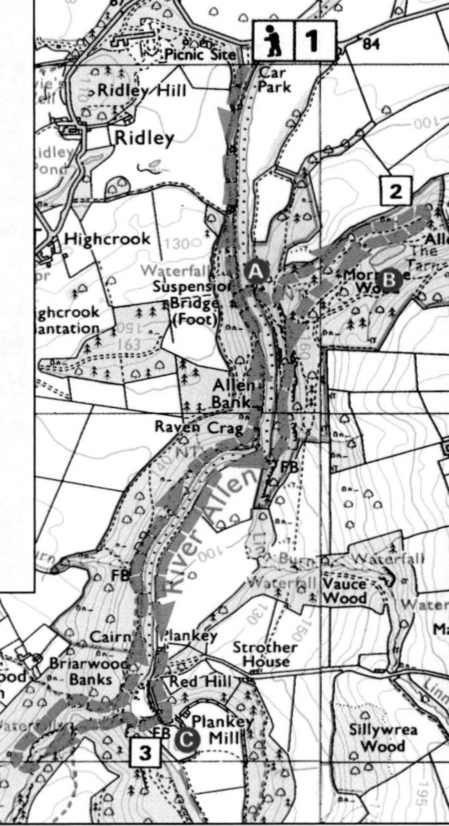

This path is much smaller and rougher than most paths in Allen Banks. After a few minutes walk, a stone step leads up to another path. Turn right and climb steep wooden steps. The path levels off then gradually descends again to join another, which leads back to the information board. From here, a good path leads for 1 mile (1.6 km) back to the car park, following the river all the way.

Briarwood Banks Nature Reserve. In 1988, the reserve was bought by the Northumberland Wildlife Trust.

About 10,000 years ago much of the landscape was covered by trees, of which only small portions of 'ancient' woodland survive today. Those that have remained undisturbed are valuable places for wildlife. The most common trees in Briarwood Banks are ash, wych elm, sessile oak and birch.

SIMON FRASER

HAZEL COPPICE

Amongst the shrubs here are holly, bird cherry, blackthorn, honeysuckle and some old hazel coppice. Coppicing was once commonly practised in an 8- to 12-year rotation, for producing firewood, charcoal and basket material. In these woods you may be able to see some roe deer. You may also see signs of the red squirrel, which is quite common in Northumberland — this county is one of England's last strongholds for this increasingly rare rodent.

◀ *About halfway through the walk is Plankey Mill, which once used the River Allen as its source of power.*

WOODPECKERS

There are a number of interesting birds here such as pied flycatcher, wood warbler, treecreeper and greater spotted woodpecker, as well as more common species such as blue tit and robin. Dippers may be seen bobbing in the river. Leaving Briarwood Banks, the path rejoins the main route along the river and continues through fine woodland scenery back to the car park.

YEAVERING BELL'S TWIN PEAKS

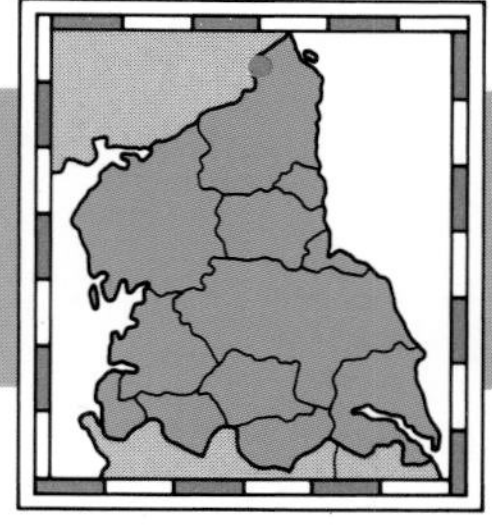

31

NORTHUMBERLAND

▲*A stone rampart encircles the twin summits of Yeavering Bell. There are extensive views from here. The wood warbler (inset) is a summer visitor, nesting in deciduous woodland.*

Upland country, a waterfall and a hill-fort in the Cheviots

The walk takes in some of the most attractive features of rural Northumberland: an ancient church; a quiet track leading to a sheltered, wooded valley; rough upland pasture and moorland; and sweeping views of remote hill country.

It begins in the beautifully situated village of Kirknewton, which nestles in a valley below Yeavering Bell, a shapely hill crowned by an extensive Iron Age fort. The village is characterized by the thick stone walls of its cottages, built to withstand attacks from Scottish border raiders. Its remarkable Early English church Ⓐ has a chancel and south transept with pointed tunnel vaults set on walls barely 3 feet (1m) high. Inside is a stone carving, believed to be Saxon, showing three kilted Magi in adoration of the Virgin.

INTO THE VALLEY

From the village, you follow a track into the valley of College Burn Ⓑ, a salmon stream whose source is on the west flank of the Cheviots, 6 miles (10km) to the south. The burn is heavily wooded, in contrast to the bare hills above. A path through rough pasture descends to the burn

FACT FILE

- Kirknewton, 5 miles (8km) west of Wooler on the B6351
- Pathfinder 475 (NT 82/92), grid reference NT 913302
- miles 0 1 2 3 4 5 6 7 8 9 10 miles / kms 0 1 2 3 4 5 6 7 8 9 10 11 12 13 14 15 kms
- Allow 3½ hours
- Some steep gradients — not recommended in snow. Unsuitable for young children or the elderly
- P In a quiet road by Kirknewton Church
- Shops and pubs 5 miles (8km) away in Wooler

SIMON FRASER

◀*The view from Yeavering Bell of the small village of Kirknewton, with the River Glen in the valley beyond it.*

THE WALK

KIRKNEWTON - YEAVERING BELL

The walk begins at Kirknewton Church Ⓐ, just off the B6351.

1 Turn right out of the churchyard gate, then left and right again to reach the edge of the village along a narrow road. This soon curves to the right and becomes a grassy track between trees, leading to open fields beyond. Follow this track past a derelict house on the left and continue curving around into the valley of College Burn Ⓑ.

2 The track continues to the southern side of West Hill and becomes more grassy. Bear right at a fork to follow a wooden 'Permissive Path' sign. Cross the stile in a nearby wall, but, instead of following a small arrow pointing left, follow the distinct footpath bearing to the right across a field. Stay at the same level (the ground and another path slope away to the right) and make for a gate in the next wall. Continue on a path through the bracken to a rough pasture and follow the traces of an old field wall to a wire fence. Follow sheep paths beside the fence until you reach a stile on your right, just before a wooded burn. Cross the stile, then turn left down a narrow path through some gorse bushes. Cross a burn and continue with woods on your right and a fence on your left, soon descending to Hethpool Linn Ⓒ.

3 Retrace your steps to cross the stile by the wooded burn and head diagonally, towards a stone enclosure, on a faint path. Soon you join a track leading to Torleehouse.

4 Continue past the house to the second cattle grid, which is set in a stone wall. Turn right and follow the track steeply uphill, passing through a new gate and crossing the wall higher up by a stile. Follow the track for a further ½ mile (800m) to reach a gate and a fence.

5 Turn left and follow a sheep track through the bracken, descending into a shallow valley, then gradually climbing. Where the track levels out, head north (directly towards Yeavering Bell Ⓓ) across the heather-covered moorland, climbing to the twin summits.

6 From the western summit, descend steep slopes in a north to north-westerly direction and cross a stile/gate in the fence at the bottom.

7 Follow the stone wall that leads from the fence down to a rough track. Turn right over a stile and descend to a barn at Old Yeavering. Pass through a gate next to the barn, turn right and follow the track to the main road. Turn left and follow the road for about ½ mile (800m) back to Kirknewton.

▼*On the descent from Yeavering Bell you pass the farm buildings at Old Yeavering before rejoining the road.*

JEFFREY BEAZLEY

at Hethpool Linn Ⓒ, a delightful waterfall in a sheltered spot.

From here, the route heads east across an open hillside, where red grouse are a common sight, to reach a track leading to Torleehouse. As you climb the hill, views open out on all sides. The Cheviots, dotted with remote farms and cut by hidden valleys, roll away to the south. To the north, the hills end abruptly as the landscape becomes a flat patchwork of fields, irrigated by the River Tweed and its tributaries.

With Torleehouse behind you, Yeavering Bell Ⓓ dominates the way ahead. The stiff climb towards its twin summits, one of 1,164 feet (355m) and one of 1,184 feet (361m), is rewarded by some fine views.

ANCIENT REMAINS

Around the summits is an extensive Iron Age settlement. A stone rampart encloses an area of 13 acres (32ha) scarred with the 'pock marks' of 130 circular stone huts, evidence of what must have been a very large community for the period.

Finally, you pass the remains of an ancient tower at Old Yeavering and return to Kirknewton.

Along Shildon Burn

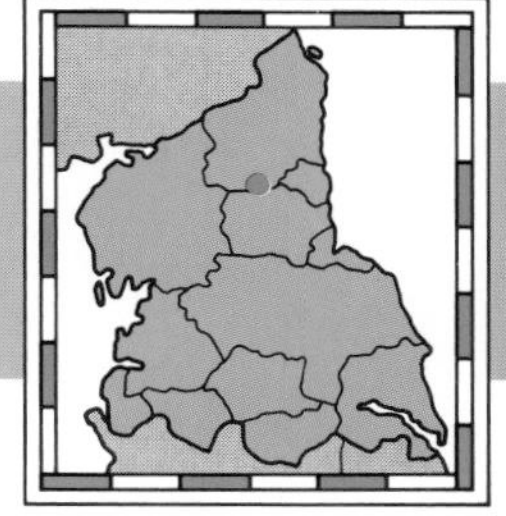

32

NORTHUMBERLAND

◀*The woods behind Blanchland mark the beginning of the tree-lined lane that follows Shildon Burn. In summer, the woods are filled with the songs of the blackbird (inset) and many others.*

SIMON FRASER. INSET: E.A. JANES/NHPA

FACT FILE

Blanchland, 10 miles (16km) south of Hexham on the B6306

Pathfinders 560 (NY 85/95) and 570 (NY 84/94), grid reference NY 964505

miles 0 1 2 3 4 5 6 7 8 9 10 miles
kms 0 1 2 3 4 5 6 7 8 9 10 11 12 13 14 15 kms

Allow 2 hours

Good tracks, footpaths and a metalled road. Gradual ascent. Wet in places in winter

P Free car park at start of walk

T Bus services from Hexham and Consett

Lord Crewe Arms Hotel and tea shop in Blanchland

WC Near road-bridge over River Derwent

I Information leaflets at the abbey and at the small shop in the main square

Explore an elegant village set in wild moorland

Romantically situated in a valley beneath heather-clad moors, the little village of Blanchland is one of the finest in Northumberland. Its pastoral elegance contrasts dramatically with the bleak moors and hills all around. Most of the village was built in the 18th century on the site of a 12th-century abbey, though the gatehouse dates from the 15th century. On a clear day, there are spectacular views of the northern Pennines from the high moors above the village.

The walk follows a quiet, tree-lined lane along Shildon Burn. In early summer, the sides of the lane are thick with cow parsley, germander speedwell, greater stitchwort, meadow cranesbill and creeping buttercup, and the woods are full of the songs of wren, chaffinch, blackbird and goldcrest.

LEAD MINING

Shildon Ⓐ is a small hamlet, lying near the ruins of an old smelt mill chimney that dates from the lead-mining days in the 19th century. Behind Shildon are spoil heaps, bare of vegetation. The site is an interesting reminder that lead was mined in Northumberland from Roman times right up to the 1920s.

North-west of Shildon, the route passes a plantation of sitka spruce and Scots pine before emerging on

▶*The heather moorland just before Pennypie House offers a panoramic view and is at its best in late summer.*

SIMON FRASER

THE WALK

BLANCHLAND – PENNYPIE

The walk begins at a car park situated on the north side of Blanchland, off the lane to Shildon.

1 Turn left out of the car park and follow the lane gradually uphill to Shildon **A**, which is visible as a row of cottages on the right above the road, with the ruins of a lead mine on the left. The road becomes a dirt track. Follow it past a conifer plantation and a barn, then on into open country. Continue until the track turns sharp right towards Pennypie House.

2 Go through a gate straight ahead. Cross the plank bridge over the burn on your left and join a rough track that runs parallel to a dry-stone wall and leads across the moor **B**. Cross a stile over a wire fence beside a wooden gate. When the track becomes a metalled road, go through a gate and continue downhill to Baybridge. In the centre of this hamlet you come to a road junction.

3 Turn right and walk past the Baybridge picnic area on your right.

4 Just before the bridge over the River Derwent, turn left along a public footpath marked by a wooden signpost. Continue along the river bank through mixed woodland.

5 Just before Blanchland **C**, cross a wooden bridge over a small burn and join the main road that leads left into the village square. The gatehouse is straight ahead, opposite the Lord Crewe Arms. A little further on is the entrance to the church.

6 After exploring the village and the church, take the road on the north side of the square to return to the car park.

open pasture-land. Northern marsh orchid, fairy flax, bird's foot trefoil and lady's mantle grow here in summer, when the beautiful, plaintive call of curlews can be heard. In winter, these birds return to their coastal feeding grounds.

Just before Pennypie House, the route crosses Shildon Burn and heads south on a rough track through heather moorland **B**. Lapwings nest here in summer and give spectacular, tumbling flight displays. There are superb views in all directions over the moors, The route descends steeply to the hamlet of Baybridge, then follows the River Derwent back to Blanchland **C**.

SIMON FRASER

◀*Once the medieval gatehouse in the village square, Blanchland's post office boasts an unusual Victorian post box.*

NORMAN ABBEY

The mellow, grey-stone houses in the centre of the village are grouped snugly around an open square that was once the outer courtyard of Blanchland Abbey. The abbey was founded in the 12th century by Walter de Bolbec for the Premonstratensian Canons, who originated from Normandy. It is thought that the village was named Blanchland, which means 'white land', after the white habits that were worn by these monks.

After the Dissolution of the Monasteries (1534), Blanchland passed into private ownership. Lord Crewe, a former Bishop of Durham, who owned the Blanchland estates, died in 1721. He left his property and land to trustees who rebuilt the village to house lead miners. The medieval gatehouse that dominates the village square was once the entrance to the abbey precincts, and now houses the village post office, with its unusual Victorian post box.

The present church was built in 1752 from parts of the old abbey church. It has several interesting features, including some fine medieval tombstones on the transept floor.

HAUNTED HOTEL

The building that today is the Lord Crewe Arms Hotel was originally the Abbot's lodge, guesthouse and abbey kitchens, while the lawn at the back used to be the site of the abbey's cloister.

Lord Crewe married Dorothy Forster in 1699. When her brother became involved in the Jacobite Rebellion of 1715, she helped him escape from imprisonment in London, and hid him in the Lord Crewe Arms. She was later immortalized in the novel *Dorothy Forster* by Walter Besant, and her ghost is said to haunt a bedroom at the hotel and to roam the lonely moors.

HISTORIC HEXHAM

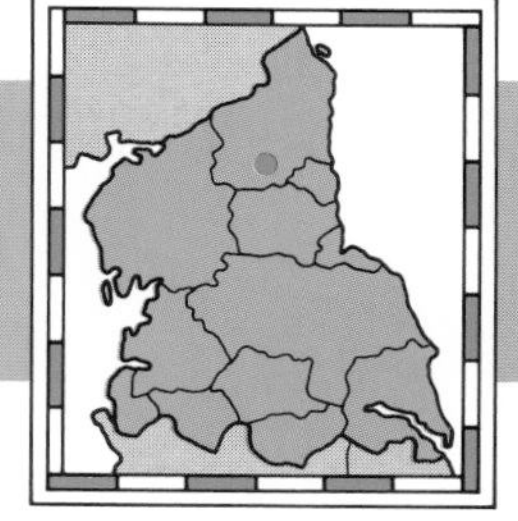

33

NORTHUMBERLAND

A walk around a small monastic town on the River Tyne

The attractive market town of Hexham, set in the beautiful Tynedale valley, is dominated by its fine abbey, which dates from Saxon times. Like many of England's border towns, it once suffered at the hands of the Scots, but now it is a peaceful, bustling place, popular with tourists visiting nearby Hadrian's Wall. There are several interesting historical buildings, a weekly market, and plenty of green, open spaces, as well as lovely walks in the surrounding countryside.

MANOR OFFICE

This walk, though, concentrates on the town itself. Near the start is the Manor Office Ⓐ, built as a prison in 1330-32 by the Archbishop of York. It was the first building in England to be specially built for this purpose, and was used as such until 1824. Today, it houses a captivating Border History Museum, and the Tourist Information Centre.

A little further on is the Moot Hall Ⓑ, which dates from the 14th century, and was once the residence of the Archbishops of York. This impressive tower house is the only defensive structure in Hexham. Its walls are 11 feet (3.3m) thick in places. An archway leads through to the Market Place and a long shelter known as the Shambles, where colourful stalls are set out every Tuesday. Hexham is the centre of a large agricultural community, and there is also a weekly livestock market, one of the busiest in the country.

On the other side of Market Place is Hexham's abbey Ⓒ, founded in AD674 when Queen Ethelreda of Northumbria gave land to her spiritual adviser, Wilfrid. The abbey is set in lovely grounds with well-kept lawns. The original building incorporated stones from the Roman fort of Corstopitum. Much of the present abbey, dedicated to St Andrew, dates

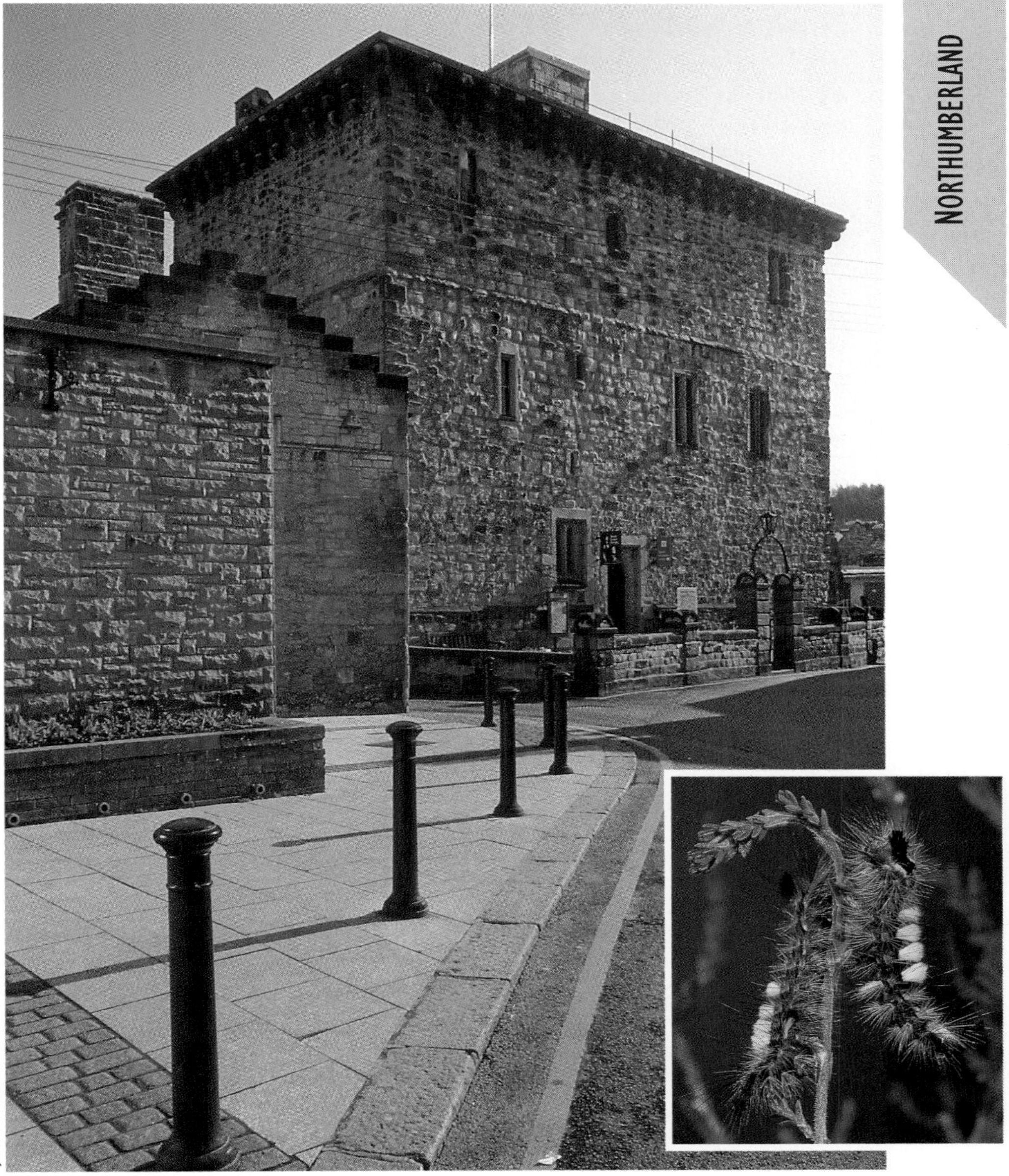

FACT FILE

- Hexham, 20 miles (32km) west of Newcastle, off the A69
- Pathfinder 547 (NY 86/96), grid reference NY 938641
- 1 hour
- Pavements and good paths
- Regular coach and train services to and from Newcastle and Carlisle
- Car park at start
- Numerous pubs, restaurants and cafés in the town
- By car park at start
- Tourist Information Centre at Manor Office

JEFFREY BEAZLEY. INSET: G.CAMBRIDGE/NHPA

▲*The 14th-century Manor Office, near the start of the walk, was the first purpose-built prison in England. The caterpillar (inset) of the widespread vapourer moth is highly distinctive.*

THE WALK

HEXHAM

The walk begins at the large car park by Wentworth Leisure Centre and Safeway.

1 Walk up the path beside Wentworth Café, and follow a sign to the Tourist Information Centre in Manor Office Ⓐ. Continue to Moot Hall Ⓑ. An archway leads through to Market Place, and Hexham Abbey Ⓒ is clearly visible on the other side.

2 After visiting the abbey, turn right out of the entrance along Beaumont Street. Turn right through the memorial arch gateway into the Abbey Grounds.

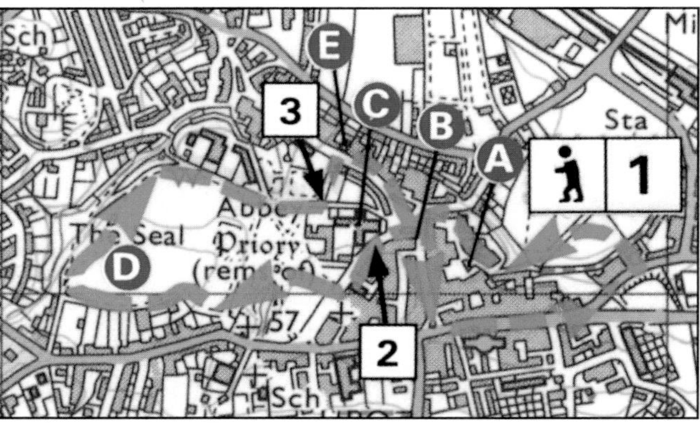

Follow a footpath towards the bandstand. Over a stream, bear left and follow a path uphill through beech trees to a gateway in the corner. Go through the gateway, and follow the path uphill, with cottages on your left and the Seal Ⓓ on you right. At the end of a stone wall, turn right along the far side of the Seal. This path bears right, and descends steps to a metalled path heading back towards the abbey, past a school on the left and a playground area on the right. Keep ahead down Cowgarth.

3 Just before an archway leading to the abbey on your right, turn left towards the Priory Gatehouse Ⓔ. Turn right along Market Street to Market Place. Cross to the Moot Hall side, and go down Fore Street to the Midland Bank. Turn left along Priestpopple. Bear left at a mini-roundabout, then turn left into a side street back to the car park where the walk began.

BOTH PHOTOS: JEFFREY BEAZLEY

▲***The Moot Hall, a 14th-century tower house, now houses a library. Hexham Abbey (below right) overlooks delightful grounds with a bandstand.***

from the 12th century, but there is also a superb Saxon bishops' chair — in which the Saxon Kings of Northumbria were crowned — cut from a solid block of sandstone.

ABBEY GROUNDS

The walk continues up Beaumont Street towards the Queens Hall, built in 1865-66 in a French-Château style. It is now a multi-purpose Arts Centre, with a theatre and a library. A gateway opposite the Queens Hall, a memorial arch to those who died in World War I, leads into the Abbey Grounds. You follow a footpath past a war memorial to reach a jolly Edwardian bandstand. There are lovely glimpses of the abbey through the trees, particularly in the spring and autumn.

The path crosses a small burn and continues right round the Seal or Sele Ⓓ, a large, gently sloping hill on the western side of the Abbey Grounds. This lovely open space, once a place of meditation for monks, is now a public park.

On the other side of the Seal, you pass through the Priory Gatehouse Ⓔ (St Wilfrid's Gateway) on the site of the original AD674-680 cathedral, which was destroyed by the Danes in AD821. The Gatehouse dates from the time of the Augustinian Canons, who built a priory in 1114-40. There was an almonry here, where the Hexham monks cared for pilgrims and the poor.

Beyond the gateway is Market Street, the old main street of Hexham, which has interesting shops and buildings. This leads back to the Market Place, where the pedestrianised Fore Street takes you to an unusual, late Victorian triangular building, with a wealth of architectural detail, which now houses the Midland Bank. At the junction, you go left down Priestpopple — which, together with Battle Hill to the right, makes up the main street through the modern town — to return to the start.

DRAKE STONE

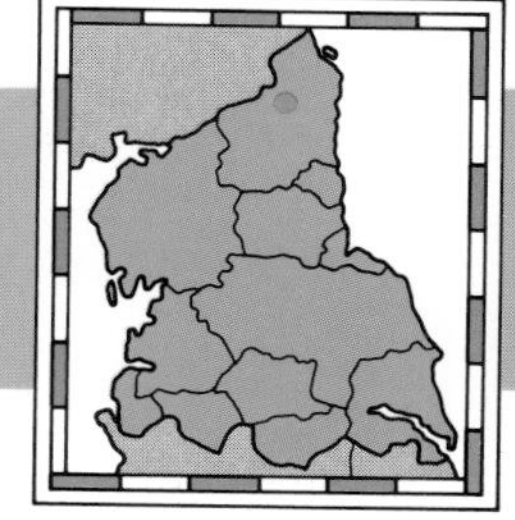

34

NORTHUMBERLAND

SIMON FRASER. INSET: ROBIN FLETCHER/SWIFT PICTURE LIBRARY

▲*On the climb to Park House you can pause to look back to the limekiln and Low Alwinton. The fox moth (right) has a caterpillar that feeds on bog myrtle.*

Woodlands, moors and a river valley at the edge of a National Park

The attractive village of Harbottle sits in a sparsely populated area at the edge of the Northumberland National Park. To the north and west are the mountain streams and pine forests of the isolated Cheviot Hills, and to the east is an exquisite pastoral landscape of rolling hills and deep meadows.

The village is built of local sandstone and is surrounded by fields and old trees. It is overlooked by a ruined castle, and the beautiful River Coquet flows nearby. High moors with craggy outcrops dominate the skyline.

The walk starts from a car park west of the village, where there is a Northumberland Wildlife Trust Information Centre Ⓐ. A track leads up the hill through the trees to the open moorland of Harbottle Crags Nature Reserve, which covers 160 acres (65ha). The hillside is covered by a mixture of heather and bracken, along with patches of bilberry, sweet gale (bog myrtle) and tormentil.

▼*Drake Stone, in the Harbottle Hills, was isolated here by a glacier.*

SIMON FRASER

FACT FILE

- Harbottle, 33 miles (53km) north-west of Newcastle upon Tyne
- Pathfinder 499 (NT 80/90), grid reference NT 926048
- miles 0 1 2 3 4 5 6 7 8 9 10 miles / kms 0 1 2 3 4 5 6 7 8 9 10 11 12 13 14 15 kms
- Allow 2 to 3 hours
- Roads, tracks and rough paths; fairly steep and strenuous in places; paths may be slippery in bad weather. Walking boots recommended
- P Forestry Commission car park at the start
- Pub in Harbottle
- WC Public toilets up alleyway to right of pub in Harbottle
- I The Northumberland Wildlife Trust Information Centre is open from June to September, 9am-6pm, but closes for lunch

DRAKE STONE

In summer, you may hear the song of the willow warbler as you climb towards Drake Stone on the horizon. A few silver birches grow beside the path, and new seedlings are taking root now that the reserve is no longer grazed by sheep. There are also a few boggy areas where sphag-

THE WALK

HARBOTTLE – LOW ALWINTON

The walk begins at the Forestry Commission car park, by the information centre Ⓐ, ½ mile (800m) west of Harbottle.

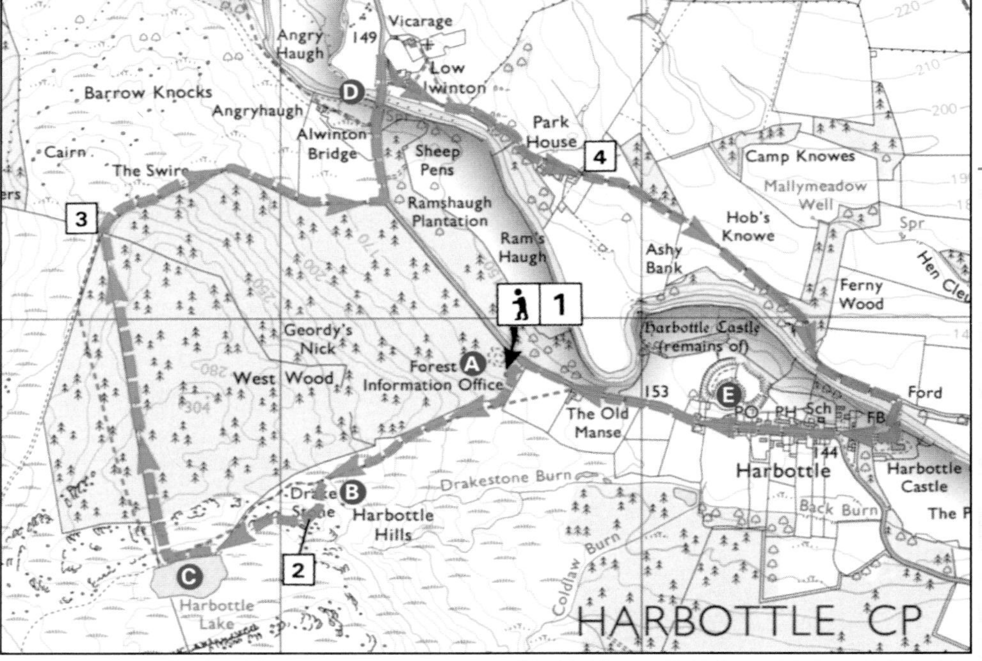

1 Ascend the steep track through the woods to a gate leading to Harbottle Crags Nature Reserve. Follow a good path uphill, with the forest on your right. By a pile of stones, the path splits. Turn left, then left again at a white marker-post. Continue on a rough, steep path through heather and boulders until you come to Drake Stone Ⓑ.

2 Pass to the right of Drake Stone, across scattered boulders, onto a small path through the heather. This leads back to the main path, and on towards Harbottle Lake Ⓒ. Cross a stile and follow the lakeside to a fence near a Range Boundary notice by the corner of the lake. Do not cross the fence, but turn right and follow the path into the forest. Continue straight ahead on this undulating path (there are some steep descents) for just over ½ mile (800m), alongside a broken wire fence, to a gate and broad crossing track.

3 Turn right onto the track. Pass through a large metal gate, and follow the track down through two more gates to a road. Turn left and cross over the river Ⓓ, then turn right at some cottages onto a narrow road across some cattle grids. Beyond a limekiln on your left, you ascend to Park House.

4 Pass the farm buildings on your right and go through a gate. Follow a rough track through two more gates down into a wood. Continue past a cottage onto a path by the river. Cross a footbridge to the modern Harbottle Castle. Turn right and follow a lane, which joins the main road. Follow this through Harbottle, passing the old castle Ⓔ, to return to the car park.

num and hair moss flourish, along with cotton grass and sundew, whose sticky leaves trap and digest insects. Wheatears and grouse are often seen among the rocks.

Drake Stone Ⓑ is named from the Anglo-Saxon word for 'dragon', and is the country's largest isolated boulder. The broad ridge of fell sandstone it stands on was laid down 280 million years ago in an ancient estuary. Layers within the blocks show how irregularly the sand was deposited in piles on the sea floor, a feature known as cross-bedding.

The rock around Drake Stone was scoured away by glaciers in the last Ice Age. Lines called 'striae', gouged in the rock by the ice, are still visible. Millstones were cut from the hard rocks here and taken downhill on horse-drawn sledges.

FINE VIEWS

The views, which are magnificent, span the Cheviot Hills, the Coquet Valley east to Rothbury, the Alnwick Moors and the Simonside Hills. Harbottle village is very clearly visible in the valley beneath you.

Beyond Drake Stone is Harbottle Lake Ⓒ, with its swampy fringe of rushes and sedges. The route follows the edge of the lake, then turns off through the forest and joins a track leading to the Harbottle-Alwinton road. Turning north, the road soon crosses the River Coquet Ⓓ, where otters are present but rarely seen.

The route follows a narrow road past a fine limekiln and up to Park House. Beyond the farm buildings, a rough track across pasture-land yields fine views across to the Harbottle Hills and Drake Stone. After descending through woodland, the route follows the banks of the Coquet to a footbridge, and you cross the river to the present Harbottle Castle, built in 1829.

From here, you walk through Harbottle, which consists of a single street lined with neat cottages that mostly date from the early 19th century. The village, whose historic name 'Hir Botle' means Army Station, originated in Saxon times, and was occupied by the Umfreville barons after the Norman Conquest.

Henry II built a stone castle Ⓔ on the site of the original Norman fortification, following the transference of Northumberland from Scotland to England in 1159. The castle ruins are on private land and visits are discouraged. A short walk along the road leads you back to the car park.

SIMON FRASER

►*The ruins of the 12th-century Harbottle Castle are on private land on the site of an earlier Norman fort.*

FROM PEEL TO PEN

35

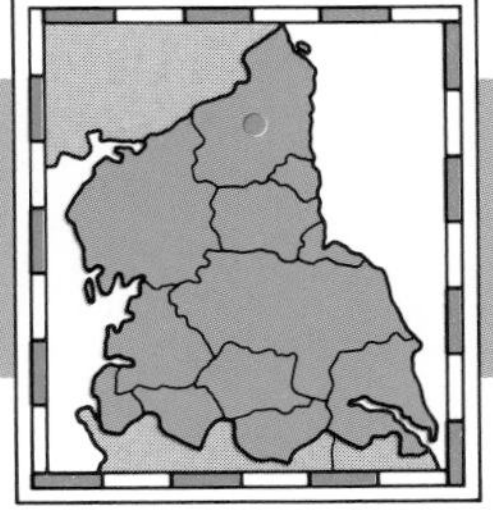

NORTHUMBERLAND

JEFFREY BEAZLEY. INSET: ANDREW CLEAVE/NATURE PHOTOGRAPHERS

A village on the Scottish borders, with a violent past

It is hard to believe that the small village of Elsdon, with its Georgian cottages surrounding the village green, was once the capital of Redesdale. Situated close to the Scottish border, this remote area was far from any centre of civilization, even by pre-industrial standards. It was terrorized by the border reivers, gangs of cattle and horse rustlers whose feuding and raiding gave the area a legendary lawlessness. It was also in the front line of more official disputes between England and Scotland. The village shows much evidence of this turbulent past.

The plan of the village, with the cottages facing inwards to the large square green, made for efficient defence. The Parish Church of St Cuthbert Ⓐ was placed within this perimeter. Built in the 14th century, it is typically Northumbrian: squat and strong with an elaborate bell-cote rather than a true tower. It was to this church that the Scottish dead were brought for burial after the Battle of Otterburn in 1388.

On the northern edge of the village, just beyond the church, stands Elsdon Tower Ⓑ. Built around 1400, it is one of the county's best peel towers. These strong, stone-built tower houses, with relatively small windows set in thick walls topped by battlements, were built as defensible residences by many of the local gentry during the troubled centuries before the Act of Union. Many were inhabited by the clergy, including this one, which was used as the rectory until 1962.

NORMAN CASTLE

The walk leads beyond the village to the top of a quiet farm track, where there are two impressive grass mounds known as the Mote Hills Ⓒ. These are all that remain of a Norman motte and bailey castle built by the d'Umfreville family

◀*This peel tower, a fortified house easy to defend, is one of many along the Anglo-Scottish border. Marsh cinquefoil (inset), commonest in the north, grows in wet places.*

FACT FILE

- Elsdon, 17½ miles (28km) east of Morpeth, on the B6341
- Pathfinder 510 (NY 89/99), grid reference NY 935931

miles 0 1 2 3 4 5 6 7 8 9 10 miles
kms 0 1 2 3 4 5 6 7 8 9 10 11 12 13 14 15 kms

- Allow 2 hours
- Easy walking, but country sections may be muddy. Some gates may be bound shut but have plank fencing at the sides, which is easily climbed
- P Round the village green
- The Bird in Bush pub at the start
- WC At the bottom of the track to Mote Hills
- The grounds of Elsdon Tower are open Apr-Sept, 10am-6pm

THE WALK

ELDSON

The walk starts from the Bird in Bush pub in Elsdon.

1 Follow a narrow lane to the church **A**, then continue on the lane to Elsdon Tower **B**. Keep right to bend round the churchyard to a road.

2 Turn left and cross the bridge over Mill Dean. As you leave the bridge, turn right onto a farm track and keep left to pass between a pair of cottages and a stone barn. Follow the metalled track to the top of a short rise. The Mote Hills **C** are to your left.

3 Continue through a stone gateway into a farmyard, then pass through the gate ahead by a green oil tank. Go slightly right through a second gate, then head for a line of trees to the right of a small disused quarry at the top of the field.

4 At the trees, pass through the left-hand gate of two onto a sunken track. Follow this straight ahead, staying close to the fence on your right, for about 200 yards (180m). Go through another gate onto a metalled farm track and bear right to a fork just beyond a white cottage.

5 Turn right. Follow the road downhill. At the bottom, go through a gate and bear left to the main road (B6341).

6 Turn left over Mill Dean Bridge. At the corner of the churchyard, fork left, then left again, and go past a row of Georgian houses to the stone cattle pen **D**.

7 Take the road signposted 'Morpeth and Newcastle'. At a fork, keep left over a bridge **E** and go uphill for ½ mile (800m) until the road bends sharp left. From this point **F**, the view is particularly good.

8 Do not bend left on the road; instead, turn right through a gate onto a farm track. Follow the track for nearly ¼ mile (400m). Before reaching a farm gate ahead, turn right through another gate in the fence into a field. Walk straight ahead to another pair of gates. Take the left-hand one and follow the fence downhill. At the bottom, a small gate to your right and a second one in the main fence lead onto the road.

9 Turn right. At a T-junction, turn left. Follow the road back to the start.

shortly after the Conquest.

After making a loop around the fields above the village, the route returns to the bottom edge of the village green, where there is an old, stone cattle pen **D**. With walls 5 feet (1.5m) high, and only one narrow opening, it doubtless made a useful defence against sneak thieves trying to rustle a herd of cattle quickly and quietly at the dead of night.

Leaving the village again, this time on the road going south, the walk passes over a small but elegant double-arched stone bridge **E** before climbing a hill to a viewpoint **F** that gives a fine perspective of the varied landscape. Elsdon stands close to where the craggy sandstone topography to the north gives way to the gentler limestone belt running south. Here there is hilly but tame

▲*The view from St Cuthbert's Church and its graveyard across Elsdon's village green. The Mote Hills (left) are the remains of a motte and bailey.*

BOTH PHOTOS: JEFFREY BEAZLEY

moorland, with rough grazing on tussocky grass in the valley bottoms and heather-clad tops. Wild rabbits abound, and the plaintive call of the curlew, the symbol of the Northumberland National Park, can sometimes be heard overhead.

From here, you follow a farm track past an old sheep wash at Shaw Cleugh, then head downhill and follow surfaced roads back into the village and your starting point.

CRAGS AND CONIFERS

36

NORTHUMBERLAND

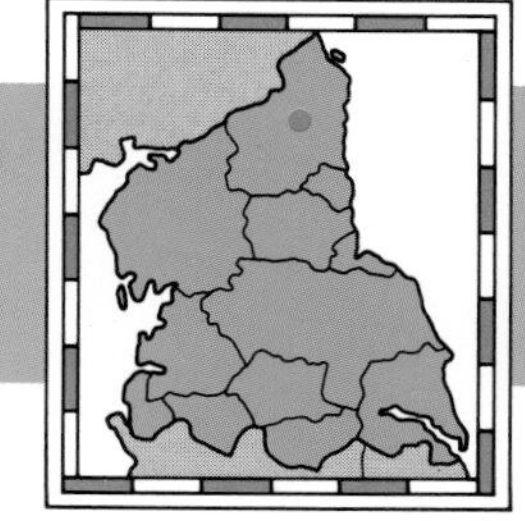

JEFFREY BEAZLEY

▲*The climb up Simonside is worth it for the extensive views over moors and woods to the Coquet Valley's farms.*

A dramatic hike through the remote Simonside Hills

To the south of the Coquet Valley is a small but dramatic upland area, the Simonside Hills. It is one of several small ranges formed from an arc of fell sandstone sandwiched between the Cheviots and the limestone lowlands.

This rock is noted for producing dramatic crags and heather moorland. It is also well suited to the cultivation of conifer plantations, although the Forestry Commission is now planting deciduous species such as silver birch and rowan among the pines. The area has escaped human influence for many centuries. As a result, it contains some precious prehistoric remains.

Starting from a remote forest car park, the walk sets out along a quiet moorland road to visit the Lordenshaw Iron Age hill fort Ⓐ. Surrounding the ditched mound are signs of an even earlier civilization. A number of Bronze Age cairns can be seen, and there are cup-and-ring marks, saucer-shaped depressions surrounded by circles, on the rocks. Although they are fairly common in Northumberland, no-one is quite sure of the significance of these marks, which are associated with the Beaker folk of the Bronze Age, though they are believed to have had some ritual significance.

The mounds and ditches of the hill fort are clear enough, but the cairns and cup-and-ring-marked rocks are less so. Both are marked on the Pathfinder map, however, and there is an example of each on the

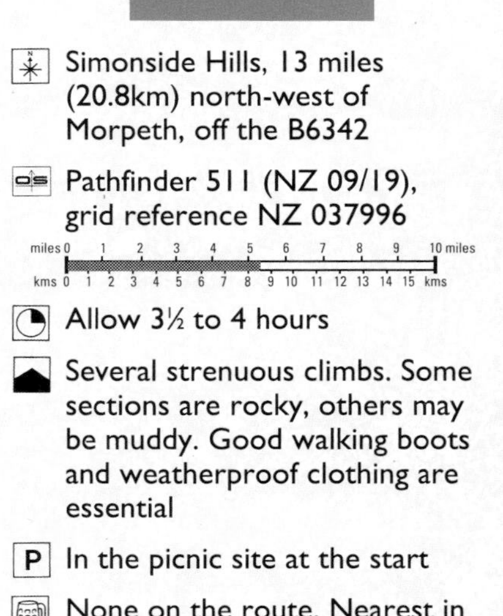

FACT FILE

Simonside Hills, 13 miles (20.8km) north-west of Morpeth, off the B6342

Pathfinder 511 (NZ 09/19), grid reference NZ 037996

Allow 3½ to 4 hours

Several strenuous climbs. Some sections are rocky, others may be muddy. Good walking boots and weatherproof clothing are essential

P In the picnic site at the start

None on the route. Nearest in Rothbury, 1½ miles (2.4km) north-east of the start

▼*The silver birch, often planted with conifers, grows well on heather moors.*

A. JOHNSON/SCOTLAND IN FOCUS

THE WALK

THE SIMONSIDE HILLS

The walk starts at the car park at the Lordenshaw picnic site. To reach it, take the B6342 out of Rothbury. After 3 miles (4.8km), turn right, signposted 'Simonside Forest Walks'. The picnic site is 2 miles (3.2km) along on your left, clearly signposted.

1 Walk back onto the road and turn right. After about 1 mile (1.6km) there are footpaths leading both left and right off the road. The one on the right has a ground-level footpath sign.

2 Take the left-hand path to a gate in a wire fence. Take a line diagonally right beyond the gate for about 500 yards (450m), to the right-hand edge of the hill fort Ⓐ. Return to the road and cross over to take the signposted path, which climbs to the bottom end of an old stone wall.

3 Turn right above the wall and follow a distinct stony path, which follows the southern side of the wall for a while before diverging to climb up to The Beacon Ⓑ.

4 Continue along a level stretch to a stile, then follow the path up to Dove Crag Ⓒ. Halfway up, there is a waymarked path to the right; ignore this, but take the next right fork to make the loop around the rock.

5 Continue around Dove Crag to rejoin the main path, bearing right to carry on towards Simonside. At one point the path becomes grassy and indistinct, but the line is easy to follow by aiming for the cairn directly ahead. The summit Ⓓ gives some splendid views.

6 From the summit, follow the path left before it forks right, down a shallow gully, to a wide forest access road. Take care on the descent as some of the stones are loose. Turn right onto the road and follow it for about ⅔ mile (1.1km) into the plantation Ⓔ.

7 Where a right fork leads over the Coe Burn, follow the main track, downhill to your left. After ¼ mile (400m), turn right by an old wooden bench onto a narrow path waymarked red. Where the path forks either side of a gully, keep right.

8 Eventually this narrow path crosses a wider one. Go straight across, following the red waymarker, to return to the picnic site.

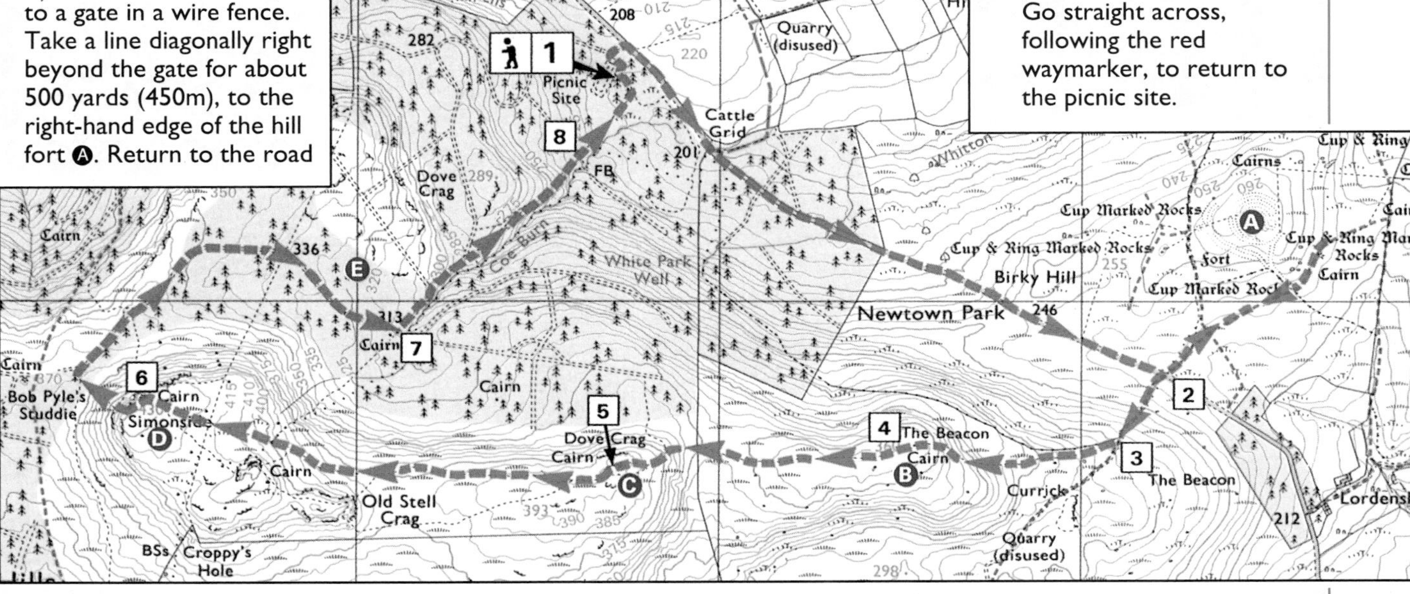

eastern side of the fort. You should enjoy the search for them.

The walk begins its ascent to Simonside on a clear path through heather and rocky outcrops. Grouse are ever present here, and the wheatear is a common sight in spring and summer. The climb follows the top of the north-facing escarpment, with superb views over woodland and the Coquet Valley beyond. There are also good views eastwards, even to the sea on a clear day, as the route leads to the fine rock formations of The Beacon Ⓑ, where there is a hollow cairn that can serve as a windbreak, and Dove Crag Ⓒ. The summit of Simonside Ⓓ provides an opportunity to take in magnificent views to the north-west over miles of Northumbrian landscape to the Cheviot Hills.

CONTRASTING CALM

A rough gully takes the route down to a forest access road before turning into the plantation Ⓔ. The contrast between the blustery tops and the cloistered calm of the wood is one of the walk's great pleasures. Red squirrels are a common sight here, and woodland finches such as the crossbill can also be seen, as well as the tiny goldcrest, said to be the commonest breeding bird in the area. Should you decide to eat on your return to the picnic area, you are very likely to receive the attentions of friendly chaffinches.

▶ The road from the car park provides views over the forest to Simonside.

JEFFREY BEAZLEY

Bridges and Bagpipes

37

NORTHUMBERLAND

L CAMPBELL/NHPA

JEFFREY BEAZLEY

◀*The sandstone arches of Telford Bridge cross the gentle River Wansbeck on the eastern edge of Morpeth. Hawthorn (above) is in blossom along the route during the month of May.*

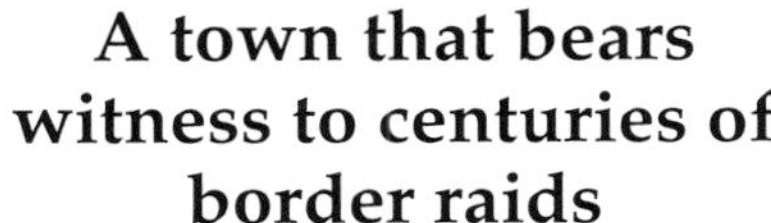

A town that bears witness to centuries of border raids

At the time of the Norman Conquest, the area where Morpeth now stands was a minor river crossing in the wilds of the north country. Once William I was established he set about consolidating his hold on the northern parts of his new kingdom, building up defences against the possibility of an invasion by the Scots.

In 1080, he granted the baronetcy of Morpeth to the de Merley family, who built a motte and bailey castle on the south side of the River Wansbeck to guard the crossing. From those early beginnings, Morpeth became part of the extended northern defences of Newcastle, and grew into a town of some importance. Today, it is the county town of Northumberland.

The town suffered greatly from disputes and cross-border raiding during the Middle Ages. It is said that Scottish brigands entered Morpeth with the regularity and impunity of men going to market. As a result, some of the town's earliest buildings are now only ruined shadows of their former selves, requiring some imagination to see them as they once were.

Fortunately, there is still much to see on this walk around the town, beginning on the northern bank of the river at the Chantry Ⓐ in Bridge Street. Originally part of All Saints' Church, the Chantry was founded in the 13th century. One of its early functions was to collect the tolls for the bridge crossing.

It was later used as a grammar school, and now houses the Tourist Information Office, a craft centre, the Northumberland Wildlife Trust shop and a particularly interesting bagpipe museum. Here, you can follow the history of bagpipes from around the world with special emphasis on the Northumbrian small pipes (see box on page 110)

The original bridge has now gone, and a Victorian footbridge rests self-consciously on the old stone piles. Modern road traffic crosses the river a little way downstream on an elegant stone bridge built by Thomas Telford in 1831.

FACT FILE

- Morpeth, 15 miles (24km) north of Newcastle, off the A1
- Pathfinders 523 (NZ 08/18) and 524 (NZ 28/38), grid reference NZ 200858

miles 0 1 2 3 4 5 6 7 8 9 10 miles
kms 0 1 2 3 4 5 6 7 8 9 10 11 12 13 14 15 kms

- To include a visit to the museum, allow 3 hours, or 4½ if you divert to Mitford
- Easy walking, suitable for all ages, though can be muddy in parts
- P Several long-stay car parks in the town. Parking may be difficult on Wednesday, market day
- T BR local services and regular buses from Newcastle
- Several pubs, restaurants, tearooms and cafés in the town
- Chantry and Bagpipe Museum open Mar-Dec, Mon-Sat, 9.30am-5.30pm; Jan-Feb, Mon-Sat, 10am-4pm. Newminster Abbey open by landowner's concession during daylight hours until 5pm
- I Tourist Information Office at the Chantry at the start, Tel. (01524) 414110

THE WALK

MORPETH – MITFORD – OLDGATE

The walk begins at the Chantry Ⓐ, at the eastern end of Bridge Street.

1 Cross the Telford Bridge and continue ahead for 200 yards (180m), to the Courthouse Ⓑ on your left and Carlisle Park Ⓒ on your right. Continue uphill on a raised pavement on the right-hand side of the road. Where steps divide the path, go uphill onto a lane, which runs beside the remnants of the castle Ⓓ. Beyond the start of some houses, take the first track left, downhill to a road. Walk past the Sun Inn to St Mary's Church Ⓔ. A short path runs from the tower to a gate in the churchyard wall next to a small stone building.

2 Go through the gate and turn right onto a narrow lane. At its end, cross a stile onto Morpeth Common and follow an indistinct path to the rear of the houses to your right. The path swings left along the garden boundaries to a wire fence, then turns right to a kissing-gate in the corner of the field.

3 Go through the gate and follow a short path to a road. Turn left along Swansfield to a T-junction. Cross diagonally left and take a paved path between houses, across a green. Where it forks, bear right to a kissing-gate marked 'No Bicycles'.

4 Go through and follow a distinct grassy path which heads along the top of the abbey meadow, then curves right, downhill to a stile. Do not cross; turn right along the fence line to Newminster Abbey Ⓕ. This is a concessionary path, from which you should not deviate. Return to the stile. Cross this and a second stile onto a well signposted public footpath. (If you wish to make a diversion to Mitford, you should turn left here and rejoin the walk at stage 5.) Turn right. Pass through a kissing-gate and follow the tarmac drive to the main road, where you turn right.

5 Where the road bends left across a bridge, go straight ahead onto another tarmac drive. Just before a private drive, turn left onto a gravel path. Go left again alongside a wooden fence to the riverside. Cross the iron footbridge and continue to a road.

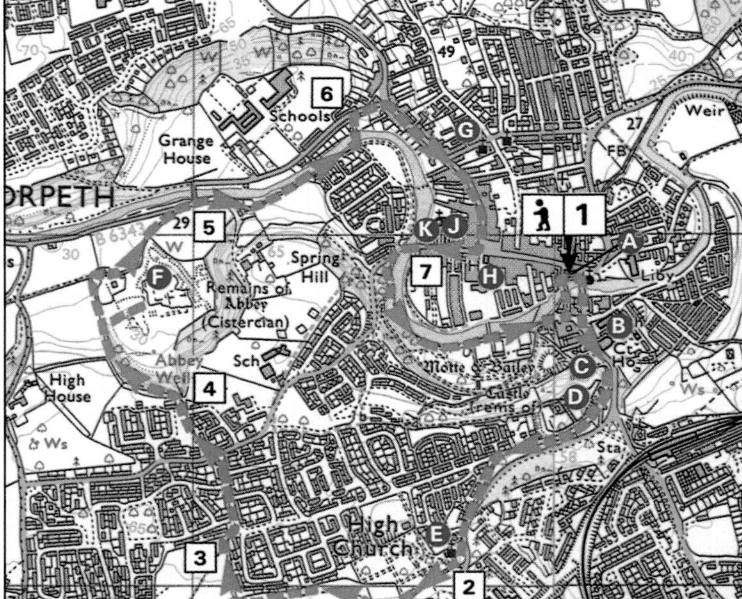

6 Turn right, uphill to a junction, then right again, downhill towards the town. The screened entrance to St James's Ⓖ is on the left before the traffic lights. Continue ahead down Newgate Street to the Town Hall Ⓗ at the bottom. Turn right along Oldgate past the clock tower Ⓙ and Collingwood House Ⓚ.

7 Cross the Oldgate bridge and turn left on the riverside path. Shortly before the first footbridge, the path leaves the bank to run alongside a bowling green. It returns to the river just beyond the bridge. Continue until the path becomes a metalled road. Turn left at The Joiners Arms pub to cross the Chantry footbridge, and return to the start.

JEFFREY BEAZLEY

◀*The Courthouse, which was once the town's prison, is opposite the fine floral displays of Carlisle Park.*

A short walk to the south of Telford Bridge is the Courthouse Ⓑ, built in 1822 by the Newcastle architect, John Dobson. It is a sturdy stone building, made more imposing by glowering battlements, and was once used as the town prison.

FLORAL DISPLAYS

Opposite the Courthouse is the entrance to the most colourful part of Carlisle Park Ⓒ. From early spring to the end of autumn, it is awash with changing colours. Its immaculate flower-beds won a national category prize in the 1989 Britain in Bloom competition. In the park is the unmistakable mound where the original castle stood.

A little further up the hill is the site of a second castle Ⓓ, believed to have been built in the 14th century. Though on a more commanding site than the Norman building, it was all but destroyed during the Civil War; only the gatehouse and some remnants of curtain wall still stand.

Further south, on the Newcastle road, is St Mary's or High Church Ⓔ, one of the finest in the county.

ALL PHOTOS: JEFFREY BEAZLEY

◀*The renovated gatehouse of the 14th-century castle is virtually all that remains of a building that was destroyed in the Civil War.*

▼*The route takes a concessionary path which runs across a lush, flowery meadow, grazed by cattle, to ruined Newminster Abbey.*

and to keep all dogs on a lead.

At this point, those with the time and inclination can leave the main route and follow the signposted footpath west along the river valley to Mitford, where a ruined castle overlooks a lovely church.

NEO-NORMAN CHURCH

The main route goes back along the river towards Morpeth, then crosses a footbridge and climbs up to the north side of the town. As you descend again to the town centre, you pass the imposing Church of St James Ⓖ, set at the end of a tree-lined drive headed by an elegant stone screen. Unlike most Victorian churches, it is built in the Norman rather than the Gothic style.

Newgate Street leads down to the Town Hall Ⓗ, designed by John Vanbrugh in 1714, when the road at the side, which runs down to the market, did not exist. Its creation has exposed the red-brick side of the building, which detracts from the elaborate stone front, but it is still an impressive sight.

ADMIRAL'S HOUSE

The route turns right into Oldgate, in the middle of which is a clock tower Ⓙ, 15th-century in origin but added to and altered later. It now stands curiously isolated, appearing conscious of the need to remain studiously aloof from the functional red-brick buildings on either side.

A little further along, on the right, is a fine Georgian house Ⓚ that was

Most of it is 14th-century, including the glass in the east window. There is an attractive lych-gate, and the churchyard contains the grave of one of Morpeth's most famous citizens, the suffragette Emily Davison, who threw herself under the King's horse at Tattenham Corner during the 1913 Derby to draw attention to her cause. She died from her injuries four days later, and is buried in the north-west corner of the churchyard close to a tall white obelisk. The epitaph on her tombstone is 'Deeds not Words'.

RUINED ABBEY

The walk swings round Morpeth Common and through the Kirkhill housing estate, before dropping down into a riverside meadow to the ruins of Newminster Abbey Ⓕ. The abbey was a Cistercian foundation, and was built in 1137 under the patronage of Ranulph de Merley. It had close connections with Fountains Abbey in Yorkshire.

Like most religious buildings in the border country, it suffered badly during Anglo-Scottish conflicts, and was finally destroyed during the Dissolution. All that remains is a rather sad, but very atmospheric collection of ruins standing among trees and undergrowth.

Access to the site, and the path leading to it, are both concessionary, and care must be taken to stay on the path when you visit the abbey

◀*The track along the top of the abbey meadow passes through the shade cast by well-grown bushes.*

The Northumbrian Small Pipes

BRITISH MUSEUM

This illuminated medieval manuscript indicates the ancient pedigree of the pipes.

The popular image of the bagpipes is largely confined to the Scottish war pipes and the uillean pipes of Ireland. However, recognizable forms of the instrument have existed in many countries all over the world.

Until the end of the Middle Ages, there were several regional variants in use in the British Isles. From the 16th century, changing musical tastes tended to confine the bagpipes to the northern and western parts of Britain. By the early 1800s, the Northumbrian pipes were effectively the only survivor in England.

Smaller and lighter than their Scottish cousins, Northumbrian pipes are usually played when sitting down. Their softer, more plaintive tone makes them more suited to indoor playing than the louder Highland instrument. There are certain technical differences that make the Northumbrian pipes in some ways more versatile.

Professional pipers were sometimes employed by public bodies or the gentry, but were more often itinerants who travelled the land making money as and when they could. One man who managed to combine both practices was an infamous rogue called Jamie Allan. Born in 1734, the son of a piper father and a gypsy mother, he became notorious for entertaining crowds while his confederates picked their pockets. He died in prison in 1810, while awaiting transportation for horse stealing.

By contrast, he was also retained as official piper to the Countess of Northumberland, and even found favour with royalty. The Prince Regent issued a free pardon to Allan just before the piper's death, but the document arrived at the prison too late to free him. The Duke of Northumberland still retains an official piper; his family are the only noble house in England to do so.

Recently, the Northumbrian small pipes have enjoyed a well deserved revival of interest. Several recordings of pipe music are now available, and concerts are held regularly at the Bagpipe Museum in Morpeth.

An 18th-century set of Northumbrian small pipes from the museum's collection.

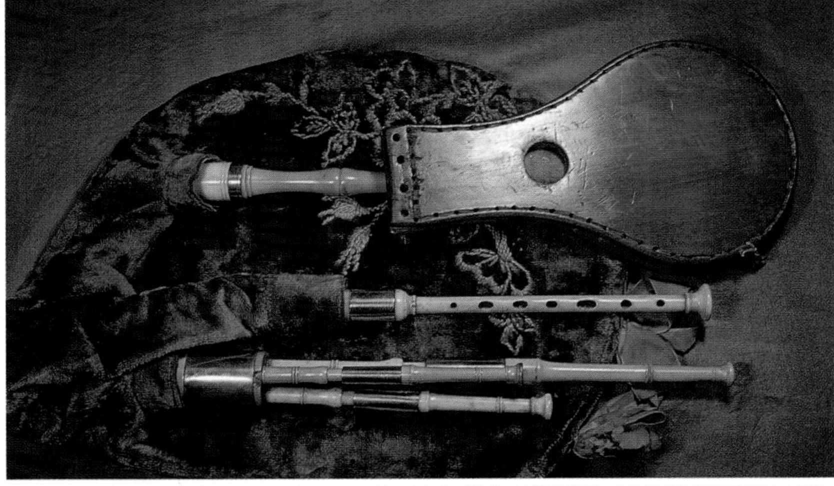

MORPETH BAGPIPE MUSEUM

JEFFREY BEAZLEY

▲*The clock tower in Oldgate is built in a fortified style appropriate to an area frequently rent by border disturbances.*

once owned by Vice Admiral Lord Collingwood, the man who took command of the fleet at Trafalgar after Nelson's death. So successful was his naval career that he is said to have spent only one year at home between 1793 and 1820.

RIVERSIDE WALK

The walk leaves Oldgate over a modern road-bridge, and turns left to follow the river. This lovely leafy path, with the gently flowing Wansbeck on one side and Carlisle Park on the other, leads back to the Chantry to complete the walk.

▼*The ruined Norman arches of Newminster Abbey's cloisters are closely surrounded by hawthorns.*

JEFFREY BEAZLEY

VILLAGE, ASH AND SPOUT

38

NORTHUMBERLAND

CAROLINE BACON. INSET: L CAMPBELL/SCOTLAND IN FOCUS

▲*As the path leads down through bracken to Linhope Spout, the air is filled with the sound of rushing water. In winter, wild goats (inset) can sometimes be seen grazing nearby.*

Prehistoric, Roman and medieval remains in wild fell country

The Breamish Valley, its broad glacial river-bed flanked by steep hills, is one of the most beautiful in Northumberland. Although there are only a few farms on the hillside today, it was not always so deserted. The landscape bears evidence of many different settlements. On the hillside above Linhope Spout is rare evidence of the earliest type of unenclosed settlement, dating from 4,000 years ago, when farmers cleared the woodland to grow crops.

As the climate grew colder, livestock replaced crops. Herders lived in groups of houses on hilltops, surrounded by wooden palisades or strong stone ramparts.

The Romans made an impact on this way of life. The peace-keeping forces they brought made some defensive settlements redundant. Round stone houses were built outside the ramparts. The walk passes many of these remains, on the sheltered, south-east slopes, including Greave's (or Grieve's) Ash.

The person you are most likely to meet in the hills today is a shepherd in his four-wheeler, but the slopes are criss-crossed with ancient tracks and informal drove roads. At Hartside Ⓐ, where the walk begins, a silver cross was found in 1861, and is said to have been dropped by an 8th-century pilgrim.

On the left of the road are curious slatted fences. These prevent snow from drifting onto the road — a necessary precaution as Linhope can be cut off for weeks in winter.

The hut on the hillside above Greensidehill is another defence against the weather. Hay from the lower slopes is stored here to feed livestock — sheep and a few cattle — when the grass is under snow.

Below Cat Crag, curlews call plaintively, and you might hear the strange hum of the wind rushing through a male snipe's tailfeathers as he dives in his courtship display. Foxes and rabbits are common here and hares also live on the hillside.

FACT FILE

- Linhope, 14 miles (22.4km) west of Alnwick
- Pathfinder 487 (NT 81/91), grid reference NT 975161
- miles 0 1 2 3 4 5 6 7 8 9 10 miles / kms 0 1 2 3 4 5 6 7 8 9 10 11 12 13 14 15 kms
- Allow 3 hours
- Occasionally strenuous walk on the lower slopes of the fells. Quality of paths varies; good walking shoes or boots essential
- P On verge near Hartside Farm
- WC Ingram, 4 miles (6.4km) to the east
- I Tourist information at Ingram

DESERTED VILLAGE

The route leads to a deserted medieval village Ⓑ. In the 14th century, a combination of border raids and the Black Death led to the abandonment of many villages in the Cheviot Hills. The remains of several houses are still visible among the grass and bracken on the fellside.

You descend towards Greave's Ash Ⓒ, a large settlement occupied from the Iron Age to Roman times. The site covers 20 acres (8ha). The sunken path by which you enter is part of its extensive ramparts. The dwelling places spill outside the walls, evidence of more settled times in the valley's history.

THE WALK

HARTSIDE FARM – LINHOPE

Park on the grass verge before Hartside Farm Ⓐ.

1 Walk back down the road to Greensidehill Farm. Immediately after, turn left through a wooden gate signposted to The Dod and Ilderton. Keeping the side of the house, then a stone wall on the left, climb the hill and go through a wooden gate in a fence. There is no clear path ahead. Keep the steep gully of Willow Burn on your right, and head for a black tin hut visible ¾ mile (1.2km) ahead, where the ground rises. Join a crossing track beyond the hut.

2 Turn right on a track through the bracken. Cross four small streams by wooden planks and continue for 600 yards (540m). A path to the right leads downhill to the medieval village Ⓑ.

3 Go back to the tin hut and continue past it to a gate in a stone wall.

4 Go through and follow the path ahead. Cross a small stream. Just beyond it, where the path turns right, go straight ahead over another small stream. After crossing a track, the path becomes indistinct; aim for the conifer plantation on the right. Soon you will see a gate in a wire fence ahead. Go past an old railway truck on the right and continue downhill, over a small stream then up a broad track to the gate.

5 Go through and walk downhill to a stone wall. Turn right and follow a track, the wall on your left, to a sunken path leading to Greave's Ash Ⓒ. Turn right along this and climb a stile into the settlement. Return to the track and continue downhill past a tin hut and onto the road through a metal gate.

6 Turn right. Cross Linhope Burn by a stone bridge and follow the road round to the left. Where it ends, go through a gate on the right, signposted to Linhope Spout, and walk uphill with the beech hedge of Linhope Lodge Ⓓ on your right. Another gate leads onto a broad track uphill. Keep the steep valley and woods on the right. Take the signposted fork right, and follow the line of the woods. At the end of the wood, go through a wooden gate and follow the main track downhill and slightly left to Linhope Spout Ⓔ.

7 Retrace your steps to the road and continue along it to the start.

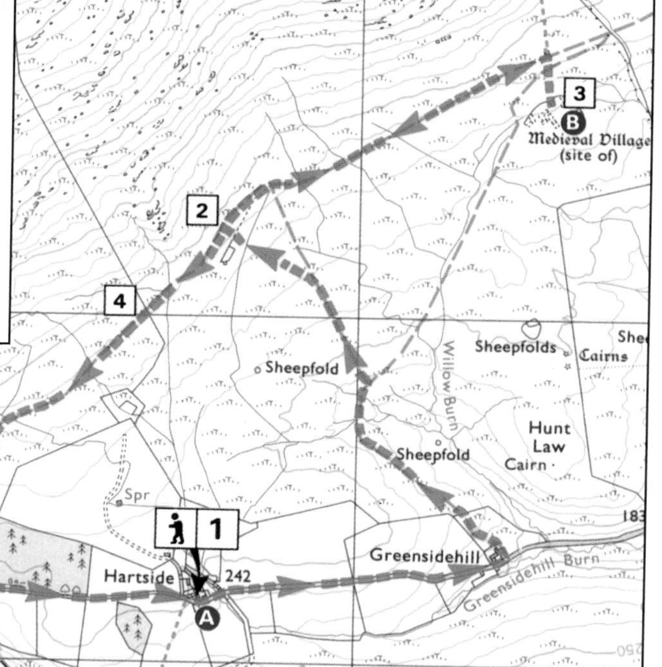

Down the hill, beyond an attractive stone bridge, is the entrance to Linhope Lodge Ⓓ, built in 1912 as a hunting lodge. After a brief interlude as an old people's home, it is now to revert to its original use during the grouse-shooting season.

A broad track climbs above Linhope Burn. In summer, the steep valley sides are purple with foxgloves, and siskins and linnets sing in the woods. The wheatear flashes back and forth across the path on the more open land.

Take care if exploring away from the main path. Adders are common, and though they slither off at the sound of someone approaching, they can be taken unawares in cold weather, when they are slow.

CAROLINE BACON

◀*Near an attractive row of workmen's cottages, the route crosses an old stone bridge over Linhope Burn.*

Wild goats, descended from domestic beasts, have bred for hundreds of years on the hills, but are rarely seen except in winter when they graze the lower slopes.

LINHOPE SPOUT

When the wood ends, a track through bracken leads to one of the loveliest waterfalls in the Cheviots. Dropping 56 feet (17m) into a basin 15 feet (4.5m) deep and 7 feet (2.1m) across, Linhope Spout Ⓔ used to be called 'Roughting Linn', from an old word for the lowing of cattle, referring to the sound of the water as it pours over the rocks.

From here, you return to Greave's Ash and follow a private road along the hillside back to Hartside Farm.

ALONG THE CLEVELAND COAST

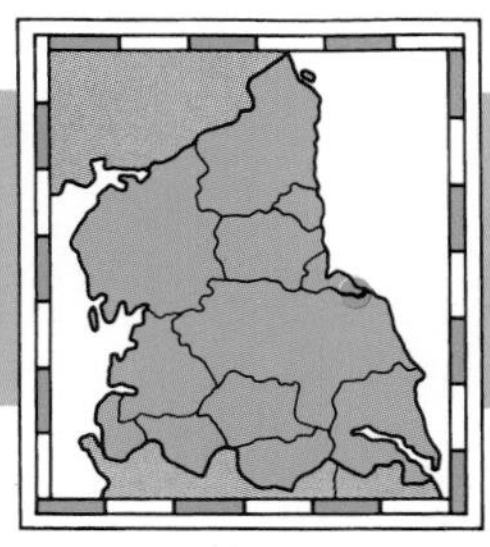

PHILIPPA SCOTT/NHPA

JOHN WATNEY

A coastal walk on the clifftop above Saltburn-by-the-Sea

Perched on the edge of the North York Moors National Park, Saltburn nestles beneath the 350-foot (105-metre) high Hunt Cliff. In Roman times the cliff was used as a lookout post for raiders, and later a small community of fishermen grew up around the Ship Inn. In 1861, when the railway arrived, a holiday resort was quickly built above the valley. Today Saltburn is quiet and unspoilt.

SALTBURN PIER

The walk begins near the pier Ⓐ, which juts out across Saltburn Sands. It was opened in 1869 and steamers moored alongside to take passengers on trips to Hartlepool, Whitby and Scarborough. It has been damaged by storms and was reduced to its present length in 1974, but it is still a well-known landmark on the Cleveland coast.

Saltburn's cliff lift Ⓑ, on the sea front, was opened in 1884 to link the growing resort with the pier. It is now the oldest water-balanced cliff railway in Britain. The valley was once spanned by a steel-framed bridge built in 1869 and demolished in 1974. It was known as the

▲*During Victorian times crowds flocked to the seaside resort of Saltburn. Holidaymakers took pleasure trips on paddle steamers from the 1,500-foot (450-metre) pier (right), and used the cliff lift to appreciate the views. The red-breasted merganser (inset) catches fish efficiently with its rough-edged bill.*

FACT FILE

- Saltburn, 10 miles (16 km) east of Middlesbrough
- Outdoor Leisure map 26, grid reference NZ 668215
- miles 0 1 2 3 4 5 6 7 8 9 10 miles / kms 0 1 2 3 4 5 6 7 8 9 10 11 12 13 14 15 kms
- Allow 2 hours
- One climb up steps to the clifftop path. Keep children under close control on the cliffs. Take great care in crossing the busy A174 road in Saltburn
- British Rail service from Middlesbrough. Bus service from Middlesbrough and Whitby
- Ship Inn, cafés, toilets and shops in Saltburn

JOHN WATNEY

THE WALK

SALTBURN-BY-THE-SEA

The walk begins at the large car park on the A174 on the side of the road which is opposite the sea.

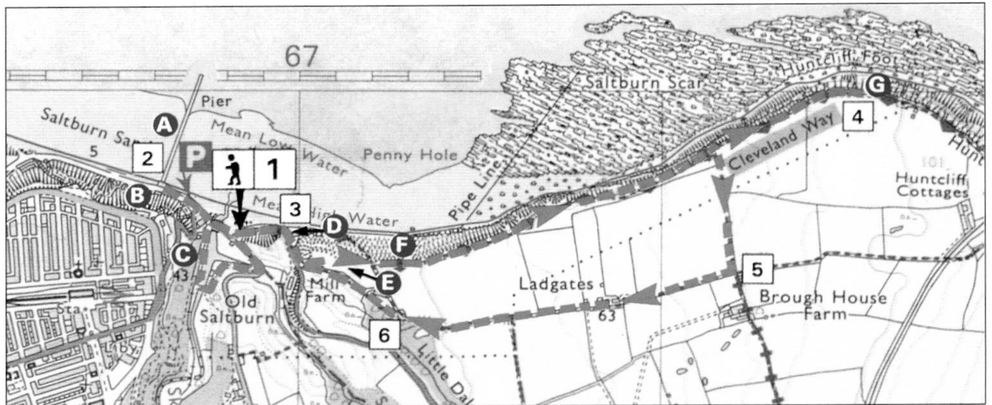

1 Leave the car park, turn left and cross the bridge. The pier **A** is ahead on the right. When the road swings left continue straight ahead through the pier car park to the start of the pier where you can see the cliff lift **B** on your left.

2 Return to the bridge, do not cross it but turn right at a sign for the miniature railway, along the valley with the stream on your left. On the hillside to your left is the toll house of the Ha'penny Bridge **C**. Just before the platform of the miniature railway, turn left over the footbridge and left again past the picnic site. Bear right to a footbridge which leads to a road. Turn left and turn right at the junction to the Ship Inn **D**.

3 Turn left beyond the inn's rear car park, signposted 'Cleveland Way' **E**. Turn left up the steps on to the clifftop path. At the top of the climb there is a good viewpoint **F** from where you can look back along the beach to the Tees Estuary. Continue along the clifftop path for a mile (1.6 km) with fine views out to sea. After crossing a stile with a Cleveland Way acorn symbol on it, continue for 50 yards (30 metres) to an information board on the site of the Roman signal station **G**.

4 Return over the same stile and continue ahead with a wooden fence on your right. When the fence ends after 500 yards (450 metres) turn left on to a path across the fields to a farm building.

5 Turn right just before the building, along the access road. From here the extensive view includes Saltburn straight ahead. Pass some farm buildings on your right and, when the access lane turns left, carry on straight ahead along a lane between hedges to a gate. Take the broad track ahead across the fields.

6 At the fork in the paths bear left, keeping a scrub-covered valley on your left and a terrace of houses on your right. Take the tarmac path which descends to a road, turn right past the Ship Inn and follow the road to return to the car park and the start of the walk.

It is at Saltburn that the 55-mile (88-km) Cleveland Way **E** joins the coast at its most northerly point. From the viewpoint **F** on the cliff-top a stretch of sand can be seen which extends as far as Teesmouth.

◀*Saltburn Sands have been used for racing cars and motor cycles, as well as for quieter pursuits. The Roman signal station, once on the clifftop (below), was a tower surrounded by a wall and a ditch.*

It was once popular for motor racing and Saltburn Speed Trials were first held here in 1908, attracting record breakers such as J. G. Parry Thomas and Malcolm Campbell with his 'Bluebird' racing cars.

At the top of Huntcliff Foot is the site of the Roman signal station **G**, built about 367 AD. It was later used to warn of the Spanish Armada and Napoleonic invasion. Most of the site has now vanished over the cliffs.

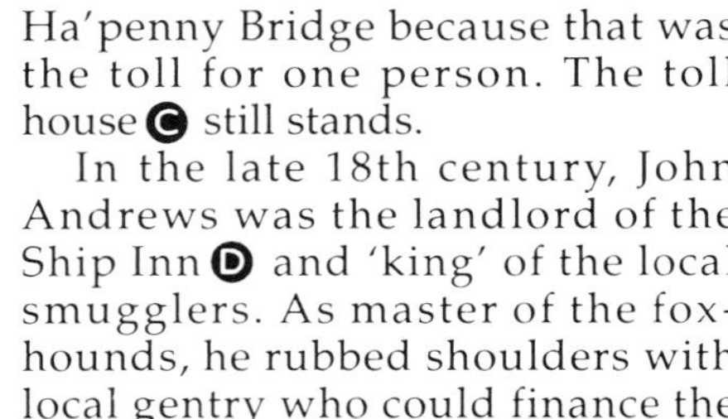

Ha'penny Bridge because that was the toll for one person. The toll house **C** still stands.

In the late 18th century, John Andrews was the landlord of the Ship Inn **D** and 'king' of the local smugglers. As master of the fox-hounds, he rubbed shoulders with local gentry who could finance the smuggling. Tea, which was expensive, was a popular commodity to smuggle as well as gin and brandy, with vast profits to be made.

BOTH PHOTOS JOHN WATNEY

THE HOLLOW HILL

40

CLEVELAND

CHRIS PELLANT. INSET: MICHAEL LEACH/NHPA

▲*Eston Moor, on the outskirts of Middlesbrough, is dotted with thick clumps of gorse. The stoat (inset) may look endearing, but in fact it is one of the fiercest of all predators. It keeps to areas with good cover.*

Above Eston Moor's old iron mine, woodland and wildlife thrive

To the east of Middlesbrough lies Eston Moor, rising from the Cleveland Plain to a height of nearly 800 feet (280 metres). The steady climb offers spectacular views over Middlesbrough and the plateau is an area rich in wildlife. The view from the summit extends far into Durham and southwards onto the North York Moors. Mining ceased here in about 1950, and nature has reclaimed the land.

In the deciduous wood Ⓐ, you may see a variety of woodland birds. With luck, there may be a nuthatch or treecreeper.

RAILWAY

Spread out below during the early part of the walk is the town of Middlesbrough. In 1829, it consisted of a ruined chapel, a few houses and only forty inhabitants. In 1830 the Stockton to Darlington Railway was extended to Middlesbrough so that coal could be put on larger ships. A rapid expansion of the town commenced, fuelled by the discovery of the Cleveland ironstone deposits. By 1881, the population stood at over 55,000 people.

KESTRELS

The plateau of Eston Moor Ⓑ is a mixture of grass and moorland with downy birch and gorse bushes. This mixed habitat may have yellowhammers, whincat and skylarks singing overhead. You may also see kestrels soaring on the breeze looking for small rodents and other mammals moving in the undergrowth. There are also pheasants and red grouse, while curlew and redshank may move onto the hill from the rich mud flats of the Tees Estuary.

Enclosing the monument is the ditch and rampart of an ancient hill fort Ⓒ. It is believed to have been built in the late Bronze Age with a pallisade for defence, the rampart and ditch were cut in the Iron Age and can still be explored. The site was abandoned when the Romans arrived. Excavations have yielded little evidence of a settlement. It may have been used only when there was the threat of danger.

A beacon Ⓓ used to stand on the hill top. It was one of a series set up to warn of the approach of the Spanish Armada. The watchers at the beacon would pick up a signal

FACT FILE

- Upsall, 4 miles (6.5 km) south-east of Middlesbrough
- Outdoor Leisure map 26, grid reference NZ 552169

miles 0 1 2 3 4 5 6 7 8 9 10 miles
kms 0 1 2 3 4 5 6 7 8 9 10 11 12 13 14 15 kms

- Allow 3 ½ hours
- About ½ mile (800 metres) of steep ascent and descent. Walking boots recommended
- P Car park and picnic site on unclassified road north of the A171 Nunthorpe to Guisborough road

▼*The walk offers a landscape that fluctuates between rugged moorland scrub and deciduous woodland filled with a variety of bird life.*

CHRIS PELLANT

THE WALK

ESTON MOOR

The start of the walk is by High Cow How 1 mile (1.6 km) north up an unclassified road from the A171 Nunthorpe to Guisborough road.

1 From the car park pass through the gate and walk up the field to a stile, keeping the hedge on your left. Turn right up the road past Rose Cottage, then turn left up some steps into the wood **A**. Eventually cross a heap of gravel and turn left on the track until you reach a stile.

2 Climb up the broad track keeping the wire fence on your right. There are extensive views to the left over Middlesbrough. At the top, cross over the stile and bear right for 100 yards (90 metres).

3 Fork left along the track that heads over the rough grass and heather moorland **B**, passing Carr Pond on your right. Climb gently up to the monument on the skyline.

4 Turn left through the ditch and rampart of the Iron Age hill fort **C**. Cross over to the monument which carries a plaque **D**. From the edge of the plateau, you can look down the hillside to the site of Eston iron mines on the right which are now covered in deciduous trees. Return to the junction and fork left on the track down the side of the wood. Eventually the path veers away from the wood and continues to descend to a former iron mine **E**.

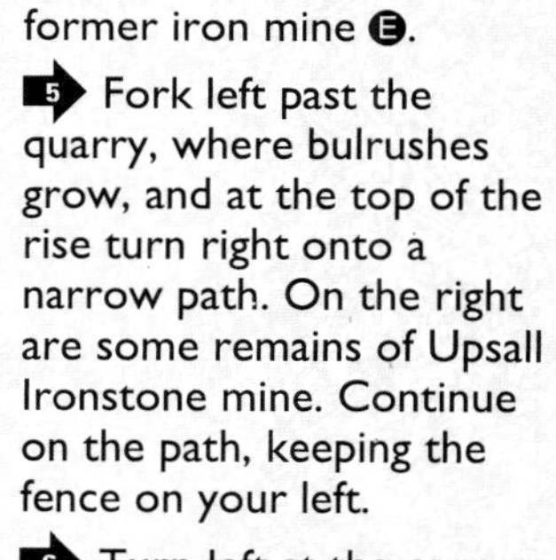

5 Fork left past the quarry, where bulrushes grow, and at the top of the rise turn right onto a narrow path. On the right are some remains of Upsall Ironstone mine. Continue on the path, keeping the fence on your left.

6 Turn left at the corner of the fenced field, then right along the path into the wood, with a stone wall on your left. After 700 yards (640 metres) you reach the stile you crossed earlier.

7 You can return down this track or bear right just before the stile keeping the wire fence on your left. The path descends steeply.

8 At the corner of the fence turn left along the path keeping the fence on your left. Just below the stile you crossed earlier bear right to the bottom of the patch of gravel. Take the path through the trees which descends to the road. Turn right, then left over the stile and descend the field to the car park.

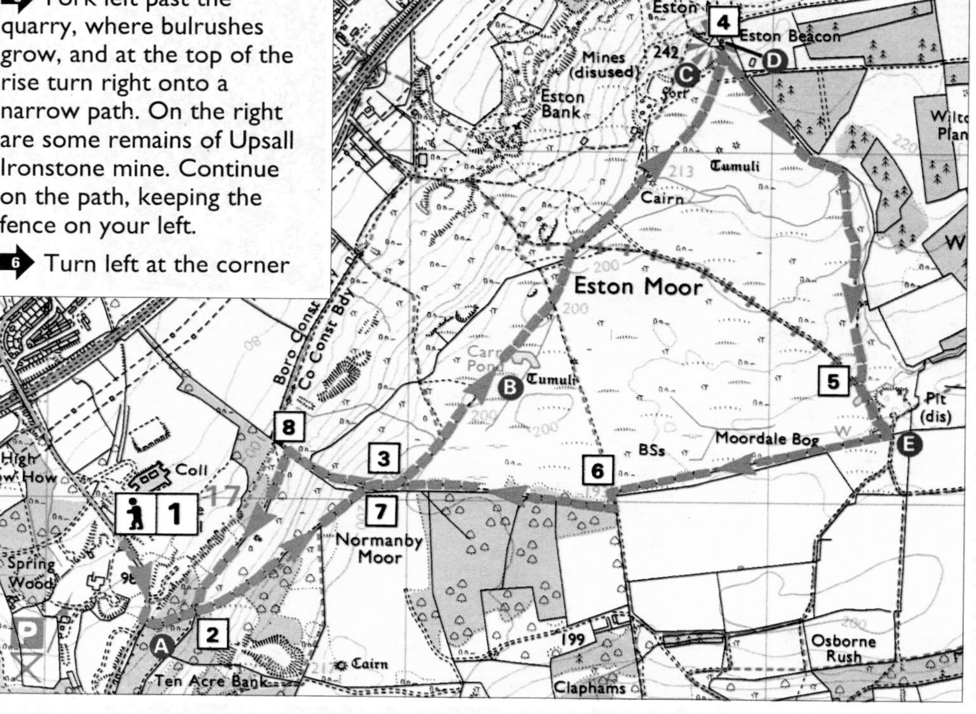

from one fired on the coast and pass it on to Roseberry Topping to the south and to the Bishopric of Durham to the north.

CAPTAIN COOK

As you leave Eston Nab, there are extensive views in front of you to the distinctive, pointed Roseberry Topping. To its left is the Captain Cook monument on Easby Moor. To the right is the line of the Cleveland Hills traversed by the Cleveland Way and Lyke Wake Walk.

In 1811, six cartloads of stone were taken from a prospective pit **E** and tested for iron. The area was said to be useless. It was 1850 before two mining engineers discovered the 11-foot (3.4-metre) thick main seam of ironstone. The ironstone was transported through the hill to the Eston mines and taken away by a railway below the beacon site. A community lived near the mine in two rows of terraced houses, serviced by a small chapel. On occasions food for the hamlet was brought through the hill and raised up the mine shaft. The seam has long since been used up and the pit is now disused. The largest mine at Eston removed 63 million tonnes of ironstone, making this a hollow hill.

CHRIS PELLANT

◀*A brick tower marks the site where a huge beacon once stood, ready to give warning of the approach of the Armada.*

Hart to Hart

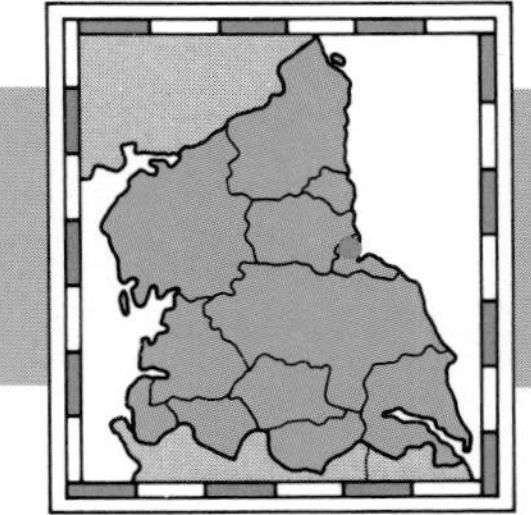

JASON SMALLEY. INSET: PAUL STERRY/NATURE PHOTOGRAPHERS

▲*The relatively low-lying farmland to the east of Hart slopes gently down to the North Sea. The speckled bush cricket (right) occurs here in hedgerows, bramble thickets and woods.*

A figure-of-eight walk centred on a church with Saxon origins

The peaceful village of Hart, which overlooks the sprawling port of Hartlepool, is reputed to be the birthplace of Robert the Bruce, whose family were lords here. This walk around the village begins near the Brus Wall Ⓐ, which was once part of the de Brus manor house.

When he murdered John Comyn in Dundee in 1306, Robert de Brus was outlawed by King Edward I, and his lands were confiscated. Robert de Clifford, the soldier-judge, was granted the title to the manor of Hart. De Clifford died in the Battle of Bannockburn in 1314, but his family rebuilt the manor and continued to live there until 1580.

The route leads along a track beside dense hedges of hawthorn — entwined with elder, dog rose and bindweed and coloured with scarlet field poppies and poisonous woody nightshade — onto rich farmland. In summer, swaying fields of barley and wheat cower beneath thunderous skies that, in this wide, level landscape, can lay a crop flat with the first heavy deluge.

The walls of Hart's graveyard are shrouded in a dense cloak of ivy, and the tombstones are overshadowed by yew and holly. In the far left-hand corner stands a proud stone commemorating Thomas Warnaby, who died aged '5 score years and six'. Close by, a memorial recalls 'Mary Thompson...cousin of the late Dr Livingstone, great missionary explorer'.

SAXON STONES

The Church of St Mary Magdalene Ⓑ has Anglo-Saxon stones embedded in the fabric of its nave and chancel arch, though much of the present building is Norman. Inside, a huge, square-headed Norman font contrasts with a 15th-century version, elaborately carved around its octagonal bowl and shaft. On the west side of the south aisle, a stone marked with a Saxon sundial has been built into the wall, confirming the church's ancient origin.

The church registers date back to 1577, and contain several entries concerning local witches, most

FACT FILE

- Hart, 1½ miles (2.4km) north-west of Hartlepool, off the A179
- Pathfinder 582 (NZ 43/53), grid reference NZ 470350
- Allow 2 hours
- Mostly level walking on roads, narrow country lanes and farmland. Long grass and overgrown hedgerows are wet after rain
- Car park at the start
- The White Hart Inn and The Raby Arms, both in Hart
- Permission to visit the windmill must be obtained from the farmhouse next door

THE WALK

HART – HIGH THROSTON

The walk begins in the car park by the Church of St Mary Magdalene in Hart.

1 Leave by the main entrance, passing the Brus Wall Ⓐ. At the T-junction, turn right along the lane, then fork right along a dirt track, to walk past North Hart Farm.

2 About ¼ mile (400m) beyond the farm, turn right over a step-stile. Head across the field to a second stile. Cross and continue ahead, the fence to your right. At the end of the field, go through a gate and turn right, keeping the hedge on your left. Go over a step-stile, then cross a footbridge and a second stile into a field. Bear right across the field to join a farm track, which you follow, keeping the fence to your left, to a gate.

3 Cross a step-stile and turn left. With the fence on your left, walk to a stile in the corner. Cross it and continue on a path between a fence and a hedgerow. Cross a stile on your left and continue across the field, with the hedge to your right, to the graveyard. Cross a stile and go through the graveyard to the front of St Mary Magdalene's Church Ⓑ. Go through the gate at the end of a gravel path onto a road. Turn left, then immediately right over a footbridge. Follow the track to a main road. Turn left past the Blue Stone Ⓒ, and follow the road across the roundabout. Continue for over ¾ mile (1.2km) to some houses.

4 Fork right into a narrow lane. Follow this to a crossroads. Turn right and continue to the entrance drive to Hart Windmill Ⓓ on your right. After visiting the windmill, return to the lane and continue walking along it to the main road.

5 Go straight ahead down a narrow lane. At the T-junction, turn right, past the White Hart Inn Ⓔ, then left onto a narrow path between houses. Continue over the footbridge to return to the start.

▲*This 13th-century stone wall, the Brus Wall, was a part of the de Brus manor house. Elsewhere in the village of Hart a painted ship's figurehead (right) adorns the wall of the White Hart Inn.*

notably Alison Lawe. Found guilty in 1582 of being a notorious enchanter and sorceress, she did penance. When she died, six years later, she was buried peacefully at Hart, as were her unholy successors, Ellen Thompson 'Fornacatrix' and Old Mother Midnight.

Just to the south of the church, the walk passes a quaint cottage named Voltigeur, after the 1850 Derby winner. The horse was born in the building, which was used as a stable. In nearby Front Street is the Blue Stone Ⓒ, a glacial hunk of Whin Sill dolerite, which was once, in the absence of a traditional village green, the hub of village festivals.

You head out into countryside again, before eventually following a lane to Hart Windmill Ⓓ. Built at the end of the 18th century to replace a medieval mill, the building has a tall brick tower, partially restored, which tapers to a massive cap. The entire crowning structure is designed to revolve, carrying the sails into the wind. Ten thousand windmills once graced the English countryside. Last used in 1915, Hart Windmill is a precious survivor.

BOTH PHOTOS: JASON SMALLEY

BONNY LASS

You return to the village, where the front of the White Hart Inn Ⓔ is graced by a beautiful, buxom wench in a long flowing skirt and tight scarlet bodice. Believed to be a figurehead from the Sunderland barque *Rising Sun*, she was washed up on the Hartlepool shore after a horrific storm in 1861, when 60 ships foundered. She had no particular connection with the pub or the village, but enterprising beachcombers no doubt thought it a shame to abandon such a fine young lady, and brought her home to their local.

Call of the Sea

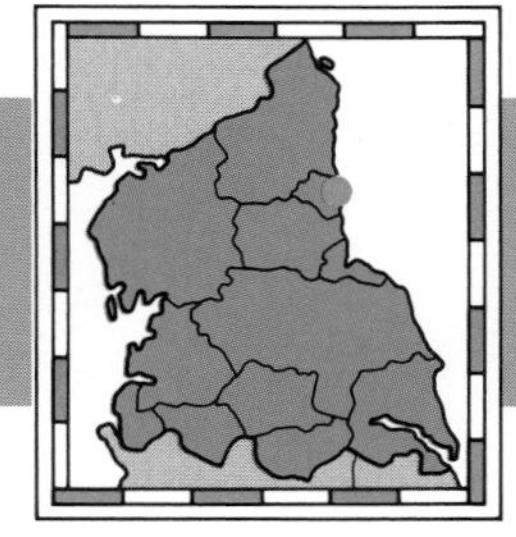

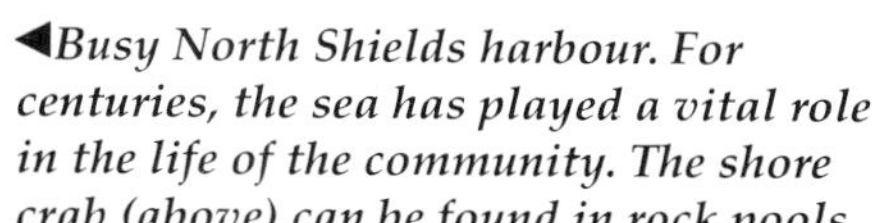

◀*Busy North Shields harbour. For centuries, the sea has played a vital role in the life of the community. The shore crab (above) can be found in rock pools.*

J.C. ALLEN. INSET: STEPHEN DALTON/NHPA

Along a river mouth from a ruined priory to a fishing quay

The walk begins at the headland where the River Tyne meets the sea, and follows the harbour entrance round to North Shields Fish Quay. On the headland are the ruins of Tynemouth Priory **A**, the burial place of the ancient Northumbrian kings. The monks from the priory took boats out from North Shields to catch fish, and so began Tyneside's fishing industry. Tynemouth Castle was built to defend the priory and, below it, the North Pier **B** stretches out to protect the harbour entrance.

Prior's Haven, sheltered by the headland, is home to a sailing club. A path leads away from Prior's Haven to the monument **C** to Admiral Lord Collingwood, erected in 1845. A local man, Collingwood took over from the mortally wounded Lord Nelson at Trafalgar and went on to win the battle.

GUIDING LIGHT

The promenade below the monument leads to the Fish Quay **H** at North Shields. The tall, white buildings topped by beacons are the 'leading lights' to guide boats into harbour. By lining up the High Light and the Low Light, the safe channels can be followed. As you walk along the cobbled streets, you pass the Low Light **D** marked by a plaque. Soon afterwards, you pass Clifford's Fort **E**, built in 1672 to defend the river against the Dutch.

NORTHUMBRIA TOURIST BOARD

◀ *The ruins of Tynemouth Priory command a prominent position on a headland above the vast North Sea.*

FACT FILE

- Tynemouth and North Shields, Tyne and Wear
- OS Pathfinder 549 (NZ 26/36), grid reference NZ 370695

miles 0 1 2 3 4 5 6 7 8 9 10 miles
kms 0 1 2 3 4 5 6 7 8 9 10 11 12 13 14 15 kms

- Allow 1½ hours; 2 hours for extension
- Mostly tarmac paths. Route includes a short, steep hill and two flights of steps
- P Car park in Tynemouth, pay and display: ticket valid for all sea-front parking
- T Newcastle Metro service extends to Tynemouth, with frequent trains. Bus service as well.
- Tynemouth: numerous pubs and cafés along Front Street. North Shields Fish Quay: grocer's shop, fish and chip shops. Wooden Doll pub above quay is on walk route
- WC Tynemouth: toilets near car park. North Shields: toilets near Dolphin Fisheries

THE WALK

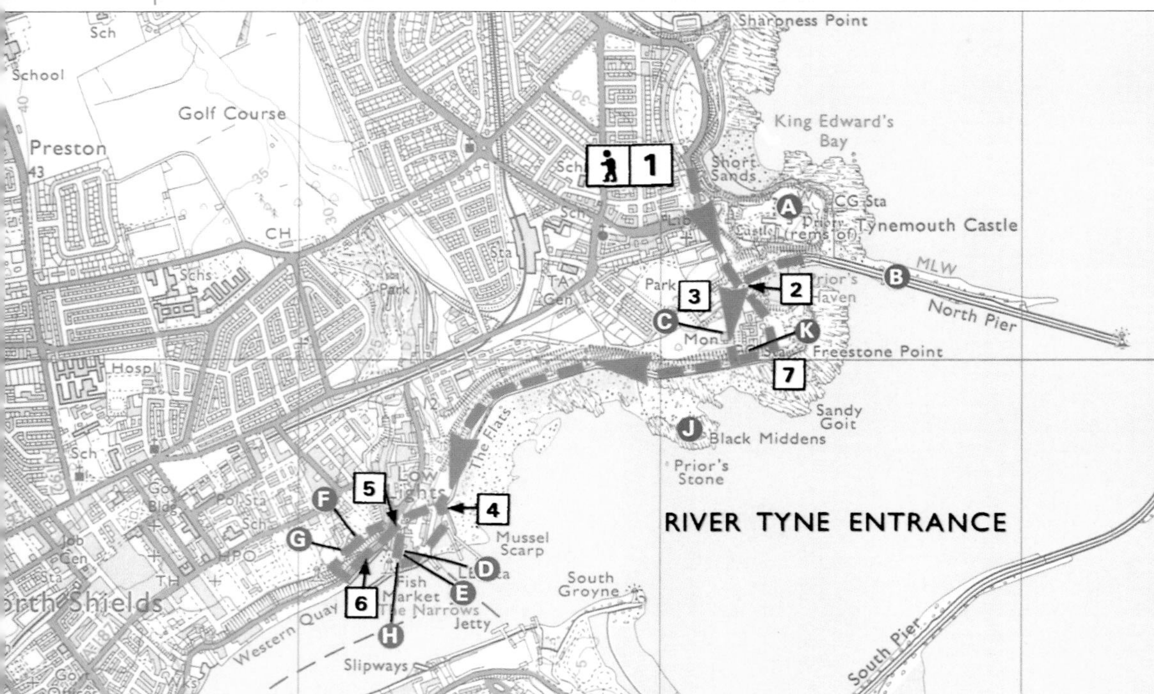

TYNEMOUTH – NORTH SHIELDS

The walk begins in the car park in Tynemouth.

1 From the car park, cross the road and turn right, past the entrance to Tynemouth Priory Ⓐ. Follow the lane downhill, and turn right where a small arrowed sign indicates the footpath to the Fish Quay, the Pedestrian Ferry and the Collingwood Monument.

2 To extend the walk by 1 mile (1.6 km), turn left past Prior's Haven and follow the road which leads below the Priory and onto the pier Ⓑ, returning by the same path.

3 At the Collingwood Monument Ⓒ, descend the grassy bank, taking care as this can be muddy and slippery, then turn right to follow the promenade towards North Shields. (Alternatively join a path along the top of the bank for good views of the river, eventually rejoining the promenade.)

4 At the end of the promenade, keep to the water's edge, passing close to the wooden jetty of the old lifeboat station, then follow the cobbled road between the buildings. Turn right, past the Low Light Ⓓ and continue along the road, passing a restored boat, the St Christopher, and Clifford's Fort Ⓔ, situated near Anchor Taxis on the right.

5 At the end of the road is Dolphin Fisheries. Turn left, then almost immediately cross the road and ascend the flight of steps opposite (avoid after dark or if alone). At the top of the steps is the Wooden Doll pub in Hudson Street. Follow the road to the left; on the right is the Old High Light and ahead is the present High Light Ⓕ. At the end of the railings with their unusual finials Ⓖ, descend the steps past the modern fish mosaic. The steps emerge by the Fisherman's Mission on the quay Ⓗ.

6 Turn left along the quay and continue along the road, turning right when you reach the New Dolphin Pub. Walk past the fresh fish shops and cross the road to return along the pavement.

7 Shortly after passing the Black Middens rocks Ⓙ, indicated by a plaque, turn left up a short steep path to the watch house Ⓚ. Continue along the path back to Tynemouth Priory and the car park at the start of the walk.

J. C. ALLEN

Steps lead up above the quay to the Wooden Doll pub, named after the succession of 'wooden dolls' — ships' figureheads and statues of fishwives — which have stood in North Shields. Along the top is the Old High Light, now a private house, and a little further on is the present High Light Ⓕ, erected when the safe channel shifted position.

Also above the quay, look out for the architectural details in the railings. The finials Ⓖ (the ornamental features at the tips) have nautical themes, for example, Jonah and the whale, and a plate of fish and chips. From here, steps lead down past a mosaic of fish to the Mission for Deep Sea Fishermen.

◀ *The four cannons at the base of the Collingwood monument are from the the admiral's ship, the* Royal Sovereign.

The return route follows the river, passing the notorious Black Middens rocks Ⓙ that have wrecked many ships. Prompted by this, the Tynemouth Volunteer Life Brigade was formed last century as the world's first ship-to-shore rescue group. In their watch house Ⓚ, you can see an interesting collection, including artefacts from the wrecks of ships that perished off the shore.

OLD NEWCASTLE

JEFFREY BEAZLEY

▲*Reflected in the exterior of a modern building is the richly ornamented, Art Nouveau facade of Emerson Chambers.*

A stroll around the medieval heart of a modern city

Newcastle is a vibrant city whose origins date back to Roman times. Its name comes from the 'new castle' built by the son of William the Conqueror in 1080. The city today still has one of the finest Norman keeps in the country, as well as medieval houses, superb Victorian architecture, modern shopping centres, an excellent Metro rapid transport system, and theatres and art galleries. A major industrial centre, it prospered in the 18th and 19th centuries from the coal trade.

GREY'S MONUMENT

The walk starts at Grey's Monument **A**, in the heart of the city, built to mark the passing of the Great Reform Bill of 1832. The 135-foot (50-m) column is open on Saturdays and Bank Holidays, and those prepared to climb its steps are rewarded with a superb view over

PAUL STEVENS/SWIFT PICTURE LIBRARY

▲*Favourite resting places for the urban-dwelling starling are ledges, telephone wires and overhead power lines.*

the city. From the Monument, Blackett Street leads between the splendid Art Nouveau Emerson Chambers, with its richly detailed facade, and the modernistic Eldon Square Shopping Centre.

The route joins the top of Newgate Street. Opposite you is St Andrew's Church **B**, the city's oldest church, with parts dating from the 12th century. The elaborate

FACT FILE

- Newcastle-upon-Tyne
- Pathfinder 549 (NZ 26/36), grid reference NZ 248644

miles 0 1 2 3 4 5 6 7 8 9 10 miles
kms 0 1 2 3 4 5 6 7 8 9 10 11 12 13 14 15 kms

- Allow at least 1½ hours
- Town walk on pavements; some steep steps
- P Various signposted car parks close to city centre; meter parking in streets
- T Well served by coaches, buses, trains and Metro
- Numerous pubs, restaurants, cafés and toilets in the city
- I Tourist information at the Central Library in Princess Square and at Central Station concourse, Tel. (0191) 261 0691

THE WALK

NEWCASTLE

The walk begins at Grey's Monument Ⓐ, at the top of Grey Street, which can be reached by taking the Metro to Monument Station.

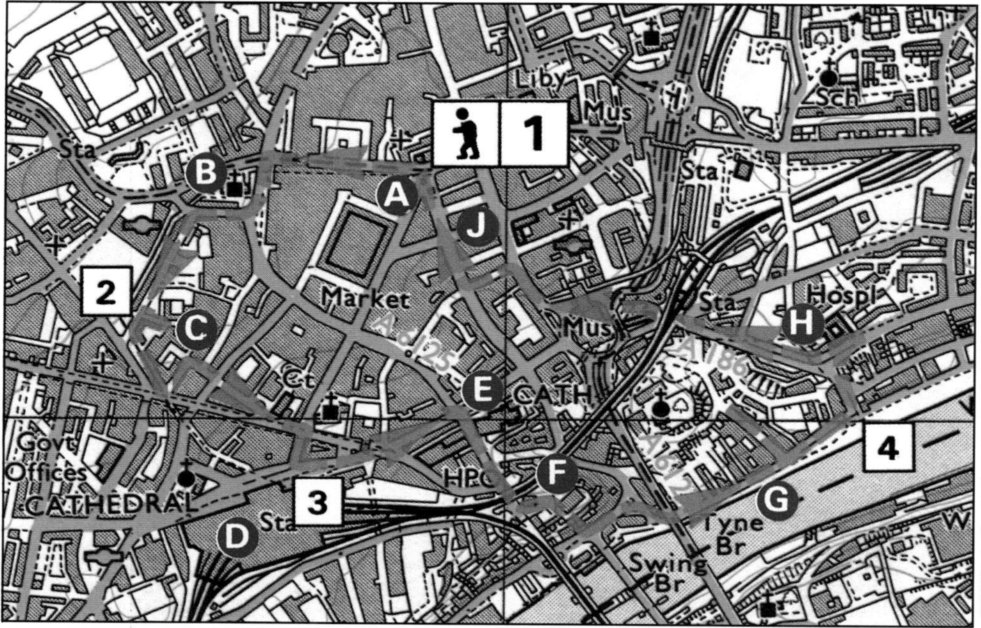

➊ Leave the square by Blackett Street, past Dillons bookshop, to Newgate Street. St Andrew's Church Ⓑ is on the other side of the road and to the left. Take the street on the right past the church (St Andrew's Street) and follow it to a public house at the top (Rosie's Bar), on the corner of Stowell Street. Just beyond the pub, turn left down a narrow alley (West Walls), and follow it to the far end at Heber Tower. Then turn left, cross Stowell Street and walk down Friars Street to Blackfriars Ⓒ.

➋ Walk back up Friars Street to Stowell Street. Turn left, then left again and walk down beside the town walls in Bath Lane. Turn left into Westgate Road, then take the first left into Cross Street, adjoining Charlotte Square. Turn right into Fenkle Street. Follow this to where it joins Westgate Road by the Assembly Rooms. Turn left to walk down Westgate Road, then right at the junction with Grainger Street to Central Station Ⓓ.

➌ Turn left down Neville Street towards the Stephenson Monument, then go straight on down Collingwood Street to St Nicholas's Cathedral Ⓔ. Turn right down St Nicholas Street, go past the Black Gate and under the railway bridge, then turn left to the entrance to The Keep Ⓕ. After visiting The Keep, cross Castle Garth and descend Castle Stairs to the Quayside Ⓖ. Follow the Quayside, past the Swing Bridge and the Guildhall. Go under the Tyne Bridge and after passing King Street, turn left into Broad Chare to visit the Trinity Maritime Centre and Trinity House. Return to the Quayside and then continue past the Law Courts.

➍ At the end of the Quayside, bear left, cross the road and go up past the Barley Mow Pub, with the Keelman's Hospital Ⓗ opposite. Cross the road here and turn left into City Road and follow this to the Corner Tower. Go under the railway bridge, cross the road via a subway and bear right in the subway to reach the Joicey Museum. From the museum, return to the subway, continuing straight on and then turning right to reach the Royal Arcade. Signs indicate the way to Pilgrim Street. Turn right up Pilgrim Street and take the next left (High Bridge). Turn right up Grey Street, passing the Theatre Royal Ⓙ, to Grey's Monument.

JEFFREY BEAZLEY

◀*Blackfriars, a substantial 13th-century Dominican abbey, now houses a restaurant and craft workshops.*

15th-century font cover is one of the finest in England. Some of the town walls are visible in the churchyard.

Further on, a narrow alley known as West Walls, just off St Andrew's Street, has the longest remaining stretch of Newcastle's 13th-century town walls. John Leland, a 16th-century historian, stated that Newcastle was one of the finest walled towns of Europe. Originally, the walls were about 2 miles (3.2km) in length and up to 25 feet (7.5m) in height. At the end of this section is Heber Tower, the best preserved of all the medieval wall towers.

Signs point the way to Blackfriars Ⓒ, founded by the Dominicans in the 13th century, and now restored with a restaurant and various craft workshops around the old cloister. Just beyond, in Bath Lane, there is an uninterrupted view of a substantial section of the town walls.

18TH-CENTURY SQUARE

From the bottom of Bath Lane, the route continues along Westgate Road and into Cross Street, leading to Charlotte Square, Newcastle's only formal 18th-century square. Between here and the Assembly

ALL PHOTOS JEFFREY BEAZLEY

Continue down Collingwood Street to St Nicholas's Cathedral Ⓔ. This was originally a parish church, raised to cathedral status in 1882. Its chief architectural glory is the lantern tower with its crown spire of about 1470, rising to a height of 193 feet (58m). There is a tradition that in 1644, during the siege of Newcastle, the Scottish army threatened to blow up the church with cannon fire, but the mayor put his Scottish prisoners in the lantern tower and thus saved it from destruction.

SQUARE NORMAN KEEP

From here you head towards the river, following St Nicholas Street to the Black Gate, the entrance to the massive castle Keep Ⓕ. The original 'new castle' of 1080 was built of wood; Henry II started on the stone building visible today in 1168. It is one of Britain's finest examples of a square Norman Keep. The roof commands an excellent view of Newcastle and Gateshead, and of the River Tyne running between.

Castle Stairs descend steeply to the Quayside Ⓖ, with good views of some of the six Tyne bridges nearby. The High Level Bridge on the right, built by Robert Stephenson in 1846-49, was a great engineering achievement for its time. The Swing Bridge, almost immediately ahead, was built in 1876 on the site of Newcastle's Roman, medieval and 18th-century bridges. Pons Aelius, the name by which Newcastle was known in Roman times, means 'the settlement with a bridge'.

This area was the historical core of Newcastle until the building of the High Level Bridge, which took away the main traffic into and out of the city. With the decrease of the city's maritime interests and the new commercial developments of Richard Grainger, the importance of the Quayside steadily declined until recent efforts to revitalize the area began. There are some fine buildings here, such as the 17th-century Guildhall, with its magnificent Merchant Adventurers' Court and Great Hall, and some tall, timber-framed merchants' houses.

TYNE BRIDGE

Passing under the 1928 Tyne Bridge, similar in shape, if not size, to the Sydney Harbour Bridge, there is a good view up King Street to All Saints, one of the finest Georgian churches in the country. In Broad Chare, beyond the Baltic Tavern, is

Rooms was the most fashionable area of late Georgian Newcastle.

St John's Church, at the junction with Grainger Street, dates mostly from the 14th and 15th centuries. Along with St Andrew's, it is one of the four original parish churches of Newcastle. Close by, Central Station Ⓓ is one of the greatest monument's to the English railway age, and was opened by Queen Victoria in 1850. A large traffic island contains a monument to the memory of George Stephenson, the prime mover behind the world's first steam railway, the Stockton-Darlington line. He was born and raised locally.

►The elegant 17th-century Guildhall is one of many fine buildings in Quayside, which, since 1928, has nestled under the impressive Tyne Bridge (below). Another showpiece is St Nicholas's Cathedral (above left), which its magnificent lantern tower, seen here from The Keep.

the Trinity Maritime Centre, a museum devoted to shipping and the River Tyne. Next door is Trinity House, with its beautiful courtyard. Returning to the Quayside, the route passes the impressive new building housing the Law Courts, then bears left towards the Keelman's Hospital **H**, built in 1701 to provide accommodation for poor, aged or disabled keelmen and their widows. The keels were the flat-bottomed lighters that brought coal from the pits upstream to the colliers in the port. Nearby is the Sallyport Tower and then, further along City Road, the Corner Tower, another fragment of the town wall, with excellent views of All Saints Church.

JOICEY MUSEUM

The route turns back towards the city centre, passing the Holy Jesus Hospital of 1681, a fine example of old brickwork, which now houses the Joicey Museum of Newcastle's social history. A subway leads to Pilgrim Street where a left turn leads to the magnificent Grey Street. In the 1830s, this area of central Newcastle was extensively developed in the classical style by Richard Grainger, who successfully completed old Eldon Square, the New Markets, several major streets and the Theatre Royal. Grainger worked closely with the architect John Dobson, who also designed Central Station.

Grey Street stretches down towards the river from Grey's Monument. Wide and generously proportioned, it is often cited as one of the most graceful streets in Europe. The Theatre Royal **J**, with its impressive portico of giant columns, is the third home of the Royal Shakespeare Company and was extensively refurbished in 1987-8. Perhaps the finest of the other notable buildings in the street is the present Lloyds Bank at the corner of Hood Street.

Between Grey Street, Market Street and Grainger Street are the Exchange Buildings, also built by Grainger. The interior was badly damaged by fire, and in 1906 was replaced by the Central Arcade, with its iron and glass roof, and tiled floor with classical motifs. A short stroll takes you back to the start.

JEFFREY BEAZLEY

▲*Central Arcade, built in 1906, echoes the classical style of the Theatre Royal (right), with its splendid columned portico, which was constructed in the 1830s by Richard Grainger.*

JEFFREY BEAZLEY

NEWCASTLE UPON TYNE CITY LIBRARIES & ARTS

Cunard's transatlantic passenger liner Mauretania *made her maiden voyage from the Tyne in November 1907.*

Tyneside Shipyards

Ships have been built on the River Tyne since the Middle Ages, most of them associated with the coal trade. Keels, or lighters, carried the coal from the mines and staithes higher up the river to the sea-going colliers. The Tyne keels were flat-bottomed, oval boats with square sails and two long oars. The colliers were made of Baltic timber, with sails of Baltic flax, and were built in many of the small shipyards along both sides of the Tyne.

Some of the first iron ships were launched here in the 1840s. In 1852, a screw-driven collier was built, capable of carrying 650 tons of coal to London within 48 hours. At this time, the river was dredged to give a deeper channel, and new quays, docks, jetties and piers were built. Newcastle's Quayside was the centre of Tyneside's maritime trade, and in its heyday, during the 19th century, was one of the busiest and most prosperous commercial areas in England.

By the beginning of the 20th century, many Tyneside companies had merged to build huge ocean-going ships such as the liner *Mauretania*, powered by steam turbines that generated 70,000 horse-power (52.2MW) and allowed an average cruising speed of 24 knots (44.5kmh). Until 1913, Tyneside led the world in the building of oil tankers. The World Wars saw the shipyards busy with naval contracts, but ever since there has been a decline. Today, some employment is provided by oil rigs brought to the yards for repairs.

INDEX